Finally, a well-crafted and ingenious text answers, in very creative ways, a fundamental question that has eluded many previous authors. That question is, "Does being identified as gifted make a difference for culturally diverse gifted individuals?" The editors of this highly stimulating text, *Running the Long Race in Gifted Education*, have gathered an impressive and highly insightful group of "ordinary" authors, who have often defied negative predictions of their own success and nonetheless have ingeniously created a profound narrative that explores the complex and sometimes conflicting positionalities, identities, and resilient behavior associated with being gifted AND culturally diverse. Although this book is intended as a college or university text in the social sciences, it is also written to attract social justice and other advocates, as well as families of ALL gifted children who may benefit from reading about the outcomes of multiple case studies concerning various and often neglected aspects of giftedness.

James M. Patton, EdD
Professor Emeritus, The College of William and Mary
Co-author of *Gifted Youth at Risk* and *Methods for Teaching Culturally and Linguistically Diverse Exceptional Leaners*

Running the Long Race in Gifted Education is a compelling read. Each chapter tells the story of a gifted student's unique path and struggle towards adult creative achievement. Collectively the narratives reveal the complexities of the relationship between race and giftedness in our society. This book is useful for a variety of audiences. It will provide inspiration and hope to students and parents. It gives educators and other professionals an opportunity to gain a deeper understanding of the challenges, particularly psychological ones, that gifted, culturally different individuals face in becoming path-breaking scholars and performers.

Paula Olszewski-Kubilius, PhD
Director, Center for Talent Development
School of Education and Social Policy
Northwestern University

A thoughtful probe into what it means to be gifted. In this one-of-a-kind book, the editors have given new meaning to the idea of "lived experience" of culturally diverse giftedness. By inviting a number of culturally gifted individuals from across a range of countries to write about being gifted, they unlock new ways to think about giftedness and cultural diversity. Chapter by chapter, the reader is exposed to new insights into what it means to be gifted and culturally diverse—insights that are heartwarming and heart wrenching.

Running the Long Race is a "must have" and mandatory reading for anyone with a stake in education—parents, teachers, caregivers, teacher educators, counselors, and community.

Ruksana Osman, PhD
Professor of Education and Dean of the Faculty of
Humanities, University of the Witwatersrand, South Africa
Convenor of the UNESCO Research Chair in Teacher
Education for Diversity and Development

Navigating through one's formative years to successful adulthood is hardly ever easy. It's harder if one comes from a family that is stressed and/or marginalized, still harder if one's heritage is African-American, and even harder for a gifted youngster who must make his or her way past barrier upon barrier. This thoroughly engaging book of narratives by strong people who have made this treacherous journey successfully and, finally, a bit proudly invites readers to look through windows into private worlds impossible for us otherwise to access. For educators, counselors, mentors, and others who want to make the paths a little easier for today's young people; for parents of such gifted minority youth and for parents of their friends; indeed, for young gifted people of whatever backgrounds themselves, this is a welcome and exceptionally valuable opportunity to develop insights into these lives—and ours.

Nancy M. Robinson, PhD
Professor Emerita of Psychiatry and Behavioral Sciences,
University of Washington

Sharing one's story is brave. A personal story, shared to benefit others, is a potent gift. *Running the Long Race in Gifted Education* embodies the bravery and generosity of the authors as they help us to understand their struggles and their triumphs. This insightful book carries the reader on individual journeys to reconcile giftedness within a challenging cultural and societal context. These journeys remind us of the powerful influence we have over students and of our sacred responsibility as educators to nurture and support the gifts of each person. They remind us that *race* matters, that we still have work to do, that our commitment to excellence for *all* must be sustained, and that if we choose, we can make a positive difference in the lives of others.

Running the Long Race in Gifted Education is an inspirational and informative must-read for all those who touch the lives of culturally different children with gifts and talents. It is a rare gift and it should be widely shared and treasured.

Mary Ruth Coleman, PhD
Senior Scientist Emeritus, FPG Child Development
Institute University of North Carolina at Chapel Hill
Director of U-STARS~PLUS

Running the Long Race in Gifted Education is a book that gives an understanding of the dilemmas of black gifted children who wish to explore and develop their giftedness and maintain the essence of their blackness. The book gives insight into the need to belong in a social group and the effects it has had on generations, such as the mother-and-daughter conversation included in the book. The interesting tie-in with the dilemmas of women, who carry two kinds of differences, gives the reader a broader concept of how the role of being black, a woman, and gifted builds or diminishes self-esteem.

Alexinia Y. Baldwin, PhD
Professor Emeritus, Education of the Gifted
Department of Curriculum and Instruction
University of Connecticut

Negotiating a world impacted by diversity issues, disengagement with peers, vulnerability, isolation and assimilation into either Black or white communities are common themes in *Running the Long Race in Gifted Education.* Just how do gifted individuals who feel differently successfully navigate through such life experiences from childhood on through adulthood? This book offers insight into questions no one has asked. The compelling narratives exemplify the importance of scholastic questioning—does being identified as gifted make a difference for the culturally different individual?

Monita Leavitt, PhD
International Gifted Educational Specialist
Author of *Building a Gifted Program: Identifying and Educating Students in Your School,* contributing author of *Exceptional Needs Standards,* 2nd Edition, and co-author of *Let It Flow*

This book is a must-read for the growing research fraternity among the Asian and African developing countries that in some instances have initiated gifted education programs and in many others seem oblivious to the fact that the loss to a nation is colossal if the gifted minds are not tapped and nurtured.

Anitha Kurup, PhD
Professor, National Institute of Advanced Studies,
Indian Institute of Science Campus, Bangalore, India
Lead Researcher, National Program on Gifted Education in India.

RUNNING THE LONG RACE IN GIFTED EDUCATION:

Narratives and Interviews from Culturally Diverse Gifted Adults

Edited by Joy M. Scott-Carrol, PhD
and Anthony Sparks, PhD

Foreword by Diana Slaughter Kotzin, PhD

BOOK PUBLISHERS NETWORK
Changing the World One Book at a Time

Book Publishers Network
P.O. Box 2256
Bothell • WA • 98041
Ph • 425-483-3040
www.bookpublishersnetwork.com

10 9 8 7 6 5 4 3 2 1

Printed in the United States of America

LCCN   2016930500
ISBN   978-1-940598-93-2

Names: Scott-Carrol, Joy M., editor. | Sparks, Anthony, editor.
Title: Running the long race in gifted education : narratives and interviews from culturally diverse gifted adults / edited by Joy M. Scott-Carrol, and Anthony Sparks ; foreword by Diana Slaughter Kotzin.
Description: Bothell, WA : Book Publishers Network, [2016] | Includes bibliographical references and index. | Contents: Part I. Identification and participation in gifted and talented programs -- Part II. Navigating adulthood and careers -- Part III. Navigating cross-cultural access, survival, and what's expected of me -- Part IV. Navigating families -- Part V. Navigating self: to belong or not to belong.
Identifiers: ISBN: 978-1-940598-93-2 | LCCN: 2016930500
Subjects: LCSH: Gifted persons--United States--Personal narratives. | Gifted persons--United States--Psychological aspects. | Gifted children--Education--United States. | Talented students--United States. | Minority students--United States--Psychological aspects. | Social perception. | Success--Psychological aspects. | Self-realization.
Classification: LCC: BF412 .R86 2016 | DDC: 153.9/8--dc23

Editor: Julie Scandora
Cover Designer: Laura Zugzda
Book Designer: Melissa Vail Coffman
Indexer: Carolyn Acheson

To Ruth (Allred) Scott
Pearlie Mae Sparks,
and all navigators of giftedness

CONTENTS

FOREWORD

Diana Slaughter Kotzin, PhD

"To Be Young, Gifted, and Black"—during one of her many concerts, Nina Simone told the story that she was inspired to write the lyrics to this beautiful song by the recent death at age thirty-four of Chicago-born dramatist Lorraine Hansberry.[1] At age twenty-one, Lorraine Hansberry became the youngest American playwright, the fifth woman, and the only Black American to win the New York Drama Critics' Circle Award for the Best Play of the Year (*A Raisin in the Sun*). In 1969, Hansberry's widower, Robert Nemiroff, published posthumously a collection of Hansberry's writings with the same title: *To Be Young, Gifted and Black*. Nina Simone's album that included this hit song was released in 1970 under RCA (LSP-4248). Not surprisingly, Nina titled her LP *Black Gold*. In 1969, I was twenty-eight years old. The encounters with Lorraine Hansberry's book and Nina's song were, I now believe, the first experiences I ever had of the two concepts being juxtaposed together, i.e., of being gifted and being Black.

In the 1940s and '50s, being smart in school usually enabled children double promotions and other school-related advantages linked to being able to apprehend information quickly and efficiently. Frequently, such behaviors were equated, due to scores on intelligence and aptitude tests, with giftedness. Fortunately, the research published in *Creativity and Intelligence* by Jacob Getzels and Philip Jackson of the University of Chicago in 1962 led us to understand that divergent, rather than convergent, thinking, for example, was more frequently a hallmark of giftedness. Persons, especially youth, who could rapidly master presented concepts and ideas and then transform them into something new and refreshing for us all to experience, and frequently enjoy, became more often acknowledged as gifted after the publication of these authors' findings. Further, their book helped us to understand the important role of the family home environment in nurturing gifted children and youth. Thanks to the research of one of Getzels's former students, Mihaly Csikszentmihalyi, we subsequently learned that problem-finding, rather than problem-solving, is a hallmark of gifted persons and that the experience of being totally "into" an activity is linked to the active expression or experiencing of gifted behavior, whether or not the "flow" or optimization of psychological experiencing is tied to a specifically artistic or humanistic life style (Csikszentmihalyi, 1990).

With the publication of this significant volume of life history narratives featuring adults about the experience of being identified as gifted, over forty years after Nina's song, we learn why Nina Simone and Lorraine Hansberry wanted to be very encouraging and supportive of youth who, as talented individuals, on one hand, hold all the promise and potential that a family, neighborhood, or community could hope for and, on the other, are potentially subject to all the disadvantages associated with race (e.g., poverty, racism) and racial stereotyping that plague economically and socially marginalized and vulnerable families and communities in the United States of America and around the world.

There is a fairly substantial literature about gifted Black youth, dating back to articles by a former protégé of Northwestern University's Martin D. Jenkins, who published on the topic "A socio-psychological study of Negro children of superior intelligence" in 1936, "Case studies of Negro children of Binet IQ 160 and above" in 1943, and "Intellectually superior Negro youth: Problems and needs" in 1950. Each of the articles can be found in the *Journal of Negro Education.* As a professor of child development and educational psychology, I kept during my career a file of some of the more interesting articles and papers, published and unpublished (e.g., Chepko-Sade 1985, Shade 1978, Stanfield 1995, Stanfield and Dennis 1995, Tidwell 1979, and Witty 1978).

Varied interests led researchers to the topic, including the then-prevailing nearly sole reliance on IQ and aptitude testing to identify gifted youth—an arena of long-standing challenges and difficulties for underrepresented and economically challenged minority groups, a focus on the causes of underachievement in otherwise identified talented youth, and the seemingly social inertia that exists to this day in our society's reluctance, even inability, to conceive that Black American youth, including youth from the African diaspora, could also be gifted and talented.

Succinctly stating the problem, Stanfield and Dennis (1995, 214–215) report:

> Historically, Blacks who stood head-and-shoulders above their White peers have been dismissed as "not really being Black," or as having sufficient amounts of "White blood" to account for their stellar achievements—-or they have simply been ignored. As Talalay (1995) and Winston (1971) note, it has been commonplace for the stunning contributions of such extraordinarily intellectually gifted Black people as George Washington Carver, marine biologist Ernest Everett Just, piano prodigy Phillipa Schuyler, and many more unsung, brilliant Blacks to be devalued, while overbearing emphasis is placed on their personal idiosyncrasies. The inability of many Americans to understand that Black children and adults can be just as intellectually gifted as athletically gifted, if not more so, is apparent in the lack of historical interest in Black gifted or exceptional education. Notwithstanding the early work of Martin Jenkins (1936, 1943) and others on African American children of superior intelligence. . . . Until very recently, Black education has been focused on the other end of the spectrum, with an emphasis on the learning disabilities and behavioral problems many Blacks experience in schools. It has been easier to attract funding for Black youth who are having or causing problems in schools than for Black youth who are exceptional learners.

The personal narratives in this book reaffirm in the voices and appraisals of the gifted youth themselves that their pathways to truly understanding the scope and depth of their own precocities were highly diverse. This book makes clear that there are many paths to acknowledgment of one's own genius. Some authors (e.g., Nicole Monteiro, chapter 12) report intense, ongoing active engagement of both parents and family in their support and development of themselves as a gifted Black child. Other authors (e.g., Marquis Bey, chapter 2) seemed to imply that they literally accidentally bumped into the challenges of formulating an identity around being gifted and Black. Marquis Bey states:

> My high school was where one's giftedness crawled into the darkest hole it could find for seven hours and twenty minutes each weekday. . . . Put bluntly, yet honestly, from my experience the school was merely a hangout spot for kids to see their homies and besties while learning the bare essentials needed to function in life. But learning remained the tertiary priority . . . next to chilling with your friends and trying various routes for ultimate coolness.

Not until he reached college did the author have an opportunity "through [his] intellect and [his] language [to] reclaim a lost Blackness."

Joy Scott-Carrol (chapter 10), the mother of a highly gifted daughter, made deliberate choices to nurture and preserve her child's Blackness while simultaneously enrolling her in predominantly white independent schools. She embraced the concept of racial and ethnic socialization to shield against the emotional rigors of racial tensions. Scott-Carrol writes:

> Though I vowed never to let race dictate my decisions, as an educator and mother of a Black child, I knew the importance of racial/ethnic socialization (R/ES), particularly if I wanted [my child] to maintain a solid sense of self in an environment that lacked the diversity she had learned to appreciate.

The narratives indicate that devoted parents use many different means to support the education of their gifted children. Scott-Carrol took a holistic approach that involved promoting learning experiences in and outside the classroom. Many of her choices stressed gifted education enrichment opportunities over the rigor of traditional gifted education in the classroom. The end goal was to facilitate the blossoming of her [daughter's] intellect and the growth of a self-respecting, well-rounded, caring, young woman.

In a recent edited volume (Slaughter-Defoe et al., 2012), my colleagues and I discuss the contemporary challenges posed by elite private and charter schools, particularly for youth and their parents. Nia Ricks and her mother, Shawn, in an important conversation, explore how moving to the desegregated suburbs posed new challenges for Nia as the gifted, better economically -resourced Black daughter of a gifted Black mother who grew up in a Black impoverished neighborhood in the city. As a reader, I thought the best message from these authors was the actual experience of parent and child talking together and really listening to one another as adults. As Scott-Carrol notes in her chapter, it is really important that parents, particularly those whose children attend predominantly White institutions, understand their own values, set appropriate goals for their children, and support them unconditionally. Citing Slaughter-Defoe et al. (2012), she addresses the complexities of parenting Black youth "when the larger societal context of race-based inequities is unconsciously perpetrated by well-intentioned authority figures such as teachers, and other school administrative staff."

From the vantage of psychological theory, I found many of the authors of these wonderful chapters reported coping in ways discussed in the research of Claude Steele (the importance of wanting to do well as a representative of the race), John Ogbu and Signithia Fordham (the importance of having to resist negativity projected by peers), and Margaret Spencer (the importance of integrating positive self-esteem and positive racial concepts), to name just a few.

However, the editors of this prescient volume are to be congratulated. It is so very important that these personal narratives are written in the voices of the adults themselves, as they reflect upon younger days and earlier times. The narratives included in this volume that have been written and contributed by gifted culturally diverse individuals who are not Black are especially valuable, given the extent of racial and ethnic diversity in contemporary American educational institutions.

The chapter authors have elected to revisit and invade the realms of what had to be challenging childhoods, teen, and young adult years to give us refreshing, new contemporary perspectives on gifted youth. I think it takes considerable emotional courage to invade your own privacy so deeply and profoundly. Educators and other professionals need to study and discuss the ideas and viewpoints of the authors. Parents who struggle with rearing similarly situated children will find new hope and support for their efforts. I know readers will both enjoy and learn from this volume as I have.

Diana Slaughter Kotzin, PhD
Constance E. Clayton Professor Emerita in Urban Education
University of Pennsylvania, Philadelphia

Notes

1. To Be Young, Gifted, and Black

To be young gifted and black,
Oh what a lovely precious dream
To be young, gifted and black,
Open your heart to what I mean

In the whole world you know
There are a billion boys and girls
Who are young, gifted and black,
And that's a fact!

Young, gifted and black
We must begin to tell our young
There's a world waiting for you
This is a quest that's just begun
When you feel really low
Yeah, there's a great truth you should know

When you're young, gifted and black
Your soul's intact

Young, gifted and black
How I long to know the truth
There are times when I look back
And I am haunted by my youth

Oh but my joy of today
Is that we can all be proud to say
To be young, gifted and black
Is where it's at

References

Chepko-Sade, D. (1985, March). *An incidence study of disadvantaged gifted students in the Midwest.* Research report prepared by the author for the Midwest Talent Search, Northwestern University, and funded by the College Board.

Csikszentmihalyi, M. (1990). *Flow: The psychology of optimal experience.* New York: Harper & Row.

Fordham, S., & Ogbu, J. (1986). Black students' school success: Coping with the burden of "acting White." *Urban Review, 18*(3), 176–206.

Getzels, J., & Jackson, P. (1962). *Creativity and intelligence.* New York: John Wiley & Sons.

Jenkins, M. (1936). A socio-psychological study of Negro children of superior intelligence. *Journal of Negro Education, 5*(2), 175–190.

———. (1943). Case studies of Negro children of Binet IQ 160 and above. *Journal of Negro Education, 12*(2), 159–166.

———. (1950). Intellectually superior Negro youth: Problems and needs. *Journal of Negro Education, 19*(3), 322–332.

Nemiroff, R. (1969). *To be young, gifted and Black: Lorraine Hansberry in her own words.* Englewood, Cliffs, NJ: Prentice-Hall, Inc.

Shade, B. (1978). Social-psychological characteristics of achieving Black children. *Negro Educational Review, 29(2)*, 80–86.

Slaughter-Defoe, D., Stevenson, H., Arrington, E., & Johnson, D. (eds.) (2012). *Black educational choice: Assessing the private and public alternatives to traditional K-12 public schools.* Santa Barbara, CA: Praeger.

Spencer, M. (2006). Phenomenology and ecological systems theory: Development of diverse groups. In W. Damon, & R. Lerner (eds.), *Handbook of child psychology* (6th ed., vol. 15, 829-893). Hoboken, NJ: John Wiley & Sons.

Stanfield, J. (1995). The myth of race and the human sciences. *Journal of Negro Education, 64*(3), 218–231.

Stanfield, J., & Dennis, R. (1995). Guest editors' comments: Not all that bright. *Journal of Negro Education, 64*(3), 214–217.

Steele, C., & Aronson, J. (1995). Stereotype threat and the intellectual performance of African-Americans. *Journal of Personality and Social Psychology, 69*, 797–811.

Talalay, K. (1995). *Composition in black and white: The life of Phillipa Schuyler.* New York: Oxford University Press.

Tidwell, R. (1979). *A psycho-educational profile of gifted minority students identified without reliance on aptitude tests.* Paper presented at the Annual Meeting of the American Educational Research Association, San Francisco, CA.

Winston, M. (1971). Through the back door: Academic racism and the Negro scholar in historical perspective. *Daedalus, 100*(3), 678–719.

Witty, E. P. (1978). Equal opportunity for gifted minority group children. *Gifted Child Quarterly, 22*(3), 344–352.

PREFACE

Anthony Sparks, PhD

Not long ago, while in the midst of a coffee break from a television project at Paramount Studios in Los Angeles, I entered into a conversation with a crew member working on another production, a television series that had yet to debut. The series, *Cosmos,* would be hosted by astrophysicist Neil deGrasse Tyson. The crew member nonchalantly expressed surprised that I was aware of Tyson and his many career accomplishments—but we continued to have a very friendly exchange for about ten minutes. He seemed even more surprised that I was a television writer-producer (and not another blue collar crew person). As we continued to chat, his fascination grew as he learned that I had recently earned a PhD from the University of Southern California. When our break ended and we prepared to return to our respective offices and soundstages, the crew member shook my hand, but it wasn't just any handshake—he gave me "dap." In other words, he gave me respect by shaking my hands with the rhythms and gestures of what some would call a "soul brother" handshake. He shook my hand the way you might see two Black men on the streets of any American inner city exchange greetings. In doing so, this white male crew member positively acknowledged my Blackness and my presence in a professional space where many people did not look like me. My colleague was friendly, yet pleasantly surprised.

This book, *Running the Long Race in Gifted Education: Narratives and Interviews from Culturally Diverse Gifted Adults,* is about the surprise and reactions that continue to greet culturally diverse adult achievers. As they journey from childhood to adulthood, many often notice a dissipation of the gifted title, but the intelligence lives on and often seems to forcibly illicit a response. In the example above, the reaction was pleasant, but this is not always the case. Sometimes the response is unpleasant and even hostile, but more than likely, it manifests as a sudden awkwardness or perhaps a studied indifference. Such negative responses, in retrospect, connect to the deficit frameworks of many culturally irresponsive teachers and administrators, especially those perplexed by intellectually gifted children who are so culturally different from the dominant standard of privilege or influence.

While many books, articles, and papers have been published about gifted children and some have included topics on culturally diverse gifted children as subjects (often from the still-vital stance of deficit thinking, underrepresentation in gifted programs), few if any have been written about the successful adult lives of culturally diverse gifted individuals negotiating family life, influential careers, advanced degrees, and more.

Publications in education and other disciplines have not adequately covered within-group diversity among racial and ethnic individuals. This work seeks to address the dearth. The color of one's skin does not dictate uniformity or sameness in cultural identity, whether acquired or passed down through generations. Our chapter authors represent diverse geographic regions, families of origin, socio-economic statuses, genders, races, specific areas of giftedness (intellectual, creative, academic, artistic, linguistic, twice-exceptional, leadership, etc.), religions, and other cross-cultural configurations. *Running the Long Race in Gifted Education* is a groundbreaking effort to address these gaps in published literature on gifted education. It does so by privileging the voices, experiences, and narratives of Black, Brown and other culturally diverse gifted adults as the basis for grounded theory and understandings.

How This Book Came About

THE SEEDS FOR *Running the Long Race in Gifted Education* were planted twenty-five years ago when Joy Scott-Carrol served as program director of Northwestern University's Center for Talent Development NU-Horizons counseling program for gifted, economically disadvantaged, and culturally diverse college-bound tenth graders. The NU-Horizons program began by canvassing Chicago's public schools for economically disadvantaged but academically gifted and culturally diverse students. For three years (1988–1990) under Scott-Carrol's leadership, approximately forty gifted students received extensive pre-college counseling and academic preparation for their likely admittance to highly selective universities. Despite challenges for securing long-term grant funding, the NU-Horizons program was a smashing success. Many of the mostly Black students were admitted to institutions of higher education, such as Harvard University, Cornell University, Rice University, Stanford University, Northwestern University, and the University of Chicago. At sixteen years old, I was one of the students in the program and went on to attend University of Southern California (USC) on scholarship.

Meanwhile, Dr. Scott-Carrol continued her work in gifted education while maintaining a long-distance mentorship with many of her NU-Horizons students. As a result, she and I connected in person twenty years later, just as I was entering my doctoral studies and after I had spent many successful years working in the arts and entertainment industries.

Reading Audiences

THIS BOOK IS ONE OF A KIND. Nowhere else will readers find such an extensive collection of narratives and interviews on the lives of low-profile, highly accomplished, culturally diverse, gifted adults. Readers will hear the voices of gifted individuals who proudly share their gifted identification, successes, family influences, trials, strategies to overcome obstacles, and strategies of reliance on higher level gifted thinking to manage discouragement. Readers from all educational, racial, ethnic, gender, economic, and cross-cultural backgrounds will find powerfully reflective narrations to guide their own lives as thriving, goal-oriented individuals.

As editors, we set out to know from the perspectives of culturally diverse adults who were either (1) officially identified by intelligence testing or other such standardized achievement testing noting giftedness or (2) recognized by teachers, the community, and/or parents as gifted based on a combination of factors such as grade level acceleration, portfolios, and national competitions and had also participated in school-related gifted programs or specialized classrooms. We wanted to know if such gifted identifications made a difference in their adult lives. There is always the option to collect self-reported empirical data and draw conclusions about a population based on numerical results; however, an exclusive use of such methodologies struck the editors as limited in its usefulness in a field of study that has not yet carved a niche within the gifted and talented field of study, namely, adulthood outcomes of culturally diverse gifted children.

We also rejected an exclusively research approach to embrace grounded theory, which would highlight, through description, the voices of those who know best what it is like to coexist with the label and identity, expectations, and responsibilities of being a gifted child who would one day grow up as a gifted adult. We wanted to know from the self-reflexive stance of an adult how they perceive life experiences many years later. What were the bases of their interpretations, and how might these interpretations have changed over time? We want to share with a wide array of audiences the interpretations and compelling insights that were unearthed because we dared to ask questions some twenty, thirty, forty years after the fact.

We recognize that a significant gap does exist in the long-term scholarship on culturally diverse, gifted learners. This awareness sparked the original idea and questions that drive the scope of *Running the Long Race in Gifted Education*:

- Does being identified as a gifted/high-ability learner or having participated in gifted and talented programs make a difference for culturally different people?
- What happens to culturally diverse students who were identified as gifted learners during their childhood?
- How do culturally diverse gifted adults view and interpret their childhood experiences in gifted education programs and classrooms?
- Does identification as a gifted learner in one's childhood significantly or descriptively impact adult life? If so, how?

Rarely, if ever, will you find a child who will say to a parent, "I am gifted, and you as a parent must meet my intellectual needs," or to a teacher, "My intellectual needs are not being met. What are you going to do about it?" And so, we asked these very accomplished adult achievers to speak from a reflective standpoint and help readers understand giftedness over time as giftedness relates specifically to culturally different adults who are not represented enough nationally or internationally. How has being identified as gifted made a difference in life outcomes? How has this identification supported career successes or aspirations, family lives, and relationships with peers? How does just being oneself affect the confidence needed to negotiate life's many challenges and surprises?

Parents are usually the first to recognize giftedness, and they play a significant role in nurturing the gifts and talents of their children. This is the case, irrespective of race or nationality, socioeconomic status, and educational opportunity. Through the narratives and non-scientific interviews, we discovered that being identified as gifted or having participated in intense, specialized, inclusive classrooms and enrichment programs does make a difference. However, that difference takes a back seat to the support and guidance of the family unit. Therefore, *Running the Long Race in Gifted Education* is a proud tribute to parents and families for nurturing the self-efficacy and internal locus of control that drives gifted children to honor their differentness and succeed in life.

What Next?

ULTIMATELY, THE EDITORS AND AUTHORS of *Running the Long Race in Gifted Education* draw upon their most powerful resources—their narratives and interviews—in order to contribute to new critical conversations in both gifted education studies and ethnic studies. In choosing to highlight the reflective adult voices of the rarely studied intersection of the culturally diverse gifted child and the lack of diversity in the environments from which that child generally emerges, this work seeks to spark an intervention. It takes a first step in expanding the foundational, epistemological dimensions where this conversation can currently take place. To date, published education literature on Black, Latino, or other culturally diverse gifted individuals is deeply engaged with discussions centered on scarcity—scarcity of representation, of inclusiveness, of economic opportunity. All these topics deserve the epistemological space they occupy, but this effort represents an abundance of new knowledge. It is a firsthand adult perspective from culturally diverse gifted individuals about acknowledged giftedness, gifted education programs, and how the interrelationship of the two plays out over time, irrespective of the place from which one begins.

Running the Long Race in Gifted Education opens a window into the culturally diverse gifted adult's personal and professional life. It gives an eye-level view of influences (family, mentors, parental struggles, teacher attitudes) that are often only discussed through a stereotypical lens. It shows, using their own words, how students who sometimes felt isolated as children learned coping mechanisms as adults. We anticipate this vital work will be useful in theoretical and case-study approaches within disciplines such as education, psychology, sociology, ethnic and race relations, women's and feminist studies, masculinity studies, narrative studies, international relations, comparative analysis, documentary research, and qualitative ethnographic research. Ultimately, our hope is that this collective work will be an initial, first-of-its-kind salvo in eliminating theoretical and in-practice gaps concerning the worldwide giftedness encountered by all individuals at one time or another.

ACKNOWLEDGEMENTS

THE EDITORS THANK our chapter contributors one by one for sharing in the commitment to produce a quality book. Thank you Sara del Moral, Traci English-Clarke, Asegun Henry, April Lisbon-Peoples, Sharrell Luckett, Ruben Martinez, Rugvedita Parakh, Shawn Arango Ricks and Nia Ricks, and Tia Shaffer. A special thank you is extended to contributors Marquis Bey, Neeraj Kulkarni, Nicole Monteiro, and Jennifer Quamina for their constant encouragement, support, positivity, generosity, recommendations, and, last but not least, modeling grit in action.

We also thank our personal mentors, colleagues, friends, and other individuals of inspiration, especially gifted education scholars and practitioners who have, over the years, provided Joy M. Scott-Carrol with the hope of realizing her dream to write this cross-generational book: Alexina Y. Baldwin (professor emeritus, University of Connecticut Education), Karen Bendelman (International Education Consultant in Uruguay), Mary Ruth Coleman (senior scientist at the FPG Child Development Institute, University of North Carolina at Chapel Hill), Diana Slaughter Kotzin (author of the foreword, distinguished professor emeritus, University of Pennsylvania), Anitha Kurup (professor, National Institute of Advanced Studies in Bangalore, India), Monita Leavitt (specialist, International Gifted Education), Azwihangwisi Muthivhi, PhD (senior lecturer, University of Cape Town), Paula Olszewski-Kubilius (director, Center for Talent Development at Northwestern University), Ruksana Osman (dean of Humanities Faculties, University of the Witwatersrand), James M. Patton (professor emeritus, College of William and Mary), Nancy Robinson (professor emerita of Psychiatry and Behavioral Sciences, the Robinson Center for Young

Scholars, University of Washington), and attorney E. Russell Tarleton. Thank you also to Sarah Banet-Weiser, Ruth Wilson Gilmore, Velina Hasu Houston, Lanita Jacobs, Dorinne Kondo, Tara McPherson, Fred Moten, Nayan Shah, and Francille Rusan Wilson for supporting Anthony Sparks along the way. Our sincere gratitude is also extended to interviewer Nadirah Angail and Miriam Kolker for their conscientious proofreading and editing.

Gratitude beyond measure is extended to inspiration from our families: Paul C. Carrol; Ruth (Allred) Scott; Anastasia, Daniel L., Isabella, and Desmond Konecky; Harriette Coret; Anita Dashiell-Sparks; and Olivia, Langston, Dashiell, and Pearlie Mae Sparks.

Thanks also to Janet L. Gore and James T. Webb of Great Potential Press for the suggestions and encouragement, which helped expand the scope of this important book.

Finally, thank you to Carolee Danz, who put us in touch with Sheryn Hara and her staff at Book Publishers Network.

Chapter contributors also wish to thank the following individuals who have played important roles in supporting their education and careers:

Hina Alam
Bryant Keith Alexander
Terence Bey
Amobi B. Christopher
Sylvan Clarke
Felicia Coward
Eden Cowart
Jami and Thelma English
Shirlene Holmes
Bernette J. Lisbon with Jerel, Samir, and Jasmine
Gilbert Ling
Deepak and Ravi Marda
Dr. Shriwallabha and Madhuri Marda
Pablo and Juana Martinez
Anthony Monteiro
Wanjiku Oladigbolu
Mugdha V. Padalkar

Satyajeet, Maitreyi, and Neil Parakh
Dr. Vijay and Anjali Parakh
Nathan Anderson Ricks
Ruby Ricks
The Late Earline Rivers
Cathy Romagnolo
Ruth (Woodruff) Williams

INTRODUCTION

Joy M. Scott-Carrol, PhD

WE DIVIDED *Running the Long Race in Gifted Education: Narratives and Interviews from Culturally Diverse Gifted Adults* into five parts to highlight a range of life experiences. In part 1, "Introduction, Identification, and Participation in Gifted and Talented Programs," the authors describe when they were identified or selected to participate in gifted/ talented classrooms, programs, or schools and what impact identification had on their adult attitudes about being labeled as gifted.

In part 2, "Navigating Adulthood and Careers," another set of authors describe social-emotional successes and challenges associated with their childhood-to-adulthood journey. Often, this includes seeking the acceptance of teachers, peers, and co-workers who are observantly different from them, their families, and their micro-cultural communities. The interplay of gifted status and cultural difference is most noticeable when entering careers where co-workers and colleagues rely on stereotypes, make men or women invisible—to be neither seen and nor heard, or suggest entrance into a position by some standard other than one's qualifications. They track and explore this changing dynamic in an incredibly visceral fashion by analyzing the complexities of key moments in their transitions from student to career professional.

Part 3, "Navigating Cross-Cultural Access, Survival, and What's Expected of Me," includes contrasting experiences described by gifted adults who may identify as culturally different based on race, ethnicity, regional differences, privilege, or country of birth. The contributors are Black and Brown American, second-generation Spanish American

Caucasian, British, and South Asian (from India). Adults born outside the United States and identified as gifted in childhood or adulthood offer insights into negotiating their giftedness. In one case, an overlooked, twice-exceptionally gifted adult poignantly reveals her lifelong experiences of dismissals because being gifted with special needs had been an unheard-of phenomenon within gifted education. Most represent cultural differences from the standpoint of having to find their way around various social, academic, and cultural systems while also learning a second language.

In part 4, "Navigating Families," gifted adult authors who are also parents of gifted children narrate lessons learned from their family of origin and from gifted programs and how a gifted identification impacts family life for generations.

In part 5, "Navigating Self: To Belong or Not to Belong," authors reflect on and analyze the central role their gifted childhoods have played in conceptualizations of self and the ongoing struggle to balance an intellectually stimulating and holistically healthy sense of self.

Data Collection

MEN AND WOMEN WHO MET CERTAIN demographic and experience criteria were invited to submit narrative manuscripts for consideration as chapters (see appendix A). The salient question studied throughout *Running the Long Race in Gifted Education* is "Does being identified as gifted or having participated in gifted and talented programs in one's youth matter for culturally diverse gifted individuals?" Answers giving multiple perspectives to this question expose the weight of the gifted identity and what it represented for chapter contributors in childhood and represents now for them as adults.

Definition

SCHOLARS, PRACTITIONERS, EDUCATORS, and others familiar with gifted education as a scholarly inquiry or practice know too well that defining "gifted" is as complex as defining individual challenges at any point on the intelligence curve, and this is especially true depending on geography. On the other hand, individuals unfamiliar with the broad range of giftedness or gifted education as a study or practice invariably ask,

"What do you mean by gifted?" or "How do you define gifted?" The editors are comfortable recommending the National Association of Gifted Children's (2014) definition:

> Gifted individuals are those who demonstrate outstanding levels of aptitude (defined as an exceptional ability to reason and learn) or competence (documented performance or achievement in top 10% or rarer) in one or more domains. Domains include any structured area of activity with its own symbol system (e.g., mathematics, music, language) and/or set of sensorimotor skills (e.g., painting, dance, sports).

Chapter contributors represented in this book have been assessed or recognized as gifted based on either a single criterion or a combination of factors, such as IQ test scores, portfolios, performance evaluations, achievement scores, teacher/school district recommendations, parent recommendations, and more. They represent diverse categories of giftedness: intellectual, creative, academic, artistic, leadership, and other areas.

Pre-narrative Screening Survey Summary

POTENTIAL CHAPTER AUTHORS WERE SELECTED from a variety of referral sources: social media, word of mouth, friends, contacts at colleges and universities, and family members. Potential contributors provided documentation on their self-reported gifted identification, such as copies of assessment reports or the name and location of the school district or gifted program. These data allowed the editors to validate shared or similar experiences with other potential authors. To minimize the possibility of editor influence or partiality, we did not require that potential authors have achieved a specific educational level or career achievement. In other words, no applicant was rejected or selected based on credentials. See appendix A for demographics.

Selected authors completed an eighteen-item screening survey (see appendix A), which aided the editors in collecting descriptive data, such as family demographics at the time of gifted identification.

Racial, ethnic and national origin demographics revealed that twelve of the final contributors self-identified as Black or African American. Other self-reported racial, ethnic, and nationality identifiers were British, South Asian (Indian), Mexican American, and White/Spanish-American. Most of the authors have earned doctorates or master's degrees and are employed as university professors, K–12 school educators/administrators, physicians, corporate or government executives, clinical psychologists, entrepreneurs, or matriculating doctoral candidates. They range in age from twenty-two to over fifty and are all either currently employed or working toward an advanced degree. While many of these voices are female, the male perspective comes through as well—five chapter contributors and the co-editor are male. Their stories are especially impactful in both the specificity of their experiences and the tragedy of their noticeably reduced presence in gifted education.

Post-narrative Survey Summary

EACH NARRATIVE CHAPTER CONTRIBUTOR was invited to complete a post-narrative survey (see appendix C). This survey, designed to collect descriptive data that would assist in knowing and articulating the authors' perceptions after writing their narratives, provided invaluable and unpredictable information about the writing process—insights not initially expected by the editors. Questions asked on the post-narrative survey reflect what is currently known or missing about culturally diverse gifted experiences compared to mainstream (dominant group, often privileged and influential) gifted learners. The post-narrative survey items captured data that may not have been revealed in a freestyle writing exercise. In addition to demographic data, we asked the authors about perceptions of the writing process and current attitudes associated with writing about the systemically contested exclusion of culturally diverse students in gifted education.

Concerned about the toll such a personal and reflective writing experience might take, we asked if writing the narrative had changed their perspectives or feelings about being identified as gifted. Over half of the authors indicated that perceptions of their giftedness changed from "somewhat positive impact" to "big positive impact." This change represented nearly a 50 percent increase in positive perception.

We wanted to know if the authors currently hold a belief that children identified as gifted continue to apply their gifts, talents, and abilities in similar ways as they mature and become adults. Over half agreed or strongly agreed. The latter response may suggest that, from the author's perspective, the gifted label and/or experiences in childhood could be a highly functional, lifelong identity. However, most disagreed or strongly disagreed that gifted children from culturally different backgrounds (race, ethnicity, language barriers, etc.) are as successful in life as mainstream gifted children. Given the professional and educational successes of the contributors, these negative responses may suggest that despite individual successes, perceptions such as societal inequalities may interfere with culturally different gifted learners achieving in the same way as mainstream gifted learners. Such insights are first noted as young children in classrooms who recognize their underrepresentation in gifted programs.

We asked the respondents about the extent to which they agree or disagree with the statement, "I would be where I am today had I not been identified as gifted or participated in gifted and talented programs in my youth." Most disagreed or strongly disagreed. Over half agreed or strongly agreed that participating in gifted and talented programs taught them how to be competitive in the workplace and aspire toward advanced education. It is clear the gifted identity and select programs helped the authors navigate the terrain of being exceptional and culturally different. The contributors' telling narratives shed light on this sometimes painful process. One author's comment captures the depths to which this process was encouraging:

> Writing this chapter has been cathartic for me. I now know that the things experienced were not unique to me, they were what many [people] like me experienced. Learning this has allowed me to release the baggage of rejection and the insecurities which accompany it that I've carried for a long time.

When asked about the major obstacles for gifted children from culturally different backgrounds, most indicated poor academic advising as the biggest obstacle. The choices were: (1) not enough culturally different students in their classes, (2) overt racism, (3) micro-aggression, (4) lack of exposure to role models, (5) poor academic advising and guidance, (6) poor culturally responsive teaching, and (7) other—please indicate. Responses indicated that our chapter contributors perceived academic advising and guidance as more significant to their success than, for example, coping with overt racism or having a critical mass of gifted students in the classroom.

Interviews

IT WAS NOT INTENDED that *Running the Long Race in Gifted Education* become a research project. After all, its data come only from a small and non-randomly selected audience (the selected chapter authors) and cannot provide generalizations about the greater population. Rather, the intent is to uncover through the narratives and interviews, a body of knowledge missing in the published literature on gifted education, especially in relation to Black, Brown, and other culturally diverse (e.g., linguistically different, socioeconomically and educationally disadvantaged) men and women. For seventy-five or more years, highly regarded scholars of psychology, education, and other disciplines have published broadly and narrowly on equity and access paradigms for these groups, and such publications have exposed and introduced ground-breaking seminal conclusions about the education of gifted Black Americans. Those writings collectively led to broadening paradigms, thus welcoming topics such as cultural diversity, inclusion, cultural pluralism, and multicultural education (Baldwin, 1985; Banks & Banks, 2001; Castellano, & Frazier, 2011; Coleman, 2005; Ford, 1996; Frasier, 1991; Grantham, 2002; Harris & Ford, 1991; Henfield, 2012; Hilliard,1976; Hoover, et. al., 2007; Jenkins,1936; Lawson-Davis, 2010; Olszewski-Kubilius, 1994; Olszewski-Kubilius & Scott, 1992; Slaughter & Johnson, 1988; VanTassel-Baska, 2010; Witty & Jenkins, 1995). Likewise, research projects, published articles, conference presentations, colloquiums, and other venues have reported on IQ and other testing inequalities, underrepresentation in gifted programs, lack of culturally responsive teaching, deficit perspectives about cultural differences, language and linguistic differences, and poverty and race (Grantham, 2002).

We broadened this collection of knowledge and included interviews from culturally diverse individuals who may not have been impacted by deficit thinking. This strategic step also allowed us to include gifted adult learners for whom writing an in-depth narrative would not be feasible. To locate potential interviewees, narrative authors were invited to recommend persons they knew to be gifted, based on such factors as being in the same gifted education classroom, competing in a national, international, or regional competition, or giftedness in adulthood, as indicated by membership in certain intellectual societies, such as Mensa International.

The selection process included a telephone pre-screening, followed by a series of screening correspondences with one of the book's editors. The interviewer, a credentialed marriage and family therapist, structured interviews around a set of questions the editor formulated to capture themes and insights that surfaced from the narratives. Ultimately, five individuals were selected to write or co-write interviews. Two of the interviewees participated in full telephone interviews with the interviewer, and the three remaining were given an interview schedule, comprised mostly of the same open-ended questions used by the interviewer. The latter allowed for participant ethnography, although on a small scale, yet useful for case studies (see full interview in appendix B).

Interview questions included the following categories: giftedness in youth, fitting in/social isolation, family life, motivations, accomplishments, careers, and adult-identified giftedness (for those who became conclusively aware of their giftedness in adulthood). These categories would ultimately assist us in collecting data on emergent perspectives similar to what our narrative contributors revealed naturally and freely without such probing or leads.

References

Baldwin, A. Y. (1985). Programs for the gifted and talented: Issues concerning minority populations. In F. D. Horowitz & M. M. O'Brien (Eds.), *The gifted and talented: Developmental perspectives* (223–249). Washington, DC: American Psychological Association.

Banks, J. A., & Banks, J. A. (2001). *Cultural diversity and education: Foundations, curriculum, and teaching.* Boston, MA: Allyn and Bacon.

Castellano, J. A., & Frazier, A. D. (eds.). (2011). *Special populations in gifted education*. Waco,
TX: Prufrock Press.

Coleman, M. R. (2005). Academic strategies that work for gifted students with learning disabilities. *Twice Exceptional Children, 38*(1), 28–32.

Ford, D. Y. (1996). Reversing underachievement among gifted Black students: Promising practices and paradigms. New York: Teachers College Press.

Frasier, M. M. (1991). Disadvantaged and culturally diverse gifted students. *Journal for the Education of the Gifted, 14* (3), 234–245.

Grantham, T. C. (2002). Straight talk on the issue of under-representation: An interview with Dr. Mary M. Frasier, *Roeper Review: A Journal on Gifted Education, 24*, 50–51.

Harris III, J. J., & Ford, D. Y. (1991). Identifying and nurturing the promise of gifted Black students. *Journal of Negro Education, 60*(1), 3–18.

Henfield, M. S., & Washington, A. R. (2012). "I want to do the right thing but what is it?":
White teachers' experiences with African American students. *Journal of Negro Education*, 81(2), 148–161.

Hilliard, A. (1976). Alternatives to IQ testing: *An approach to the identification of gifted "minority" children (Final Report)*. Retrieved from ERIC database. (ED147009).

Hoover, J. J., Klingner, J. K., Baca, L. M., Patton, J. R. (2007). *Methods for teaching culturally and linguistically diverse exceptional learners*. Upper Saddle City, NJ: Prentice Hall.

Jenkins, M. D. (1936). A socio-psychological study of Negro children of superior intelligence. Journal of Negro Education, 5, 175–190.

Lawson-Davis, J. (2010). *Bright, talented, and Black: A guide for families of African American gifted learners*. Scottsdale, AZ: Great Potential Press.

National Association for Gifted Children (2014). *Definitions of Giftedness*. Retrieved from
http://www.nagc.org/resources-publications/resources/definitions-giftedness.

Olszewski-Kubilius, P. (1994). Social support systems and the disadvantaged gifted: A framework for developing programs and services. *Roeper Review, 17*(1), 20–25.

Olszewski-Kubilius, P. M., & Scott, J. M. (1992). An investigation of the college and career counseling needs of economically disadvantaged, minority gifted students, *The Roeper Review*, 14(3), 141–148.

Slaughter, D. T., & Johnson, D. J. (1988). Visible Now: Blacks in Private Schools (Contributions in Afro-American and African Studies). Westport, CT: Greenwood Publishing Group.

VanTassel-Baska, J. (2010) (Series Ed.) *Patterns and profiles of low income gifted learners.* Volume IV, *Critical Issues in Equity and Excellence in Gifted Education.* Waco, TX: Prufrock Press.

Witty, P., & Jenkins, M. D., (1935). The case of "B"—A gifted Negro girl. *Journal of Social Psychology, 6,* 117–124.

PART I

Identification and Participation in Gifted and Talented Programs

CHAPTER 1

"You Must Be a Genius!" Crafting a Viable Identity while Managing Competing Expectations and Self-Doubt

Traci English-Clarke, PhD

IN THIS CHAPTER, I chronicle my experience as an African-American girl who, along with my older sister, was identified as gifted and attended schools for gifted youth. I touch on issues of racial and academic identity development, discussing the impact of having a gifted older sibling, the role of family, teachers, and peers, and the differing expectations that I faced along the way. In addition to illustrating my personal journey, this narrative speaks to the importance of tailoring educational experiences to students' intellectual and social needs; it is imperative that we provide youth with individualized academic challenges and supports to help them develop the competencies that will serve them well throughout life.

Getting into Gifted Education Programs

MY PARENTS ARE RETIRED Chicago public school teachers, with my mother having taught at a classical school for several years when I was young. Because she had been teaching for a long time before we were born, my mother knew how the school system operated. She was aware that in Chicago at the time, elementary schools were organized in tiers: there were neighborhood schools, classical schools, and gifted schools. Gifted schools were geared towards children who were identified as gifted and talented, classical schools were intended for children who are considered academically advanced, and neighborhood schools were open to all children. Classical and gifted schools both provided an accelerated curriculum; gifted schools focused on enhancing creativity, critical thinking, reasoning, and problem solving, in addition to core subjects, whereas classical schools focused mainly on achievement in the core subject areas of literature, math, language arts, world language, and the humanities. Students had to take a test to get into the classical and gifted schools. The test for gifted schools measured cognitive abilities, including critical thinking skills, reasoning, and problem solving, whereas the test for classical schools measured academic achievement (CPS Office of Access and Enrollment, 2014b).

In order to be eligible to even apply to take the test for the gifted centers and classical schools, children have to score high on achievement tests: several years ago, classical schools accepted students whose test scores fell in the sixth and seventh stanines, and gifted schools accepted students with scores in the eighth and ninth stanines (English, T. M., personal communication). Stanines are bands that divide a normal distribution of scores into nine sections, so eighth and ninth stanines means that your score is in the top 11 percent of students who took the test; sixth and seventh stanines comprise the sixtieth to eighty-ninth percentiles. The CPS system uses deciles (ten-percentile bands) now, but the range is about the same: a child has to score in the ninetieth percentile or above in reading and math to qualify for placement in gifted and talented schools (Keller Regional Gifted Center, 2014).

As a result of her familiarity with the school system, when my mother realized my sister Tori (a pseudonym, like all other names of individuals in this chapter; school names are real) was ahead of most children her age, my mother had Tori tested for the gifted schools. Because Tori scored highly on the test, she was put on the list of students to be enrolled in a gifted school. However, because Tori had not yet been placed in a particular school by the time the school year began, my mom enrolled her in kindergarten at Gillespie Elementary, a neighborhood school. This school shared a principal with the school where my mom taught, so the principal knew of Tori's advanced academic abilities before she arrived—and agreed to a temporary placement until Tori could be moved to a gifted school. Tori had been reading since she was two and a half years old; as a result, her reading was much more advanced than the other children in this kindergarten class, most of whom probably could not read at all. Because Tori was academically so far ahead of the other kindergarten students, she was moved to a first grade class on the third day of school. On the fourth day, they moved her to a second grade class. Luckily for all involved, on the fifth day she was assigned a spot at Annie Keller Gifted Magnet Center (now Annie Keller Regional Gifted Center), so she attended Gillespie only for a week. At Keller, Tori was put in a class with children her own age with similar reading and math levels.

Two years later, when I was five years old, my mother had to decide where to send me for kindergarten. She had realized that I was academically advanced as well and had me tested for the gifted schools, but Keller had eliminated its kindergarten class so it now began at first grade. Thus, she enrolled me in a kindergarten class within a gifted program located at Ralph H. Metcalfe School, which was taught by Ms. Poplar. When I started there, my mother had every intention of transferring me to Keller for first grade so Tori and I could attend the same school, but somehow Poplar was unaware of this—and she became very upset at the end of that year when informed that I was leaving. I was told that she railed a bit against my mother in the style of a woman scorned, "I teach her how to read, and then you take her somewhere else!" Because I could read by the time I was three and a half years old, long before I started kindergarten, Poplar's attempt at using guilt to persuade my mother into keeping me at her school failed miserably. In hindsight, I can only imagine how I would have fared at a school where after nine months of being in her class for gifted students, my kindergarten teacher did not realize (or internalized, if she did know) that I could read quite well before she met me.

Tori and I both thrived at Keller, a small school serving first through sixth grades that had only one class (twenty-five to twenty-eight students) per grade and approximately 180 students overall in the school building in any given academic year. I was a very shy, quiet child who did not often volunteer answers in class—but when called upon, I almost always gave the right answer. I was also a compliant, well-behaved child, never causing trouble of any kind and never questioning authority. Because I was so quiet and acquiescent, it would have been very easy for teachers at a neighborhood school to overlook me when thinking about their brightest students. Tori, on the other hand, was much more outgoing and vocal, and thus her academic talents would have likely been recognized in any school setting as extraordinary and worth cultivating. Because the teachers at the gifted schools are specifically trained to work with gifted students, they recognized both Tori's and my potential and had strategies to develop it, even despite our differences in personality that resulted in differences in the visibility of our strengths.

The Lesser of Two Prodigies

My sister Tori was very precocious: she talked a little with meaning at six months of age, learned to read by two and a half years, and started taking violin lessons at the age of three. As a result, many people thought of her as a prodigy, a genius. What this meant is that I was automatically subjected to extremely high expectations because in the eyes of my parents and extended family, my sister's accomplishments became the standard. At the same time, other people who knew us had lower expectations for me because there was no way that Tori and I could both be prodigies, right? And since I tended to present a reserved façade until I felt extremely comfortable in a situation, I did not share my skills and talents as readily as Tori did; as a result, people perceived that I must not be as smart or talented as my sister.

As an adult, I delved deeper into my mother's recollection of my experience of learning to read and discovered that, in fact, nobody really knows how or when I learned to read. Apparently I slept a lot as a baby, so my mom had a lot of time to work with the then two-year-old Tori and teach her to read. When I was two years old, my mom went back to work, so Tori and I started nursery school. Although my mom (and Tori) read to me in the evenings, my mom didn't have the same kind of time to teach me to read as she had had when Tori was younger. However, she recalls that at some point when I was about three years old, she informally tested me to see if I knew how to read any of the words in her coffee can (she had written about 280 words on index cards for Tori and stored them in a coffee can, so she used those words to assess whether I could read at two and a half also). I could read about seventy-five of the words at that point. Shortly after I turned four, I told my mom that I wanted to learn how to read that summer. She tested me again, and I could already read all the words in the can—without anyone having explicitly taught me any of them. So most likely I learned how to read at the age of three and a half simply by osmosis: my mother and sister read to me frequently, and I managed to figure it out from listening and observing them. It is possible to conclude that a three-and-a-half-year-old learning to read by osmosis is at least as impressive as learning to read at two and a half with lots of adult instruction. However, the narrative that was reified and told to family members and strangers was that Tori learned to read at two and a half years old. Because that narrative did not include my experience, it implied that my reading trajectory was typical of most children. In this way, Tori was positioned as the prodigy, and I was just the younger sister of the prodigy.

At home, my accomplishments were judged by my sister's accomplishments—literally. My mother compared everything about our academic and musical development at a given age: test scores, grades, violin-playing abilities, musical ear, AP classes taken during high school, spelling and writing ability, math ability, etc. For better or worse, every year when we got the results of our standardized tests, my mother would pull out my sister's test results from two years before and compare my scores to Tori's old scores. My grades were compared to her grades from two years before. My musical abilities and proclivities were compared to hers, although there was no objective way to assess much of this. Unfortunately, I never seemed to quite measure up; although I typically scored in the ninety-fifth percentile or higher on standardized tests, my scores were always just a little lower than Tori's. I read at an early age too—but an entire year later than Tori did. I didn't sing as well or play violin as well as she did. Hence, my comparatively inadequate achievements became my personal narrative: I always thought of myself as not quite as smart as Tori. Because I never quite measured up, I rejected the notion that I should try to compete with her; instead I just tried as hard as I could academically and musically. As long as I had tried my best in the areas that mattered to me, I was satisfied with the outcome.

Because of the constant comparisons (and the fact that we attended the same schools), I found that once Tori had graduated from our school and moved onto another school, I came out of my shell, found my voice, and flourished. I felt free to pursue whatever opportunities I wanted—I didn't have to appear to follow in her footsteps anymore and could just be myself. Our teachers could still make comparisons, but because I was a quiet, well-behaved, high-achieving student, they typically perceived me in a positive light. Because Tori attended Keller as well and she was my sole reference point, I did not really compare myself academically to my classmates until after she graduated from Keller. It was around this time (I was in fifth grade) that I began to realize I was among the top two or three students in my class at Keller. All of a sudden I looked around at my classmates and could only identify one or two others who scored anywhere near me on grades or standardized tests in any subject. I realized that my fellow students didn't necessarily have the same kind of educational experiences at home that I did, such as my mom giving us multiplication tests on weekends and presenting us with math word problems to solve on the way home from school, or an older sibling who could help with homework, so I didn't attribute my relative academic success solely to my own intellectual prowess.

On one hand, I was outperforming the other students in my class at Keller, and on the other hand, I still didn't measure up to Tori's academic performance. But I didn't feel smarter than the other students in my class—I recall thinking that maybe they just didn't pay as close attention in class or that they didn't spend as much time studying or thinking about academic subjects as I did. In fact, I don't remember ever spending a significant amount of time or energy comparing myself academically to anyone with lower grades and/or test scores than I had—I tended to compare myself primarily to people who were outperforming me (even if those people were in a higher grade or attended a different school). I had developed an orientation to look upwards in addition to evaluating whether I had done my best, rather than to look down from a lofty perch, gloating about the number of people that I had surpassed. The downside to this sort of orientation is that the feeling of success is fleeting, as—in the world that I was exposed to at home and through the schools I attended—there was always someone doing better than I was. The benefit of this orientation is that it kept me humble and always gave me something more to strive for, regardless of what I had already achieved. In this way, it has served me well.

Diversity at Keller

KELLER IS A VERY DIVERSE SCHOOL; although it is located in the Mount Greenwood neighborhood (which is a primarily White area) on the Southwest Side of Chicago, it is a magnet school that pulls students from across the city who live in a variety of neighborhoods, ranging from the racially diverse to more homogenous ethnic and racial enclaves. The student population is not monolithic in any sense; in my class were Blacks, White Americans, Latinos, and Asian American students. As a result, I did not associate intelligence with certain races, as I could see firsthand that there were smart people of various races. Additionally, the teachers at the school were racially diverse, even though the administrators and office personnel were all White.

However, Keller's diversity did not mean that it was immune from racism. For example, my mother told me about how a few students taunted (or bullied) a dark-skinned Black friend of mine—they repeatedly called her a gorilla while riding with her on a school bus. I never found out whether the perpetrators were Black or another race or whether the school did anything to address the issue, but it certainly was a horrible experience of anti-Black racism for our friend. Unfortunately, she eventually left the school as a result of these incidents.

Despite its focus on gifted students, Keller was also not immune from academic issues that plague many schools, such as teacher preparation. One day during a fourth grade math lesson, my teacher, Mr. Elm, was trying to teach us how to do long division. In the course of the lesson, he admitted that he wasn't sure if it was right—he had never learned how to do long division. Luckily for me, my mother was a math teacher, so I made sure to ask her when I got home from school that day—and she was easily able to teach me everything I needed to know about long division. Although Elm was good at teaching many other topics, his math knowledge was not sufficient to help us to learn math ourselves. Math content knowledge may have been an issue for other teachers at Keller as well; to alleviate the problem, the school hired a math specialist teacher, Ms. Oak, the next year to teach math to all the upper grades (three through six).

With her creative and energetic teaching style, Oak quickly became my favorite teacher. I could tell that Oak really liked me and thought I was smart. She loved math and made everything fun—and along with my mother, Oak helped to sustain my love of math and to develop in me a strong math knowledge base that formed the foundation for my future work.

Beyond Keller: The Transition to Seventh Grade and Beyond

BECAUSE KELLER WAS A kindergarten-through-sixth-grade school at the time (it now extends to eighth grade), we had to change schools after sixth grade. Our main options were the Academic Center programs, selective enrollment for seventh and eighth grade programs located at a handful of high schools in the city. Academic Center programs serve gifted and talented students, providing an accelerated college preparatory program that enables students to amass high school credits before entering ninth grade. Thus, students who have attended Academic Centers are one or two years ahead of the prescribed curriculum upon beginning high school (Chicago Public Schools Office of Access and Enrollment website, 2014). For example, Academic Center students take ninth grade language arts, algebra, biology, etc. in eighth grade, and language courses like Spanish I (typically taken in ninth grade or later) as seventh graders. This accelerated curriculum allows students to either graduate from high school in three years or take several AP courses in many different subjects during the traditional four years of high school. It provides a significant advantage either way because colleges look favorably upon high AP scores and challenging courses, and if a student wants simply to be done with high school after three years and officially start college a year early, he or she can easily do just that because of the high school credits earned during seventh and eighth grades.

Keller Gifted Magnet Center was considered a feeder school for Morgan Park High School's Academic Center program. I think the reason for this relationship was proximity: Morgan Park was the closest high school with a seventh and eighth grade Academic Center program. Morgan Park was a good school, but it was certainly not one of the best schools in the city. It is currently ranked sixtieth in the state of Illinois and has a Silver ranking from *U.S. News and World Report* (*U.S. News & World Report*, 2014b). Unlike several other Academic Centers in the Chicago Public Schools system, Morgan Park's Academic Center program is currently not ranked in the top fifty middle school programs in the state of Illinois (FitzPatrick, Golab, and Schlikerman, 2014). Keller's faculty at the time were so focused on funneling us into Morgan Park that when informing students about the test for all of the city's seventh and eighth grade Academic Center programs, they referred to it as "the test to get into Morgan Park." It was just assumed that we would go there after graduating from Keller, even though Keller was a magnet school, so other middle schools might have been closer to students' homes and several other schools in the city had better reputations and more challenging programs.

Because my mother was a CPS teacher she knew a lot about the options for our seventh and eighth grade education—in fact, she informed my sister and me of our right to go elsewhere when the Keller faculty presented no other educational options and portrayed the seventh and eighth grade test as serving only for admittance into Morgan Park's Academic Center program. Our mother, however, decided we were going to the Academic Center at Whitney M. Young Magnet High School when we were accepted—we were given no other choice. Yes, all our school friends were going to Morgan Park, and it was also closer to our house, but that did not matter to my mom—Whitney Young was a much better school, and that was that.

In hindsight, that was one of the best decisions my mom ever made for us. In the 1990s, Whitney Young was considered the best public high school in the city, and its Academic Center was considered the best middle school program in the city. In recent years, a few new Chicago public schools have provided some competition, but Whitney M. Young Magnet High School is still considered an elite, top-ranked school. It was recently ranked number four in the state (*U.S. News & World Report*, 2014), nine in the country (*Business Insider*, 2014) and its Academic Center has been repeatedly ranked number one in the state by the *Chicago Sun Times* (Selective Prep, 2014). The Academic Center curriculum was accelerated and rigorous, and although it provided a challenge, we had been well prepared to achieve in this type of environment.

As you might imagine, Tori and I enjoyed a fair amount of privilege—our parents, although first-generation college students, both attained master's degrees and were able to earn a decent wage. Because of their jobs as teachers, they had significant knowledge about the Chicago Public Schools system. As a result, they were aware they could get us tested for gifted programs, valued the affordances of being identified as gifted, and had intimate knowledge about the advantages and disadvantages of attending certain schools. They knew that in order for us to be competitive as college applicants, we needed to take lots of honors and AP classes and become involved in various extracurricular activities. Although many other students at Keller and Whitney Young were the children of teachers and other professionals, some of our fellow students were not from middle-class backgrounds and thus did not enjoy these same advantages.

One special challenge at Whitney Young was that in addition to being quiet and shy, I was very soft-spoken. In seventh grade, I was in a math class with other "Ackies" (as the students in the Academic Center were affectionately called), taught by a man named Mr. Aspen. He basically took it upon himself to try to get me to speak up more in class by acting as though he couldn't hear me when I gave answers to his questions. Aspen would stand next to my desk and tell me that he still couldn't hear me. It reached the point where every time he called on me, he would end up telling me to shout out my responses. It was frustrating at the time, because I could hear myself quite clearly so I thought everyone else could hear me too—and I became self-conscious about it because I was repeating myself over and over again in an attempt to get him to "hear" me. Other students got into the act as well, telling me to shout during that class when I was sure that they had heard me just fine. Somehow I didn't feel silenced or discouraged from offering answers in his class—after all, it seemed as if he really wanted to hear what I had to say. Oddly enough, no other teacher ever seemed to have such a problem hearing me. In retrospect, I wonder whether he had embarked on a covert mission to build in me the confidence to loudly assert my opinions and to see them as worth hearing by everyone.

My seventh and eighth grade and high school years seemed fairly normal to me—probably because I was among other students who were just like me in terms of academic achievement. During high school, however, there was definitely a sense that we were different from the regular admittance students at the school. Being a former Ackie was seen as something special within the school because it was a highly selective accelerated program within a larger high school that was also accelerated. But because there were so many of us (both Ackie and non-Ackie) taking advanced classes, it was relatively easy to blend in among like-minded peers. Because it was a selective enrollment school for which applicants had to score above a certain point to be considered for admission, even the regular tracked students at Whitney Young were more academically oriented, on average, than regular students at most neighborhood high schools.

Although I think I started seventh grade in the middle of the pack (I'm guessing I was ranked between forty and fifty out of one hundred students upon arrival—there were no official class ranks at that grade, so it's a little unclear where I stood), by the end of eighth grade I had decided I could do better. I concluded that I was at least as smart as some of those people who were doing better than I was, so I challenged myself to get the best grades I could in order to rise to a class rank that accurately reflected my abilities. This meant that I could afford to take only honors and AP classes during high school (except for gym and art). My eighth grade social studies teacher placed me in regular world history class for ninth grade, and before the school year began, I was worried that it would be a bad fit, even though I didn't like studying history—and I was right. The other students seemed to be disinterested in learning and typically were not very attentive during class. There was no lively productive discussion as in my other classes, and it was annoying that the teacher (who taught my sister in AP history that same year) had to devote energy and time to managing the handful of people who made it abundantly clear that they didn't want to be there. My perception was that this disengagement was fairly standard for regular level classes (and perhaps for honors level classes at many public schools). Additionally, because it was a regular level class, it was going to bring down my GPA even if I earned an A; to earn a high rank in my class, I could not afford to take regular level social studies for another year. Needless to say, I made sure that I worked hard so the teacher placed me into honors level for my tenth grade social studies class, and I never took another regular level class again.

Whitney Young—The High School Experience

AS A LIGHT-SKINNED BLACK who is often assumed to have one White parent, I felt unsure of my racial identity in high school. At the time, Whitney Young was a 60-40 school: 60 percent Black, 40 percent other races. Most of the Black students were middle-class, as were we, but somehow I was not able to relate to them culturally. I had a very literal view of race categorization at the time; although I was aware of my family's extensive racial mixture, I didn't realize that most Blacks are racially mixed (Gates, 2013), so I was unsure of whether the label of Black accurately described us. We lived in a predominately Black neighborhood and, like most other Black families, emphasized close relationships with immediate and extended family. However, my nuclear family engaged in extracurricular activities that are typically associated with European American culture, such as playing classical violin and listening to classical and soft rock music. We did not listen to hip-hop or rap, even though they were starting to develop into mainstream genres at the time and were very popular among our peers. Unlike many of the parents of Whitney Young students, my parents refused to buy trendy name-brand clothes and bags, so we had difficulty relating in these superficial ways to many of our middle-class Black school peers. I recall distinctly feeling race-less and culture-less during this time, a feeling that many Whites report when asked about their racial identity (McDermott and Samson, 2005). So while a majority of students at my school were high achieving, middle-class Blacks, I didn't particularly feel as though I fit in with them—and while I knew I wasn't White, Latina, Arab American, or Asian American, I didn't feel as if I was Black either.

How does this relate to being gifted? I took almost all honors and AP classes in high school.[1] There were several other Blacks in these classes as well, so I didn't have the sense of being "the only African American in the room." Likewise, the culture at Whitney Young is focused on achievement, so I faced no ostracism for taking honors and AP classes (Tyson, Darity, & Castellino, 2005). However, in the only regular-level class I took (the ninth grade world history class), all the students were Black. That was probably the only class I took (in my entire schooling experience) in which all of the students were Black. And even though some of those students had been in my seventh and eighth grade program (for gifted students), it seemed to me that they had decided to

participate in the culture of underachievement, disruption, and disengagement that manifested itself in that class . . . and I couldn't wait to
move up to a (racially diverse) honors class where the students were
actually trying to learn. Thus, it seems as though I had internalized negative academic stereotypes about Black students, and perhaps my fellow
students had as well. But because of how I conceived my racial identity
at the time and the overall school culture, I didn't feel that I needed to
perform that stereotype—instead, I felt it just didn't apply to me. This
type of experience is not uncommon among Blacks in majority-Black
schools and other school contexts (Spencer et al., 2003; Tyson, Darity,
& Castellino, 2005).

By the end of senior year, I was ranked thirteenth in my class of
499. Somehow, though, I didn't really think about the proportional
meaning of such a rank or the number of people behind me—I only
compared my numerical rank to my sister's rank two years prior and
that of the twelve people ahead of me. My sister was in her second year
at Harvard (along with four of her Whitney Young classmates—all former Ackies), and I just knew that I wasn't as smart as she was. After all,
at the end of my junior year, I was ranked fifteenth, and she had been
ranked eighth at that point; it was clear to me that I was not going to
get into Harvard. I had gotten straight As only once while at Whitney
Young, and I perceived that I was nowhere near as talented, academically or musically, as my sister. I aimed my sights at Brown University
instead (of course Brown isn't an inferior school, but I felt it was more
in line with my particular record of excellence).

While I was fairly certain that I had a good chance to be admitted
to Brown (through comparing my GPA and standardized test scores
with the average GPA and scores earned by Brown students), other students at my school did not necessarily think I was smart enough to
be admitted to this Ivy League school. During senior year, after I had
received my acceptance to Brown, one of my fellow former Ackies came
up to me one day and asked incredulously, "*You* got into Brown?" I
experienced this comment as a racial micro-aggression, a small, subtle,
verbal expression of racist ideology that can have a negative psychological effect on the person experiencing it (Sue, Capodilupo, & Holder,
2007). Even though this particular student, a White male, was very
smart, he had spent a significant amount of time during our high school

years smoking pot outside the school instead of working as hard as he could in school. I took his question to mean that he was surprised I had gotten into Brown because he had not and he thought I was intellectually inferior to him. However, because I had already been accepted and because I thought there was no way that he could have possibly gotten into Brown due to his less than stellar academic record, I was able to shrug it off and not really let it bother me.

In the end, I decided to apply to Harvard just to see if I could get in. I had no intention of actually going because I really didn't think I would get in, and I was convinced that Brown was the best fit for me. Even when I did get into Harvard, I didn't really think I would go (this probably had to do with doubting whether I would do well there). It was only upon visiting Brown and feeling as if I didn't belong there that I considered Harvard as a viable option. I had applied to only three schools total, and the other school, Williams College, was just too small for my liking (it was smaller than my high school, so I would always be on display and could never fade into the background to observe, as I enjoy doing sometimes). As a result, Harvard turned out to be my only viable option. But what an option!

Off to Harvard

Harvard was a fascinating and sobering experience. Incoming students took a placement test in math upon arrival, for which they instructed us ahead of time not to study. So over the summer, I didn't study or review any of the math concepts that I had learned during twelfth grade. I later came to realize that what they meant by "don't study" was really, "don't try to learn any new material." I scored borderline on the placement test, meaning that I could either take the remedial calculus course or take the standard freshman math course, Math 1a. After some discussion with my advisor and with the instructor of the remedial calculus course, I decided that it could only benefit me to take the remedial course. Now keep in mind that I had scored a 5 on the exam for my AP Calculus BC class in twelfth grade (and I remember mentioning this fact to my advisor and the instructor when talking to her to decide what to do). By two weeks into the semester, I realized that the remedial course was going to be a waste of my time, but it was too late at that point to switch to Math 1a. So I remained in the remedial calculus course and devised a plan to take Math 1b, the next course in the sequence, the next semester. The main problem with this plan was that I didn't have the same math preparation as those who had taken Math 1a, so I was at an extreme disadvantage. The other problem was that my section of Math 1b was taught by an East Asian graduate student with a very strong accent. There were some words he said that I never deciphered and others (unfortunately very common words in calculus, like derivative) that I only decoded towards the end of the semester. I was too shy to ask this instructor to clarify or repeat himself, as well as to ask for help from any other source, so I resigned myself to trying to learn two semesters' worth of math at once—primarily from the textbook. I managed to pass the class, but I didn't do very well. And the next year, I decided that since math classes were bringing down my GPA and I didn't need them for my major (sociology) anyway, I would just stop taking them, even though I loved math.

In hindsight, if I had consulted my older sister before making a decision about my freshman year math courses, I would have taken Math 1a without hesitation. Math was the only subject in which I had always done better than my sister, and she took Math 1a as a freshman—so if I had talked to her about it or taken her experience into consideration, I would never have taken the remedial calculus course. And quite frankly, I wonder whether the advice from the math instructor and my advisor were based on low expectations of me as a Black woman from a public high school—even though I had scored a 5 on the AP Calculus BC exam, the harder of two AP options, the previous spring. The AP tests are nationally standardized, so a 5 on the AP test meant that I did very well compared to everyone else in the country who took this college-level course. My hesitation in making this decision was based on my self-doubts about my intelligence, especially relative to the other Harvard students—and the advice from my advisor and the math instructor confirmed my own self-doubt. I may have been unconsciously trying not to confirm the negative stereotype about Black students' academic underperformance, but by not taking Math 1a (for which I worried that I was underprepared), I took the remedial class followed by Math 1b, for which I *was* then underprepared because I had not taken Math 1a. By trying to avoid confirming the stereotype, I made decisions that created a situation in which I would confirm the negative stereotype at a later point (Steele, 1997).

Societal beliefs about the academic inferiority of Black students (and of students from inner-city public schools) may have exacerbated my preexisting self-doubt during my first year at Harvard. Many of my fellow students had attended elite preparatory schools and/or boarding schools, and even some of the Black students had had this type of secondary school experience that prepared them for an elite education. Although my school was the premier public school in Chicago, the expectations were that my education was not quite the same (or as good) as at an East Coast prep school. Meanwhile, although my combined highest SAT math and verbal scores were about average for Harvard undergrads, each of my total SAT scores was lower than the Harvard average. In doubting my qualifications, I also hypothesized that I had received extra consideration by the admissions committee because my sister was a student there. However, when I shared this theory with Tori, she disagreed with me, as she knew that at least two of her classmates had siblings who did not get admitted. Ironically, the math class debacle showed me that I was no less smart or academically prepared than other Harvard students—my math preparation as an incoming first-year student was on par with most other first-year students, and I was intellectually capable enough to earn a passing grade in a math class despite significant barriers to my success. So, it affirmed that I belonged at Harvard.

At the start of my first semester of college, my mom told me not to expect to get As in my classes. When asking her later why she had given me that advice, she said that it was because of my older half-sister's experience at a community college: she expected to get As and didn't, and she was so disappointed and discouraged that she ended up dropping out. Additionally, my sister Tori was very accustomed to getting As so was quite disappointed when she did not get all As in her first year at Harvard. In my mom's attempt to make sure I was not setting unrealistic expectations for myself (or setting myself up for failure), she created even more self-doubt within me. In my mind, her statement conveyed a belief that I was not smart enough to get As at Harvard. While I was not completely discouraged by this message, I recall not trying as hard as I could have in my classes during my first semester. However, at the conclusion of the first semester, I realized that I could have worked harder in my classes, and I was able to take the feedback I received from my professors and apply it in future classes. As a result, I earned better grades every semester during college and even graduated with honors— an accomplishment (however common at an Ivy League school in the 1990s, due to widespread grade inflation) that I thought impossible after receiving my first semester grades. As Tori had graduated without honors, this provided a significant boost to my academic sense of self.

The H Factor

BEING A HARVARD GRADUATE comes with one distinct disadvantage: the H-bomb. Known to shut down conversations and intimidate potential suitors (especially among underrepresented minorities), the H-bomb is the mere expression of the identity of your alma mater: telling someone that you attended Harvard. When asked the dreaded question, "Where did you go to college?" most of my fellow Harvard graduates skirt around the issue, demurring, "In Boston" or "In Massachusetts." I, however, come right out and say it nonchalantly: "Oh, I went to Harvard." After a two- or three-second pause during which the person is usually trying to decide whether he or she heard me correctly (and for some folks, whether I meant to say Howard), most people are impressed . . . at which point I typically downplay its significance or divert the conversation away from Harvard, occasionally saying something like, "It's just a school like any other school." I have found that people dwell more on the H-bomb when given the demurred name-dodge (which almost always results in a follow-up question and hence more focus on the name) than if I answer the question directly. Most people who went to other colleges don't skirt around the topic when asked where they went to college, so I don't either. If it intimidates others, that's their problem. I go in with the assumption that they can handle it—and I don't mind informing them of the range of diversity among Harvard grads.

Aside from the silence and awe, people sometimes express surprise when I tell them I went to Harvard. Admitted to such an esteemed institution, I have never had anyone outwardly doubt my ability to succeed, for example, saying, as a White co-worker did to my sister once, "Did you *graduate?*" but people have told me that I'm not what they expect. Apparently Harvard grads are typically thought of as a pretentious, White, male, wealthy lot who reference their Harvard experience at every opportunity. Hence some people are taken aback to hear that I—this quiet, unassuming Black woman who almost never refers to Harvard by name unless making a specific point for which its reference is essential—am one of "them."

Every once in a while, people are a little star-struck by the name, saying, "You must be a genius!" This comment is especially tough to stomach because I have met some geniuses, and I'm certainly not one. Generally, I think of geniuses as rare, outstanding people like Albert Einstein, Benjamin Franklin, Mozart, Michael Jackson, Martin Luther King Jr.—people who have an amazing talent or skill that makes them stand out among others in history. (I would definitely consider one or two of my fellow Harvard classmates to be geniuses, and I would also consider one particular friend of mine—a professional musician who plays the clarinet with such deep clarity and emotion that listening to his music sends chills down my spine—to be a genius as well.) I, on the other hand, may be good at many things, but there are so many others like me in the world—and so many who are better than I am—that I don't feel special in the least. Maybe if I had not attended school at every level with other bright, gifted individuals, I might have felt like a genius. But when I compare myself to the other people around me, I seem average.

My success in college definitely boosted my self-confidence, at least for a while. During graduate school, those familiar self-doubts started to creep up again. Even after earning my PhD in education from another Ivy League institution, the University of Pennsylvania, I tend to think of myself as being only of average intelligence, and as a result, I sometimes feel I am not as smart as most others in my field. This "imposter phenomenon" is a common and well-documented occurrence among high-achieving women, and several researchers have investigated this phenomenon among Blacks and other underrepresented minorities, especially in higher education (Clance & Imes, 1978; Ewing et al., 1996; Holmes et al., 1993; Trotman, 2009).

To some extent, I have created situations in which my self-doubt flourishes. Instead of pursuing an academic career immediately after earning my PhD, I took a few years off to raise two beautiful children as a stay-at-home mom. As a result, during that time, I thought of myself as just a stay-at-home mom, which was not commensurate with my achievements or training—and was not personally fulfilling, despite being a wonderful, enlightening bonding experience. Some people are cut out to be stay-at-home parents; I am not one of them. To feel good about myself again, I had to go back to work in my field. I am now embarking on the journey back into academia and rebuilding a professional sense of self. Maybe one day I will see myself as gifted, but for now I'm just the low woman on the totem pole . . . and as a result of being identified early as gifted, my high-status education has provided me with the means to move up.

Conclusion

I THINK THAT, given my personality, I definitely benefited from receiving a gifted education, one that was designed to support and challenge me intellectually while exposing me to others with similar capabilities. For me, it was useful to have the experience of being a big fish in a small pond, which then emptied into a large pond with other big fish. Suddenly I didn't feel so big anymore, which provided me with the challenge to perform at an even higher level because I was competing with others who were just as smart as I was, if not smarter. If I had remained in schools where I was consistently the highest ranked student, I might not have realized that there was more that I could do, that I could work even harder and perform at an even higher level. Because of my exposure to others with similar (and greater) academic prowess, I challenged myself to complete things I had never even considered before then, much less thought I could do. Although my self-confidence is still probably not commensurate with my reality, it has been built up over time by repeatedly experiencing success in the face of challenge.

My mother, by enrolling Tori and me in gifted schools as well as insisting that we go to the schools that would most benefit us academically, had a major impact on our trajectories and separated us from our peers to a large extent. Her position as a teacher afforded her certain kinds of knowledge that privileged us in our academic lives, as well as prepared us to attain a high level of education. While we were growing up, she frequently told us that, because we were smarter than she was, we should go further than she had in school—so she also set an academic bar for us based on her perception of our abilities compared to her own. She then tried her best to guide us toward the opportunities that would help us to rise to the challenge, and by saving and investing their modest incomes, my parents created the financial means for us to aim for the stars without being constrained by financial considerations. This amazing combination of supports that my parents put into place for us allowed us to reach our potential—and provided us with an advantage that was rare even among children of middle-class backgrounds.

Being put in schools where I was not always the top performer challenged me to try harder, to do better, and to push the boundaries of what I (and others who knew me as a child) thought I could do. The success that I experienced in gifted schools encouraged me to try my best to succeed academically, even though I did not measure up to the standards that my sister had set. The combination of these two aspects laid the groundwork to attend two Ivy League universities and to earn an advanced degree—as well as to examine the supports that enabled me to get to this point. Therefore in my research, I focus on the challenges and supports (including cultural and family influences) that affect math learning, especially among Blacks. My goal, both as a researcher and as a parent of two young sons, is to build on the strengths of our children, our families, and our communities in order to challenge our youth to achieve to their highest potential.

As an education researcher who focuses on math education, I have heard differing opinions about gifted education. Some of my colleagues argue that every child deserves an excellent educational experience and that gifted and high-achieving children can be served adequately in inclusive classrooms and schools by providing them with the opportunity to teach other students what they know about various topics in small discussion groups. While I agree wholeheartedly that every child deserves rich and challenging educational experiences, I argue that it is important to ensure that we provide a challenge to those youth who want and need to be challenged academically and can handle the challenge. While youth typically considered underperforming can benefit from exposure to more advanced peers, so too can youth who are already academically successful, as well as those who have advanced critical thinking skills, reasoning, problem solving, and mental control. I argue that we should continue to push all youth beyond what they know and are able to do currently, rather than simply reinforcing the knowledge and skills that gifted and high-achieving youth already have. In educating all youth to reach their potential, it is our responsibility to ensure that we cultivate the skills and challenge the capabilities of all of our youth, even those at the top. In providing additional academic challenges to youth with outstanding capabilities, we may push them to achieve at even higher levels, and thereby maximize the capabilities of our society as a whole.

Notes

1. At Whitney Young and many other high schools, honors and AP classes are given extra weight in GPA calculations in order to encourage students to challenge themselves instead of taking easy classes in which they know they will get As. At Whitney Young, a grade of C in an AP class and a grade of B in an honors class are both equivalent to a grade of A in a regular-level class.

References

Chicago Public Schools Office of Access and Enrollment. (2014). *Selective enrollment elementary schools: Academic centers*. Retrieved from http://www.cpsoae.org/apps/pages/index.jsp?uREC_ID=72695&type=d&termREC_ID=&pREC_ID=151354.

Chicago Public Schools Office of Access and Enrollment. (2014b). *Selective enrollment elementary schools: General questions*. Retrieved from http://cpsoae.org/apps/pages/index.jsp?uREC_ID=72695&type=d&termREC_ID=&pREC_ID=121684.

Clance, P. R., & Imes, S. A. (1978). The imposter phenomenon in high achieving women: Dynamics and therapeutic intervention. *Psychotherapy: Theory, Research & Practice, 15(3)*, 241–247.

Ewing, K. M., Richardson, T. Q., James-Myers, L., & Russell, R. K. (1996). The relationship between racial identity attitudes, worldview, and African American graduate students' experience of the imposter phenomenon. *Journal of Black Psychology, 22(1)*, 53–66.

FitzPatrick, L., Golab, A., & Schlikerman, B. (2014, October 31). Chicago dominates top of state list with elite schools, with a catch. *Chicago Sun-Times*. Retrieved from http://chicagosuntimes.

com/news/chicago-dominates-top-of-state-list-with-elite-schools-with-a-catch/.

Gates, H. L. (2013, February 11). Exactly how 'Black' is Black America? *The Root.* Retrieved from http://www.theroot.com/articles/history/2013/02/how_mixed_are_african_americans.1.html.

Holmes, S. W., Kertay, L., Adamson, L. B., Holland, C. L., & Clance, P. R. (1993). Measuring the imposter phenomenon: A comparison of Clance's IP scale and Harvey's I-P scale. *Journal of Personality Assessment, 60(1)*, 48–59.

Keller Regional Gifted Center. (2014). *About page.* Retrieved from http://www.keller.cps.k12.il.us/about.html.

McDermott, M., & Samson, F. (2005). White racial and ethnic identity in the United States. *Annual Review of Sociology, 31*, 245–261.

Selective Prep (2014). *Whitney young academic center profile.* Retrieved from https://selectiveprep.com/6th-grade-program/academic-center-profiles/whitney-young.html.

Spencer, M. B., Cross, W. E., Harpalani, V., & Goss, T. N. (2003). Historical and developmental perspectives on Black academic achievement: Debunking the "acting White" myth and posing new directions for research. In C. C. Yeakey (Ed.) *Surmounting all odds: Education, opportunity and society in the new millennium* (273–304). Greenwich, CT: Information Age Publishers.

Steele, C. (1997). A threat in the air: How stereotypes shape intellectual identity and performance. *American Psychologist, 52(6)*, 613–629.

Sue, D. W., Capodilupo, C. M., & Holder, A. M. B. (2008). Racial microaggressions in the life experience of Black Americans. *Professional Psychology: Research and Practice. 39(3)*, 329–336.

Trotman, F. K. (2009). The imposter phenomenon among African American women in U.S. institutions of higher education: Implications for counseling. In G. R. Walz, J. C. Bleuer, & R. K. Yep (Eds.), *Compelling counseling interventions: VISTAS 2009* (77–87). Alexandria, VA: American Counseling Association.

Tyson, K., Darity Jr., W., and Castellino, D. R. (2005). It's not "a Black thing": Understanding the burden of acting white and other dilemmas of high achievement. *American Sociological Review, 70*, 582–605.

U.S. News & World Report. (2014). *Whitney M. Young Magnet High School overview.* Retrieved from http://www.usnews.com/education/best-high-schools/illinois/districts/chicago-public-schools/whitney-m-young-magnet-high-school-6551?int=c0b4c1.

CHAPTER 2

Ballad for a GhettoNerd: Growing Up Too Black and Too Smart

Marquis Bey, PhD Candidate

IF "THEY"—THAT EVER-PRESENT SPECTER of ethereal and unlocatable authority—were to write a book about me, I'd demand that it go something like this:

> Once upon a nowhere,
> There was a quiet kid with too much on his
> mind.
> Too many thoughts too big for most—
> so he kept them inside, hoping
> one day to unleash those words
> on everyone who thought he had nothing to say.
> Those words that could one day carve hieroglyphics
> in stones and erect golden pyramids of unspoken
> revolutions, so
> quiet as they're kept
> in lock-jawed dormancy waiting

for that Toussaint-type rebellious uprising
those words
rising up,
in a tide of Black ghetto intelligentsia
caught between
Philly slang and Ivory Tower.

I was always the smart one in my family and my social circles. In my early years, it was usually a mark of a peculiar penchant for silence and cogitation that caused others either to remark that I needed to talk more or to avoid me altogether. From the beginning, my life of the mind and the premium I placed on my intellect—that is, my ability to think deeply—was constantly perceived as inconsistent with how I was supposed to behave. Something was always off about me. Gradually, I came to understand.

I grew up in Philadelphia, Pennsylvania, in a working-class home. I lived with my mother, a stern, working woman with the bark of a rabid dog and a bite to back it up; my grandmother, a quiet, simple, arthritic woman who needs only a bag of potato chips and *General Hospital* to be content with her life; and my brother, three and a half years my senior and the epitomization of street-smart and girl-crazy. (I leave out my nine-year-old sister intentionally only because she was not around for the early years of my life.) Although unique and eclectic, my family was not a beacon for much intellectual stimulation.

To give an accurate depiction of the formative folks in my life, I cannot confine myself only to my immediate household. My father has played a special role in contributing to my giftedness, namely my love of words. While my father never married my mother and never lived with me under the same roof, I have been close with him since my birth. Spending each weekend and major holiday with him, I took a radically different intellectual form than my brother, who has a different (and absent) father. Aside from my father's peculiarities of staunchly believing in the existence of Bigfoot, the Loch Ness Monster, and UFOs, my father is perhaps the person who nurtured my early intellectualism most. He instilled in me a curiosity for language in a rather odd way: despite his not completing high school until he was twenty-one—the same age I entered my PhD program—he would ever-so casually drop scholarly word-bombs on me. "You gon' be a real perspicacious person, Marq," he said to me once. Or, "I'm sorry, Big Man, I didn't mean to hurt your feelings. You got me feelin' all contrite now." In retrospect, I can see now that these uncommon terms he would often use imbued within me an admiration and passion for acquiring words. Back then my vocabulary was only in its inchoate phase. I sought to expand my lexicon in order to speak into existence the aspects of my identity—namely, my seemingly incompatible Blackness[1] and intellectualism—that elided my understanding. My words would become the vehicle through which I manifested myself—all of myself; my Blackness, my giftedness—and it was in my writing that my words reached the apogee of my self-expression. When my intellect was able to speak itself through me, I really started digging the whole Black intellectual thing.

And so began the cultivation of me, a GhettoNerd.

High School: Authentically Being Someone I'm Not

We real cool. We
Left school. We
. . . .
Jazz June. We
Die soon.
—*Gwendolyn Brooks, 1959*

MY HIGH SCHOOL was where one's giftedness crawled into the darkest hole it could find for seven hours and twenty minutes each weekday. I went to Academy Park High School, a 70 percent Black public school in Sharon Hill, Pennsylvania, a town right outside Philadelphia. Put bluntly, yet honestly, my experience of the school was that it was merely a hangout spot for kids to see their homies and besties while learning the bare essentials needed to function in life. For most of the students, learning remained the tertiary priority (if you can call it a "priority") after chilling with your friends and trying various routes to ultimate coolness.

If I had to pick one word to describe the aspirations of most of my high school's students, it would be "cool," hands down. Everybody wanted to be cool; everybody wanted to be, to quote Outkast, "the coolest motherfuckers on the planet." In fact, one can imagine the chorus of Outkast's "So Fresh, So Clean" (2000) emanating from the attitudes of these ambassadors of cool:

> Ain't nobody dope as me I'm dressed so fresh so clean
> (So fresh and so clean clean)
> Don't you think I'm so sexy I'm dressed so fresh so clean
> (So fresh and so clean clean)
> Ain't nobody dope as me I'm dressed so fresh so clean
> (So fresh and so clean clean)
> I love when you stare at me I'm dressed so fresh so clean
> (So fresh and so clean clean).

It is interesting, then, to note the historical Black roots of the notion of cool. Contemporary understandings of cool derive from jazzmen and a break-the-rules instinct. Jazz saxophonist Lester Young coined the term after wearing sunglasses inside during a performance, setting in motion a mentality of masking Black rage under the guise of nonchalance. This mentality became consolidated into a posture, a "cool pose," as Richard Majors and Janet Mancini Billson have termed it. Cool pose acts as a coping strategy, as "the black man's last-ditch effort for masculine self-control" (Cohen, 2014; Ross, 2004, 92).

It seemed that everyone in my high school was high, not only on certain illegal narcotics but also on cool pose as well. What's more is that this cool pose carried with it a compulsory Blackness, a Blackness that was narrowly scripted; thus any deviation from its ascribed tenets invalidated the epidermal darkness or the authentic Blackness of its deviant. What seemed to be the case, then, was that authentic Blackness was defined in large part as anti-intellectual. The general consensus was that being smart was for White folk. In a strange appropriation of the historical proscription of Black people from educational spaces, intelligence, and everything that it connoted was codified as White and thus non-Black, even anti-Black.

I recall a moment in an English class freshman year where one student, Roland, a nerdy Black kid with a love for anime and Pokémon, displayed a genuine interest in improving his vocabulary and verbal diction. Witnessing this, another student commented, "You Oreo—tryna talk all

White. I thought you were supposed to be Black." Here, the other student critiques Roland's Blackness and ultimately invalidates his Blackness because an attribute he has deemed un-Black and thus White—academic words and adhering to grammatical rules—simply cannot coexist with epidermal Blackness. Because one's language is the vehicle through which one claims a kind of worldly affluence, Roland's pursuit of linguistic dexterity was equated with a pursuit of Whiteness. With this logic, affluence equals Whiteness while penury equals Blackness.

Despite how Roland wanted to portray himself, he was "perceived as a Black man trying to transcend his 'natural' state, elemental and unsophisticated;" he was "perceived as a Black man who is trying to pass for white, not based on appearance but in the metaphoric drag of linguistic performance and wearing the garments of academic accomplishment" (Alexander, 2006, 74). Roland embodied himself as a particular image—that of a Black person who could increase the quality of his diction—but, in effect, was returned to himself, disembodied, as a static, always already a foreclosed racial template. Philosopher George Yancy speaks directly to this point. The return of Black bodies to themselves repackages Black subjectivity as

> a *fixed entity*, a "niggerized" Black body whose epidermal logic ha[s] already foreclosed the possibility of being anything other than what was befitting its lowly station. [The return of the Black body is] the voice of a larger anti-Black racist society that "whispers mixed messages in our ears," the ears of Black people who struggle to think of themselves as a possibility (Yancy, 2005, 219).

Roland's dark skin fixed him in the static racial mold that the other student assigned to him. The possibility of his Blackness and passion for linguistic dexterity was immediately foreclosed, and his Black self was returned to him in likeness to the student's constricting delineation of authentic Blackness. In the image of Blackness created he Roland; Black and White created he them.

This observation affected me profoundly. As one who also enjoyed language, a passion instilled in me by my father, I began to bury that interest. Something had to take the back seat. I've always been Black, so that would have been tough to shake—instead, my words had to take a blow and be stuffed in the back of my intellectual closet. This, however, was an imperfect system. Feeling an urge to think and to speak my thoughts, I often demonstrated too much intelligence for my Blackness. In that environment I was too smart to be Black. So in order to preserve the sanctimoniousness of their definitions of Blackness—definitions upon which they've constituted their own identities as Black—they had to dismantle the threat I posed.

The scrutinizing gaze of my peers chipped away at the validity of my comingling intelligence and Blackness, rewrapping my giftedness and returning it to me as inconsistent with my Blackness. Their critiques were aimed not only at the perceived insult my intelligence lent to the purported inherent cool pose that was equivalent to them with Blackness; they were also aimed at the presumed Whiteness my intellect connoted for them, thus clashing with my epidermal hue. The critiques were incisive jabs to my erudition:

> Look at that li'l nerd nigga writing poetry and shit;
> Look at them wack ass books he read;
> Look at them big ass words he be usin'.

Eventually it became evident that Blackness was largely a matter of one's embodiment. To *be* Black and cool was to *do* Black and cool. It was a matter of stylization. One performed authentic Blackness by dressing this way, speaking that way, emphasizing mythical Mandingoes, walking in this manner, physically dominating another, outperforming others in sports. Once I made this discovery, I utilized its performative basis to my own advantage, as well as my own downfall.

Playing the Game

> It is through my body that I understand other people, just
> as it is through my body that I perceive *'things'*.
> *The meaning of a gesture thus 'understood' is* not behind
> it, it is intermingled with the structure
> of the world outlined by the gesture, and
> which I take up on my own account.
>
> —*Maurice Merleau-Ponty, 1945*

EVERY HOLLYWOOD FILM about high school football players is a dead-on depiction of my high school. I was no different. Football was not only a performance on the gridiron; it was also a performance during school. Because of the denigration of Black intellect, thus the denigration of *my* intellect, I often exaggerated my own physicality to compensate for whatever aspects of my Blackness were marred by residual intelligence. While I was not a very large high schooler, even by senior year, only five feet eight inches, 155 pounds at my biggest, I sculpted my physique in a way that gave me a desired imposing aesthetic. I was typically the first one to enter the weight room during off-season workouts and the last to leave. Although I was relatively small for a football player and played a position that does not require incredible size or strength (wide receiver), I prided myself on being the strongest player on the team.

Thus I sought to display my value and validity as Black through performing physically in football. In her book *We Real Cool*, bell hooks speaks directly to this point:

> This need to prove their value through performance is one of the reasons so many black boys look to sports as a site of redemption and affirmation. Given the history of black male success in the arena of sports, an arena deemed "manly" by patriarchal standards, black boys learn early on in their lives that by excelling in sports they can gain both visibility and a measure of respect (2004, 94).

It was this athleticism that I played up; it was my physical musculature and strength that I emphasized, cutting the sleeves off most of my shirts to display my arms, stylizing myself with my football "1000 lb. Club" shirt—a testament to my being able to bench press, squat, and power clean a cumulative weight of over a thousand pounds—and crafting my persona as the athletic, muscular football player. Perhaps the most obvious testament to my success in performing my physical Blackness was my high school nickname, a name earned after a 265-pound bench press my junior year: Roids. I was so strong, it was thought, I had to be on steroids. But not only was I super strong and super buff, through this emphasizing of my strength and physical stature, I was also, consequently, super Black.

Through my strength, I masqueraded as authentically Black, which worked to the detriment of the possibility of my intelligence being a contributing factor to my Blackness and thus altering the predominant discourse that constituted Black as an embodied cool pose. I played the part assigned to me, the role of a Black dude, and to keep my role, to be believable, I had to read from the script. There was no room for artistic, creative expression if I was to remain wholly Black.

Let me be clear. I did not begin to purposely fail tests and stop all homework assignments in order to maintain my Blackness. I performed what I saw were the tenets of authentic Blackness, while deem-phasizing and downplaying the *existence* (from Latin *exsistere*, meaning literally to "stand out") of my intellectual giftedness. My giftedness was less overtly performed, thus seemingly nonexistent, proffering an image of myself that utilized the performativity of racial identity as a way to survive high school.

I finished high school over-performing my Black embodiment, and it wasn't until college that I began to see the historical parallels between Blackness and intellect.

College Boy

> At exactly which point do you start to realize,
> that life without knowledge is death in disguise?
> —*Talib Kweli, 1998*

COLLEGE WAS WHERE I FLOURISHED. I attended Lebanon Valley College in Annville, a very White, very conservative region in central Pennsylvania. I began college as a biology major, but after quickly discovering that I had no interest in lab work or adenosine triphosphate, I decided to change majors, ultimately becoming a triple major in philosophy, American studies, and English. Two classes made my decision apparent. The first was my introduction to philosophy class. As one who has always lived a life of the mind, in retrospect it seems obvious that I would gravitate to a major in philosophy. But not knowing that philosophy was even a subject that one could study seriously, I never labeled myself a philosopher. That was all to change soon.

Only two weeks into the semester, we were asked to read Plato's dialogue "Euthyphro." At one point in the text, Socrates asks a question about piety: "Is the rock pious because of the gods' love, or do the gods love it because it is pious?" That question blew my mind. For some reason, that escapes me to this day. The formulation of that question warped my entire view of the world—it fomented questions of ethics and causality, and destabilized my naïve epistemic foundation. The question was absolutely brilliant to my seventeen-year-old mind, and at that moment, thoughts, words, and questions—the seeds of intellect, of *my* intellect—began to emerge from the hiding place it had been in for the past few years. The vibrancy of thoughts, the power of words, and the vitality of questions overcame me.

The second class that contributed to my change was a first-year seminar entitled "Man Up/Act Like a Lady." It was an American Studies course taught by an English professor that introduced freshmen to the subject of feminism, gender roles and norms, and the insidious scripting of racially and gendered marginalized bodies. While the class content enlightened me to the appalling gender oppression plaguing American society and eventually led me to identify myself as a feminist, it was the professor, Cathy Romagnolo, who was the real impetus for my intellectual transformation. Despite being a small White woman, her tenacity regarding race and gender and the broader concept of the history of marginalized identities, her English background, and, perhaps most important, her willingness to mentor and nurture my gifts gave validity to the simultaneity of my Blackness and giftedness.

It was Cathy who made me aware of writers like W. E. B. Du Bois, James Baldwin, Toni Morrison, Zora Neale Hurston; poets Lucille Clifton and Langston Hughes; and philosophers like Judith Butler, Jacques Derrida, and Slavoj Žižek. Her validation of my Blackness and my intellect provided the space for an important shift, namely the possibility of my Blackness being expressed and performed through the very things that I previously thought were antithetical to it: language, intellect, and the mind.

I ain't start writing shit down to survive until
around sophomore year of college,
a late start for most,
yes,
but when that
pen
hits
that page
it don't just bleed ink, it rips through its bowels
and vomits up my internal sickness,
crafting an Alcatraz of majestic tapestries.

Frederick Douglass believed the road to freedom was paved with education. His idea provides the template for the way I structure my pursuit of knowledge—as a means of unshackling myself from the fetters of myopia, anti-Black discourse, and ignorance. My intelligence and my Blackness—since the two are inextricable for me—are vehicles of fugitivity. There is something ever-elusive, always too hard to grasp about Blackness. This is Blackness's fugitive ethos. On the subject of Black fugitivity, Fred Moten, Black studies scholar and performance theorist of Black radicalism, provides an incisive illustration. He characterizes Blackness as that *extra*, that never-quite-locked-down "thing." Blackness, for Moten

is tantamount to another, fugitive, sublimity altogether. Some/thing escapes in or through the object's vestibule; the object vibrates against its frame like a resonator, and troubled air gets out. The air of the thing that escapes enframing is what I'm interested in—an often unattended movement that accompanies largely unthought positions and appositions (Moten, 2008, 182).

What Moten suggests is that the "thing" that eludes confinement and imprisonment is Blackness. To purloin the theistic words of Anselm of Canterbury, Blackness is that than which nothing more elusive can be conceived.[2] I am a fugitive evading the imprisoning judgments of my former high school peers who, by disallowing intellect to speak to an authentic Blackness, facilitated a "dismissal of [a particular] possible claim regarding the essence or even the being of blackness (in its irreducible performativity) [which] becomes, itself, the dismissal of blackness" (Harney & Moten, 2013, p. 48). I reclaimed and altered the given, narrowed definition of Blackness from high school and refashioned it through a historico-philosophical lens as a break from the constricting impositions cast upon my subjectivity. My Blackness is indeed precisely what Moten speaks to in *The Undercommons: Fugitive Planning & Black Study*:

> in between that impropriety of speech that approaches animality and a tendency towards expropriation that approaches criminality, lies blackness, lies the black thing that cuts the regulative, governant force of (the) understanding (and even of those understandings of blackness to which black people are given since fugitivity escapes even the fugitive) (Harney & Moten, 2013, 50).

Thus, through my intellect and my language I reclaim a lost Blackness, a historically fettered subjectivity that I now have the immense privilege of incorporating into the fabric of my identity. And this reclaimed Blackness, while still a source of pain stemming from the wounds of my ancestral past, manifests itself most vigorously through the written word and allows me, as a Black male, to slowly heal.

> I write through that pain
> I slay that hurt with the only blade that
> can create rather than destroy
> And my pen—
> my pen—
> knows no limits
> That sable, self-actualizing hue marks the page with my skin,
> marks the world with my curse of Canaan
> And I ask: who's enslaved now?
> 'Cause the lines I write ain't boxes but an infinite series of
> paths all leading to exactly who I'm becoming, the infinite
> possibility of who's really me—
> *I write so I can exist unchained.*

My writing is my own means of rewriting and redacting my racio-gendered script. It is a liberatory practice that allows me to rewrite myself as Black as I wish—and to have all that I write be just Black enough. The simple exercise of writing, for all Black folk, is, quite frankly, really dope. It is almost beyond comprehension that someone like Thomas Jefferson said that Phillis Wheatley's poetry was beneath the dignity of criticism or the German philosopher Immanuel Kant, commenting on the work of David Hume, to remark that

> the Negroes of Africa have by nature no feeling that rises above the trifling. Mr. Hume challenges anyone to cite a single example in which a Negro has shown talents, and asserts that among the hundreds of thousands of blacks who are transported elsewhere from the countries, although many of them have been set free, still not a single one was ever found who presented anything great in art or science or any other praiseworthy quality, even though among the whites some continually rise aloft from the lowest rabble, and through superior gifts earn respect in the world (Gates & Smith, 2014, xxxviii–xxxix).

For me to write, and write well, then, is already an act of resistance, always an act of reclaimed Blackness, forever an act of speaking my historically erased truth into the world.

Notes on the State of My Language

It is imperative that how I view writing be made clear. To write, for me, is the epitome of living. Writing is how I understand life, and life understood *is* life lived. Since language defines our reality, since, as Heidegger says, "It does not serve to represent the objects of the world or beings as a whole, but rather it is a means through which the world reveals itself," the act of writing, of language, reveals the world to myself, shaping the very way I see and approach the world. Or better yet, the act of writing—my writing—*creates* the world. Radical, I know. This is precisely why Jacques Derrida states that everything is a text: everything that exists is legible, is written, and can be read and interpreted, i.e., has meaning derived from it. Consequently, then, we can rewrite the world.

I can then rewrite the confining scripts of Blackness; I can write Blackness over and over again—indeed, my act of writing *is* my Blackness. Derrida also writes:

> To write is to know that what has not yet been produced within literality has no other dwelling place, does not await us as prescription in some *topos ouranios*, or some divine understanding. Meaning must await being said or written in order to inhabit itself, and in order to become, by differing from itself, what it is: meaning (Derrida, 1978).

If the former imposition of a cool pose Blackness had to be produced into literality, to use Derrida's words, via speech and language, then I can produce a new literality of Blackness.

So I write to create the world for myself. It is a constant enacting of language to proscribe the dissipation of my reality. It is my way—our way, I think—of grabbing hold of and controlling, through creation, the world. What's more is that writing allows me to speak. It is not true that written words are dead or static. They are very much alive. My writing lets me speak myself into existence in a world where I am constantly denied a full voice. Instead of being talked over, accused of talking back, written off for talking too loftily, or purported to be talking nonsense—ways to discredit my language and thus my reality—I can talk uninterrupted.

So I write, and I write fearlessly. When I write, I am the archetypal *parrhesiastes* as I risk myself when I write. (*Parrhesia* is borrowed from the Greek παρρησία meaning literally "to speak everything" and by extension "to speak freely," "to speak boldly," or "boldness.") I—the Black, gifted I—write because it is the only way I can speak my full self, my full, perennially changing, fugitive self. In writing is where I can exist boldly, unapologetically; it is where I can exist in all of myself. I write because it is a realm in which I can be who I am always becoming: myself.

It was college—with Cathy's encouragement, canonical authors in my backpack, and a confidence in my intellect—that most profoundly shaped my mind. With those forces propelling me forward, I ultimately won Lebanon Valley College's H. Anthony Neidig Award, granted to the top student in the graduating class who demonstrates superior scholarship, leadership, character, and service. Further, I was accepted to and decided to attend Cornell University for my doctoral degree in English. The most astounding feeling was knowing that my gifts—my intellect and my Blackness—had been rewarded and had been validated.

Almost daily I am reminded of the words of Toni Morrison: "We die. That may be the meaning of our lives. But we do language. That may be the measure of our lives" (Allen, 1997). My language and my intellect—my gifts—have been the most profound tool in my expression of my racial identity. Á la Du Bois's influential book, *The Souls of Black Folk* (1903/2007), my journey and struggles with my race and my mind were a sort of unreconciled striving between an intellectual and a Black. Indeed, my intellectual pursuits became an effort to marry the Du Boisian, unreconciled strivings of being not "an American; a Negro" but an intellectual, a GhettoNerd.

I need to write

I got words.
These words
Are climbing up the rungs of my trachea
Itching to breathe the bitter smell of
White America's air.
These words are stupid.

I need to write

For so long I couldn't even spell.
Now I got this ink blade
In my hand ready to twist, twist
The dance of creation,
Because in the Beginning was the
Word.
These words are Life.

I need to write

They said it's illegal, that I'm not capable,
And my words wrote that.
They said I was less, that I was different,
And my words wrote that.
They said I had no power,
And I wrote that.
These words are destiny.

I need to write

I need to live
I need to breathe
I need to see
I need to be.

When I write, my words tell me who I am.
And I am what I write.

I need to write

Because only then am I me.

Notes

1. I capitalize "Blackness" because I maintain that Blackness is akin to fugitivity and is thus a political concept. As much more than simple skin color, Blackness, for my purposes, is an act of subversion, an act of rebellion against the status quo (Whiteness). It is political because its characteristics are constructed toward a particular political end. As Henry Louis Gates Jr. says, "'Blackness' is not a material object, an absolute, or an event, but a trope; it does not have an 'essence' as such but is defined by a network of relations that form a particular aesthetic unity" (Gates, H. L. [1989]. *Figures in Black: Words, Signs, and the "Racial" Self.* New York: Oxford University Press). "Blackness," then, is, by definition, political. Consequently, I also capitalize "Black" because of the already

fugitivity of Black skin in a socio-cultural milieu that privileges and normalizes Whiteness. Black skin in white spaces is always already political.

2. Anselm's ontological argument averred that God was "that than which nothing greater can be conceived." Here, I insert Blackness, implicitly deifying it but pointing to the perennial elusiveness and thus fugitivity of Blackness.

References

Alexander, B. K. (2006). *Performing Black masculinity: race, culture, and queer identity.* Lanham, MD: AltaMira Press.

Allen, S. (Ed.). (1997). *Nobel lectures in literature: 1991–1995.* Singapore: World Scientific Publishing Co.

Brooks, G. (1959). *We real cool.* Retrieved December 9, 2014, from http://www.poetryfoundation.org/poetrymagazine/poem/17315.

Cohen, P. (2014, March 19). In Washington, 100 examples of the epitome of cool. *New York Times.* Retrieved from http://www.nytimes.com/2014/03/20/arts/artsspecial/in-washington-100-examples-of-the-epitome-of-cool.html.

Derrida, J. (1978). *Writing and Difference.* Chicago, IL: The University of Chicago Press Books.

Du Bois, W. E. B. (1903/2007). *The souls of Black folk.* New York: Oxford University Press.

Gates, H. L., & Smith, V. A. (Eds.). (2014). *The Norton anthology of African American literature* (Third edition). New York: W.W. Norton & Company.

Harney, S., & Moten, F. (2013). *The undercommons: Fugitive planning & black study.* San Francisco, CA: Minor Compositions.

hooks, b. (2004). *We real cool: Black men and masculinity.* New York: Routledge.

Moten, F. (2008). The case of blackness. *Criticism, 50*(2), 177–218.

Outkast. (2000). So fresh, so clean. On *Stankonia* [CD]. New York: RCA Arista Records.

Ross, M. B. (2004). *Manning the race: Reforming Black men in the Jim Crow era*. New York. NY: New York University Press.

Yancy, G. (2005). Whiteness and the return of the Black body. *The Journal of Speculative Philosophy, 19*(4), 215–241.

CHAPTER 3

A Father's Dream

Ruben Martinez, PE, SE
Recorded telephone interview conducted and edited by Nadirah Angail, MFT

Background

LONG BEFORE HE EVEN KNEW IT, Ruben Martinez had purpose. It was a gift from his hardworking father who left his hometown of Venado, Mexico, to pursue a better life for himself and his unborn children. A migrant worker, Martinez's father sometimes worked on college campuses and was always impressed by their beauty. He wanted his children to have the opportunity to witness that same beauty but as students, not workers. It was this fervent desire, this longing for something better that was poured into Martinez from birth. It molded him into the accomplished high achiever he is today.

Martinez grew up in an external environment that left much to be desired, but it was his internal environment that influenced him most. In the Martinez household, excellence was not only encouraged but also expected. As the youngest of six children, he was surrounded by examples of greatness. He saw in his brothers and sisters what he knew he contained within himself. Guided by his loving parents, Pablo and Juana, Martinez had no choice but to achieve. He said, "My parents would always tell me, 'You have to study; you have to study.' We never fell into that trap in the Hispanic community where people sometimes think you have to work instead of study."

Martinez owes much of his success to his parents' drive and compassion. He never had to search any farther than them to find role models. Martinez is thankful he was reared with vision and direction. He was taught to see beyond the common paths Hispanic young adults are sometimes expected to take. He learned not to focus on their income, their dangerous South Side Chicago neighborhood, or even the highly frequented bar they lived next to. In his family, their focus, the entirety of their hope and energy, was placed on educational attainment and securing a bright future. "As a kid growing up," Martinez said, "I heard the story. I understood it. My father didn't speak much, but we knew where he stood. . . . It was just something we knew. He didn't have to talk about it every day." What Pablo Martinez could not accomplish, his children certainly would. It was this simple yet profound belief in his children's potential that fueled Ruben Martinez's later successes.

Early Signs of Giftedness

FROM THE BEGINNING, Martinez performed well. He was an agreeable child who did what he was told and almost always exceeded teachers' expectations. On a grading system that included U for unsatisfactory, S for satisfactory, and E for excellent, his early report cards bore many Es. Because Martinez's parents expected excellence, he did not see his above-average grades as anything special. He had older siblings who also did well in school. Why would he be any different? To him, he was just doing what he was supposed to do, meeting a common expectation.

As Martinez grew older, he began to enter science and math competitions, and he did well—very well. In fifth grade, he entered a school math competition and won. He beat two sixth graders and caught the attention of a math teacher, Mr. Winters, who noticed the boy's intelligence and took him on as a mentee. "He was the first person who wasn't my teacher that took me under his wing for this math thing," Martinez recalled. He went on to compete at the district and city levels. Though he did not win in the finals, he made it very far.

When Martinez was in sixth grade and his older brother Pablo Jr. was in eighth, Winters recommended that Pablo Jr. apply to Whitney M. Young High School. At the same time, Winters gave Pablo Jr. an application for Ruben to apply to the gifted program at Whitney M. Young's Academic Center, a citywide resource for academically gifted children. Emanuel, their older brother who already attended Whitney M. Young as a senior, also provided support to both Ruben and his parents in this process. Thanks to Pablo Jr.'s help and Emanuel's encouragement, Martinez was tested and accepted into the Academic Center for seventh and eighth grade. Later, in high school, Martinez took many advanced placement classes and consistently made the honor roll. He graduated at the top of his class and went on to attend the highly selective research institution Rice University.

Gifted Program Experience and Recommendations for Improvements

"I HAVE NO BAD MEMORIES of anyone in the program," Martinez said fondly. "Everybody was talented, and it was good to be in an environment where success was expected." The teachers did not merely teach from a syllabus. They pushed the students to develop their individual abilities. "They knew they had good, talented kids to work with. . . . I definitely benefitted," he recalled. The students fed off each other's academic energy and respected that they were all talented in different ways. It was a humbling experience to be around so many other talented students. Now, years later, Martinez is still in contact with many of the friends he made there.

Aside from the comradery and stimulating setting, Martinez appreciated the diversity of the students in his class. "Being in inner-city Chicago, it was quite diverse, and I think that was only of benefit. We came from all parts of the city," he explained of the program. Being part of such a diverse group and living in an English-optional neighborhood allowed him to feel comfortable in his environment. Martinez never had to worry about being "otherized." He never had to adjust to being different. They were all different, all liked.

The other children in the program were not the only kind ones; so also were the other children in the school. Given that the gifted program students were middle schoolers attending class in a high school, the potential for mistreatment was considerable. Still, there was no bullying or anything of the sort. "We didn't get that," Martinez said plainly. "I kind of considered myself a nerd (and still do), but not in a bad way. We got along with everyone." Years later, when the gifted students entered Whitney Young as actual high schoolers, everyone knew who they were. The general student body knew which students had participated in the gifted program years earlier, but there was no distinction made when it came to treatment. "We were 'that group.' We may have been a bit more nerdy than everybody else, but it wasn't this ever-present burden that people thought we were nerds." It was a friendly environment that never sought to punish him for who he was.

Martinez's warm and gratifying experience with racial and cultural diversity in his gifted program is foreign to some gifted children of color. Some feel subtle or outright discrimination or both that makes it hard for them to fit in and excel in the way they normally would. To eliminate these types of experiences, gifted programs and universities should work to increase the diversity and cultural appreciation among their students. As a volunteer at his alma mater, Rice University, Martinez sees how the school seeks out students from varying racial or ethnic backgrounds. They value diversity enough to actively seek it out, rather than passively allow it to happen—or not happen. More colleges, gifted programs, and other educational institutions should follow suit. Now an adult, Martinez looks back on his gifted program experience with joy and appreciation. Every student should have that opportunity.

Gifted Siblings

BECAUSE MARTINEZ'S SIBLINGS were older than he was, he did not grow up with most of them in the home. However, he did grow up with the examples they set. Martinez's parents showed him that their natural expectations for him were high, but it was his siblings who showed him he possessed the real potential to actually reach those expectations. Not all of them took a traditional path through formal education and the professional realm, but they have all established themselves in their careers and families.

Martinez's eldest sister, Elena, received her PhD in epidemiology in 1994 (one week to the day after he received his BS from Rice). She is currently a professor at the University of California-San Diego. She travels the world presenting and lecturing and has two daughters and three granddaughters. Martinez's eldest brother, Federico, has completed some college but left school early to take a different path. He decided to go directly into the work force as a mechanic/machinist. He has raised four wonderful children. Martinez's next oldest sister, Luz, also left college to work, but she ultimately went back to school and received her bachelor's degree in 2011. A mother of two sons, she currently works as a collections manager at the University of Chicago. Martinez's next brother, Emanuel, went to medical school after getting his undergraduate degree from the University of Illinois. He is a psychiatrist with his own practice for many, many years. Proud and emotional, Pablo Sr. teared up at Emanuel's medical school graduation. "Imagine if I had never left Venado," their father used to say. "Emanuel would have been herding sheep or something and not have become a doctor." Martinez's last brother, Pablo Jr., received a photojournalism degree from Columbia College in Chicago. After graduation, he interned and then worked at the *Chicago Sun-Times* and later the *Detroit News* before moving to Washington, DC, to join the Associated Press. He is the proud father of a son and received a Pulitzer Prize in 1999 for his work on President Clinton's impeachment.

Both directly and indirectly, Martinez's older siblings acted as guides along the path to success. His sisters, in particular, played an especially strong role in his growth and development. They were not just sisters; they were more like second mothers. Elena and Luz helped Martinez in every way they could. For example, when he was in high school, Luz would give him rides to school. It was not something her parents had to force her do. She willingly offered. Elena, who lived in Houston at the time, encouraged Martinez to apply to Rice. He had not heard of it prior to her recommendation. Like many other college-bound Chicagoans, his focus was on local schools, like the University of Illinois, Northwestern, and the University of Chicago. He had not even considered out-of-state schools, but he quickly became excited about the prospect of Rice. His sister's suggestion allowed him to expand his mind and consider options that were previously beyond his scope. He was able to imagine himself doing nontraditional things and applying his intelligence in great ways. "One of the most exciting moments of my life was when I read the letter of acceptance from Rice," Martinez said with happiness in his voice. "Elena, although she had two of her own kids, would always let me stay with her if I needed to when I was at Rice. . . . Sometimes, too, she would need a babysitter. Surprisingly, she would let her idiot college brother take care of her kids," he said with a laugh.

Though Martinez and his siblings are scattered across the country, they are still close because of regular communication and yearly

Christmas get-togethers with their mother. "We always try our best to do whatever we can for each other and to keep in contact as spread out as we are," he explained. It is his family ties that have pushed him to excel and kept him strong during times of weakness.

Social Experiences and Culture Shock

"I grew up in a Mexican neighborhood right next to a Black neighborhood. It was very diverse," Martinez said. In fact, he described it as a place where you did not need to speak English if you did not want to. Despite the positive aspects of his South Side Chicago neighborhood, "it was the biggest source of problems and concerns for [his] family." It was dangerous, and that made it a potential obstacle for Martinez as a child and teen. His family relied on public transportation and lived in an area with heavy foot traffic from people who were often intoxicated.

At an early age, Martinez exhibited an emotional maturity that kept him focused and out of trouble. He could have fallen in with the wrong crowd or spent most of his time indoors, hiding from potential danger, but he made better choices. He was determined not to let his surroundings prevent him from doing what he needed to do. Looking back, Martinez is sure his parents worried much more than they let on about their children, but it was Pablo and Juana's custom to focus on the good. No matter the obstacle, Martinez was thankful and focused. "I had everything I needed," he said. Today, Martinez is able to provide his children with so much more, but he recognizes that it is a result of the work ethic he developed in his humble beginnings.

Dangerous though it may have been, Martinez's neighborhood was all he had ever known. It was his home, so it did not take much to adapt to it. "My friends and I had a system," he explained. "Whenever we'd drop someone off, we would wait for the other person to get inside the house and wave before driving off." It was their way of keeping each other safe.

Martinez's high school was just as racially diverse as his neighborhood. He was accustomed to people of color being the majority, but that changed in college. He said:

Whitney Young was about 60 percent Black, 20 percent Hispanic, 10–15 percent Asian American, and the rest was White. . . . When I got to college, it was quite a culture shock for me because the script was completely flipped. If I would have let it, it could have been an obstacle. I just was not used to that. It was quite different, but I think it was necessary. I was living in a little bubble, thinking the rest of the world was like Whitney Young. I could have told myself, "I can't succeed here. I'm not comfortable," but I knew what I had to do.

Martinez did not allow the markedly different racial terrain to deter him. Instead, he did the same thing he had done back in his childhood neighborhood: He adapted and learned to thrive in the environment. Once Martinez got over the initial shock, he was able to find friends and comfort. "I made friends with everyone, but my good friends were still students of color. About two-thirds of my friends were Black. I felt closest with people I was most used to. I made fewer but deeper relationships with people."

Looking back, Martinez is thankful for his experiences at Rice. Though it was initially uncomfortable, he benefitted from being dropped into a new and different environment. He learned how to interact with people whose racial and cultural backgrounds do not match his own. He later went on to learn from and work with people of all types, and he probably would have struggled with that had he not had that exposure at Rice. He is now able to share space and ideas with anyone from anywhere. Martinez knows that differences do not have to be a hindrance and should never get in the way of educational, personal, and professional growth.

Not only does Martinez embrace cultural diversity in his professional life, but he also embraces it in his personal life. His wife is a native-born Pakistani. They married in Pakistan in 2001, and it was a truly enlightening experience to witness such a different culture. "So much was different there, and yet so many things were similar," he said. "I did not understand what people were saying (until they broke out their English), but we were so warmly welcomed by all the friends and family." Martinez credits his upbringing and diverse experiences for his openness. He is thankful that he is able to receive people on an individual basis without saddling upon them stereotypes and preconceived notions that could prevent a true human connection.

Rising above Academic Challenges

Martinez's intelligence did not make him exempt from academic struggle. He worked hard for every good grade he received and never felt he could simply coast through. However, as a freshman at Rice, he was forced to wonder if his hard work would be enough. He started college as a physics major. It seemed only natural after the wonderful experience he had with high school physics. However, he quickly found that high school physics and college-level physics are quite different. He said:

> Second semester of freshman year and first semester sophomore year were probably my toughest. I ran into [physics] classes that were a bit more than I could handle, but I worked my way through it. . . . I eventually found what I wanted—I found engineering.

Though he had a natural knack for math and science, the weed-out physics classes challenged him in a way other classes had not. Despite his struggle, he maintained a high work ethic. He realized consistent effort would take him much farther than plain natural ability would. Martinez is fully aware that there are many people with high IQs who never apply themselves. He did not want to be among their ranks. "I knew I was surrounded by people smarter than I was. I just had to put the work in to stay ahead," Martinez said. He always remained humble and driven, even in challenging situations that left him stressed and unsure about his career path. Ultimately, the struggle Martinez experienced with physics worked in his favor. It led him to discover his love for engineering and design.

Career Building and Entrepreneurship

When Martinez originally decided to enroll in graduate school, it was mostly because his classmates were enrolling, too. Why not, he thought. Then Martinez met an adjunct professor who worked for his dream engineering firm, Walter P. Moore (WPM). The professor informed Martinez that WPM accepted only applicants with master's degrees. That was it. He knew then he had to apply. Martinez ended up at the University of Michigan-Ann Arbor, where he earned his graduate degree in civil engineering.

When he officially inquired about WPM, it was not hiring, so he took a job at another firm. Though it was not his first choice, he enjoyed it because he learned a lot in his first year out of school. The following year, he got a tip from an old classmate that WPM was hiring. She suggested that he call her father to schedule an interview. In 1997, Martinez got the job and soon moved to Houston to start his new career. "I had an incredible mentor and loved what I was doing. I put in a ton of hours," he said of his then-new position at WPM. Martinez loves learning and producing, so his heavy workload was exciting and fulfilling. He worked so much that he had practically no time to socialize, but that, too, worked in his favor because he ended up meeting his wife at work. "All the chips fall a certain way. Now I have a family and two wonderful kids I'm so proud of," he said.

A few years into Martinez's new job, he and his wife moved to Austin to help open a new WPM office. They had no children yet, so they were ready and willing to make a career move. In 2003, they moved again, to Chicago this time. He had the opportunity to work on a project at the well-known McCormick Place. Being from Chicago, it felt as if he had come full circle. It was a special treat to be able to live and work there again. During his temporary stay, his first child was born. He is proud to tell his daughter she is a Chicagoan, just like him.

As Martinez grew in his craft, so did his responsibilities. He was given more and more freedom and authority to work independently. Just four years after graduation, he was given an assignment that he would soon classify as his greatest career accomplishment. His firm was commissioned to design the International Arrivals Building at Intercontinental Airport in Houston. It was a $250-million construction project covering 780 thousand square feet. From the very first client meeting to design, construction, and completion, he managed the entire process. He got to watch his two-dimensional idea become a three-dimensional reality. Now, any time he travels internationally, he passes through the International Arrivals Building. It is a tangible reminder of what he has achieved. He is proud to say to his children and himself, "I designed that."

In 2009, the recession hit, and "things got lean. The size of staff shrank, so those of us who remained were being stretched. We made it together. We persevered until the economy rebounded," Martinez said.

In the nearly two decades Martinez worked for WPM, he rose from graduate engineer to project manager and then senior project manager to principal (i.e., part owner). After seventeen years of loyalty, quality work, recognition, and praise, he earned the opportunity to partner with WPM as the president of his own firm. As of March 2015, he is an official business owner and is ready to enter into new and unfamiliar territory. Martinez said:

> I am only a few weeks into the business, but I'm very excited and feel prepared. I didn't go to business school, and I don't have an MBA, but I'm the head of a business that does the type of work I like doing. . . . Seeing what you worked so hard for go up in front of you is really rewarding.

Bigger Picture

ASIDE FROM BEING A BRILLIANT ENGINEER and president of his own company, Ruben Martinez is a husband and father. He is the son of a man who had clarity of purpose and a woman who still, to this day, shows unconditional love. He is the brother of loving sisters and supportive brothers. He comes from a family that knows the true meaning of sacrifice, a family whose members won't hesitate to drop everything to be by each other's side. These are the things that matter most.

Neither of his children has been officially tested for giftedness, but they both show signs of promise. His daughter, a fifth grader, is a voracious reader whose report cards look even better than his did at her age. "She reads like nobody's business. I certainly could not keep up with her. My wife and father-in-law are prolific readers, and they didn't read as much as my daughter does when they were her age," he said with pride. She was recently accepted into a highly selective junior high magnet school. She is consistently praised by both teachers and neighbors. It is clear her personality shines just as much as her intelligence. Martinez's son, a highly spirited five-year-old, has been playing with Legos (the small ones) since age three. He works very hard on them and enjoys being creative in his play. He is very independent and does not let the age gap with his sister stop him from trying to be like her. He rode a bike at an early age because he saw his sister do it first. He will set his mind to accomplish almost anything if he sees his sister do it first. "We don't think he's ever going to give up on anything," Martinez said of his son. It is no coincidence that his children have drive. They have been born into the same type of purpose-driven environment that produced their father. This is promising news because intelligence without dedication is wasted potential. So, rather than focus on his children's individual accomplishments (which he is definitely proud of), Martinez finds gratification in their work ethic—a trait they inherited from their father and grandfather.

PART II

Navigating Adulthood and Careers

CHAPTER 4

The Sword and the Shield: A Narrative on the Evolution of Black Giftedness, from Childhood to Adulthood

Anthony Sparks, PhD

IT IS NOT A NEW IDEA, but it is a subtle one. And if we look closely, we will see that it is an idea that has been expressed repeatedly throughout the twentieth and early twenty-first centuries. "To be young, gifted, and Black," sang the spectacularly talented musician and activist Nina Simone in tribute to the talented playwright and activist Lorraine Hansberry. "This is a song for the genius child," wrote the incomparable man of arts and letters, Langston Hughes. These famous words from two Black literary and artistic giants explicitly name, celebrate, and defend the notion of the abundant existence of gifted learners among the millions of Black children who strive within and against the US educational system each and every day. However, if we read and listen carefully, the words of Simone and Hughes also offer a warning.

Simone, in the same composition referenced above, implores the listener to "Open your heart to what I mean/There are billion boys and girls/Who are young, gifted, and Black/And that's a fact!" The exclamation at the end of the verse ("And that's a fact!") suggests that there are many for whom the words "gifted" and "Black" are an oxymoronic formulation that invites disbelief—one she works to dispel by inviting the listener to first "open your heart." Of note is that Simone does not ask the listener to open his or her mind, for she knows that it is the mind that constructed the idea of race, gave it meaning, and maintains the material reality of racism in order to justify the unequal distribution of resources (Bennett, 1988; Gilmore, 2007; Omi & Winant, 1994). Instead she invites us to open our hearts—and in so doing tap our mutual humanity and highest morality. Hughes tells us to sing the song for the genius child "softly" and later in his composition, states as plain as can be that "Nobody loves the gifted child/Can you love an eagle, tame or wild?" Taken together, the words of Simone and Hughes reveal a fundamental tension between the presence of Blackness and the perception of the lack of exceptional ability, between Blackness and the vision of a life without racial limits, between Blackness and the acceptance of an intellectual and creative giftedness that moves from potential to realization. It is a tension that speaks to and challenges both the stated and promoted core equality of the American creed.

For those who begin life on the margins of society and fight against continued marginalization, the questions and warnings that Langston Hughes and Nina Simone articulate are what many Black professional, intellectual, and artistic trailblazers have come to know all too well, that is, that the lives of the relatively few Blacks who are identified by their school systems as gifted learners are, at best, complicated. In predominantly White settings, the identification of a child as a gifted learner is, overall, usually embraced as a most positive development. This is also true in most Black homes and communities. But this positive development, this label—gifted—is not necessarily a simple proposition for Blacks. Those given a designation of "gifted" do not necessarily find an easier existence than those who display less noticeable intellectual gifts or possess even lesser opportunity to develop those gifts. In fact, as I suggest through my narrative, the gifted Black child who gains access to appropriate educational opportunities faces a complex, ever-shifting, and too often hostile societal terrain—particularly as those educational opportunities turn into career opportunities. It is a terrain that seems all too ready to ask a question implicitly laden with the hidden-but-not-so-hidden hierarchy of a society whose past and present remains saturated in the logics, laws, policies, and practices that suggest a White supremacist ideology still at work (Alexander, 2010; Ford 2010, Lipsitz, 2006; Omi & Winant, 1994; Sparks, 2009). Namely, that all-too-ready question can often be summed up as an unstated but deeply felt variation of "Negro, just who the hell do you think you are?"

The sensitive nature of the gifted child has been described and understood as a challenge, as something of a double-edged sword (Edmunds & Edmunds, 2005; Edmunds & Edmunds 2014; Lawson & Davis, 2010). Likewise, the matriculation of supremely educated Black adults into previously unattainable professional workforces has also, due to intellectually impoverished debates about Affirmative Action, been described as a double-edged sword (Hale, 1982). As a gifted Black adult who was identified and educated as a gifted Black child and now works both in academia and as a television writer-producer in the Hollywood culture (two extraordinarily critical workspaces), I have come to a slightly revised interpretation of that visual metaphor. It is true that the low expectations teachers and other educational agents often have for Black children acts as a primary barrier to the Black gifted learner's intellectual and psychosocial needs being met (Day-Vines, Patton, & Baytops, 2003; Ford & Grantham, 2003; Townsend & Patton, 1997). For me, this clash produces the metaphor of the double-edged sword mentioned above, where either a student goes unrecognized and remains undereducated, or the student's abilities are recognized but his or her psychological, cultural, and social needs are undernourished.

In focusing on a framework that highlights the little-discussed journey of the gifted Black adult, specifically the gifted Black male adult, I now propose that the experience of the gifted Black child who grows into a gifted Black male adult be viewed as a kind of "sword and shield" experience. Black giftedness does not simply cut both ways, as the double-edged sword metaphor suggests. Rather, I first see the existence of giftedness in the Black body and the identification of high academic potential within a Black child as a weapon, as a sword that can thrust forward, cut through, and create new educational space and possibilities. It attempts to advance through the thicket of institutionalized racism and individualized biases that work together to deny or diminish the educational opportunities that all gifted children need in order to reach their highest academic and artistic potential. Even the possibility of Black giftedness becomes a weapon against the quotidian manifestation of systemic racism in elementary school education because it is tool of justification. It lends legitimacy to a parent or invested school teacher's advocacy (or pleas) to take one more look at a child whose entire life trajectory might be positively enhanced or changed if the Black child in question were properly assessed, identified, and educated as a gifted learner.

Unfortunately, within the very justification that it often takes for the identification process of a gifted Black child to occur lies a kind of ticking time bomb that threatens to destroy the potential of that same gifted Black person once he or she enters adulthood and the professional work world. That hidden explosive is the very fact that the gifted Black child usually needed extraordinary justification in the first place in order to gain what for many others was ordinary access to an education that matches the child's academic potential. Ironically, the extraordinary effort required to place many Black children in gifted programs suggests that the Black student isn't expected to penetrate those spaces without special assistance or without some gatekeeper's nod towards a reductive notion of Affirmative Action or local diversity politics. In other words, a Black child's and especially a Black male child's placement in a gifted program or school can often feel tenuous and provisional. As a result, I came to think of my escape from the deficit lens of the typical school system as an escape, akin to running from the antebellum South to the North. Thus, Black students and their parents learn that they must always be ready, like free Negroes before the Emancipation Proclamation in 1863, to "show their papers." That is, through various means, the student absorbs that he or she is expected to be able to prove the right to occupy a seat in a gifted education program or school. In my case, "my papers" were my enthusiastic willingness to discuss my competitive test scores whenever asked. No upper-middle-class sense of discretion about such matters would do for me. I even, for a time, learned to keep my scores nearby, either in my locker or backpack. Alternately and perhaps more commonly, a gifted Black student's "papers" may be shown through the continuance of extraordinary and easily visible over-achievement and model behavior. The emotional vicissitudes of typical adolescent behavior carries too great a risk for the gifted Black child, lest they be sent packing back to the educational plantation known as the school-to-prison pipeline.

Through my narrative, I posit that the intense, active effort it often requires for a Black child to access gifted education also works to plant permanent questions that carry the potential to undermine a student's confidence and performance. These questions—What are you doing here? Are you really in the right place?—must be answered perennially through words, deeds, and achievements. In response to the ever-present question, I eventually discovered that my identification as gifted student shifted from functioning as a weapon or tool that created space for educational opportunities for me when I was a child to, as a Black male adult, functioning as a self-preserving shield that helped to implicitly and sometimes explicitly justify my presence in those higher-education and work-force spaces that are considered elite realms. In my case, as an adult, the question posed by society seemed to change. No longer was it "Who do you think you are?" Instead, it became "I know what you are and what you can't do, so how did you get in here?"

The narrative, ethnographic vignettes I present here also broadly track the doors that advocates of my particular set of gifts have helped open in my life. My trajectory is one that moved from learning in traditionally academic arenas to working in artistic settings and then to working and learning in both fields. My journey thus far has been somewhat unusual, but what centers the variety of experiences and spaces I discuss in this chapter is that they each represent an arena that is considered to be an elite space. As a result, this narrative begins to offer a comparative analysis by highlighting the differences in how Black giftedness functioned in a majority Black space during my childhood and how it has functioned thus far in majority White spaces during my adulthood. Again, I emphasize that in the case of the Black gifted adult, giftedness no longer functions primarily as a provider of opportunity as much as it serves as a self-protective shield. This is a shield that helps the gifted Black adult keep the opportunities he or she has acquired and, more important, maintain a healthy sense of self-worth and capital that has been achieved over many years. Writing specifically as a gifted Black male adult, in a political moment where many feel the need to assert that "Black lives matter," the shield I speak of in this chapter is one that speaks to a sense of one's right to exist, self-determine, and thrive beyond the assigned place that history tells us is perpetually indexed by the inhabitants and gatekeepers of Successful, Elite America.

Black Giftedness as a Child (The Sword)

> A man's gift maketh room for him.
>
> — *Proverbs 18:16, King James Bible*

That Black giftedness could be utilized as a weapon and tool to help create educational opportunities, battle systemic bias, and advocate on my behalf first made itself known to me just a few years after kindergarten. I wouldn't know this, however, until the end of the sixth grade. By the end of the sixth grade, I was in the habit of using my extracurricular and recess time to work as a teacher's assistant for my teacher, a Black woman by the name of Ethel Young. I even went to school on holidays to help Young complete her various administrative tasks. Yes, I was *that* kid—a proud teacher's pet who would rather help my teacher organize her files than spend it at home rereading my Story of America cards or dodging, with varying amounts of success, fights for being the "smart boy" on the playground.

I didn't realize it at the time, but in retrospect I can see that Young had surveyed the landscape, judged it hostile to a student such as myself, and was actively attempting to protect me from one of the first complications of my identification as a gifted Black student. By giving me a job to do during recess and on school holidays, she was removing me from the dangerous physical and psychological taunts of my schoolyard and neighborhood peers who interpreted my bookishness as evidence that I was "acting like a girl" or alternately "acting White." Obviously, at eleven years old, I wasn't aware there was a growing body of research that had analyzed this kind of bullying and compulsory racial performance as a sadly common occurrence (Johnson, 2003; Whiting, 2009; Young, 2007). I simply knew that in 1980s Chicago to be accused of being a White girl was a problem when you are a Black boy (Henfield, 2012; Neal, 2005; Young, 2007). While I could more than hold my own in schoolyard fights (I was the rare nerd who could and did scrap with the worst of my elementary school bullies), I hated that I was compelled to defend myself in the first place. By the sixth grade, this far South Side of Chicago's school playground had long ceased to be a welcome place, and I am thankful that Young provided me refuge and encouragement.

So it was not a surprise that in sixth grade I found myself helping my teacher during spring-break week. What was a surprise is that the opportunity to see my entire school record presented itself. My curiosity then, as now, knew no bounds, so I happily took that opportunity to read my elementary school records. However, the more I perused them, the clearer several problematic childhood and school-related memories became.

The Triangle in the Square

I DISCOVERED THAT WHEN I FIRST BEGAN John D. Shoop Elementary School on Chicago's far South Side in the late 1970s I was placed in what was considered their remedial kindergarten class. This information came as a surprise to me because my older brothers had already taught me to read before I began kindergarten. I was also surprised by this information because by the sixth grade I had been identified as a high potential/gifted student and was generally considered by several teachers and peers to be one of the smartest students in the entire school. It's the primary reason I found myself in the middle of a lot of schoolyard fist fights! In fact, as a result of grades, awards, and test scores, I had successfully competed with thousands of sixth grade students across the city to be admitted to one of only three highly coveted public school gifted education programs available in Chicago at that time. I was already scheduled to leave Shoop School at the end of sixth grade and would be traveling 90–110 minutes each way every day to attend seventh grade at what was considered to be the most prestigious of the three programs: the accelerated middle school and high school program at Chicago's nationally renowned Whitney M. Young Academic Center and Whitney M. Young Magnet High School. I was one of only approximately one hundred students across the city of Chicago to be granted admittance that year to Whitney Young's seventh grade class. Thus, by the end of sixth grade, it seems I had already traveled a great distance in my educational journey because when I began kindergarten at my neighborhood school I had been described as a remedial student.

I stood there dumbfounded. How could I have been misidentified and categorized as in need of remedial schooling at the beginning of kindergarten? Then I remembered: A few days before starting kinder-garten, I was taken to the school for what, in retrospect, must have been a placement test disguised as what we would now call a play date. I was given a toy with various shaped blocks and expected to place the shapes into the appropriate slots. I picked up a triangle-shaped block, and though I knew the triangle would normally fit into the triangle slot, I recall that I became fascinated with the blocks. I became determined to get the triangle-shaped block into the square-shaped slot. I shoved and shoved the block until I managed to lodge a part of the block into the mismatched slot. I was proud of myself—but apparently, this did not seem to go over well. After the play-date/testing assessment, I was assigned to the remedial kindergarten class. Without my mother or me knowing it, at five years old, I had been "tracked." Granted, a play-date kindergarten assessment was a thin portfolio of information on which to base such an important decision—but then, as many studies have shown, it doesn't take a whole lot of convincing for a Black male student to be assessed as academically deficient or in need of special education (Moore, Henfield, & Owens, 2008). It would be several years before my tracking level would be upgraded. And it would be a fight—not by me but for me.

Not long after the start of my third grade year, at least three of my neighborhood school's teachers began to congregate in the hallways during their students' regulated restroom breaks. I began to notice that on several occasions these three teachers would engage in passionate discussions—discussions that were often punctuated by emphatic ges-tures towards me. It was clear they were often talking about me. I was confused, but I knew I wasn't in trouble for violating rules, so I enjoyed the attention. Still, I didn't know exactly why they were talking about me. Nor did I understand why the conversations were often so heated. But now, years later, with my school record in front of me, the general thrust of those conversations began to make sense. The combination of my third grade teacher's perceptions of my academic potential, an excel-lent school report card, and my above grade-level test scores were doing battle with an entrenched bureaucratic system that was suspicious of a Black, male remedial student who seemed to suddenly have the highest test scores in his class year after year. The teachers were discussing "what to do about him"—meaning me. According to the notes in the record, there was a debate whether I should be double promoted or at least academically upgraded in my tracking. I was too young to know exactly what the process entailed, but I do know that suddenly I was spending a lot of time with Mrs. Bennett, my older brother's fourth grade teacher. She seemed to become my advocate.

Mean Mrs. Elaine Bennett (as my brother called her) was a Black woman with a serious demeanor and her own sense of style. She wore her hair in a natural Afro style, though Afros had not been in vogue for more than a decade. She also wore huge glasses and often kept a couple of pens or pencils buried in the back of her massive mound of hair. She was smart, she was tough, and she was determined that I would be educated under her tutelage. By the middle of my third grade year, Bennett began coming to my third grade class almost every afternoon to escort me to her class. There, I would study language arts and mathematics with her fourth and fifth grade students. My school, which served an all-Black, working-class population, did not offer a gifted program, so this was the best it could offer. Even so, during my elementary school years, my unofficial identification as a gifted learner began to motivate my teachers to clear space and carve out opportunities for me. Their advocacy of my giftedness was able to cut through years of categorical sediment. Without my knowing exactly what was happening until years later, the label of a remedial student was removed dictating my education and my future because three conscientious, committed, Black, female teachers got together in a hallway over several days and decided that I was not exactly who the system said I was.

Like so many others, I had been a victim of a limited and narrow assessment criteria that failed to account for a child's creativity and determination as a sign of cognitive development or potential (Lawson-Davis, 2010). Worse, it was a flawed process that did not even consider the possibility that I might already know how to read and spell above my kindergarten grade level. No one asked or challenged me to read a book or to explain the story sequence in a picture book. It was a classic case of a deficit framework (Ford & Grantham, 2003) applied to a five-year-old from, literally, the other side of the tracks (an Illinois Metro commuter train station was located directly in the back of my childhood home). It was a brief assessment that took four years of schooling to start a correction process. Fortunately for me, these were

teachers who cared, teachers who took seriously the revolutionary man-
tle that I believe the education of a capable Black child to be. Fortunately, my kind of academic ability was one that showed up noticeably
and consistently on standardized tests. This fact, plus the quality of my
schoolwork, gave these three neighborhood school teachers the ammu-
nition and motivation they needed to find ways to poke holes in the
system. They surrounded me and created an educational village in the
midst of an educational environment and system that has historically
been slow to recognize giftedness in Black children and did not, at that
time, readily endorse grade skipping or double promotions when ability
was identified.

Out of My "Place"

BEFORE FINALLY BEING ACCEPTED and preparing to attend Whitney
Young Academic Center and High School for seventh grade, I was invited two years prior to apply for admission to the Annie Keller Gifted School on the far South Side of Chicago. Based on its location in
Chicago (west of Western Avenue, for many years the city's unofficial
racial geographical barrier) and on who showed up that day to take the
entrance exam (I was one of very few Black students), the Keller School
at that time seemed to cater to a majority White student population.
That fact didn't bother me, though I was taunted by a Black student
at my neighborhood school when I made the mistake of mentioning
that I might transfer to a gifted school. The student practically hissed
at me. "You think you're so smart. You wait. Those White kids gonna
show you something!" Still, I was excited beyond belief. Being invited
to apply to Keller Gifted School was the first confirmation outside my
neighborhood school that I might be able to compete on a larger scale
as a gifted student.

I was unbelievably excited the day my mother escorted me to the
school in order to take the entrance exam. I had just turned ten years
old, and I wore my favorite pair of oversized blue khaki pants. I was also
a fan of magicians at the time, and while waiting for my turn to take the
exam, I entertained my mother and the other parents in the waiting area
by performing magic tricks with a set of magician cards I had received as
a Christmas present. Finally, it was my turn to take the exam. I walked
down a long hallway and found the classroom. I was the only Black in a

room full of White students, a situation I had never experienced before that day. The test was also in an unfamiliar format. I didn't feel intimidated, but I also wasn't as comfortable or quite as confident as I usually felt when I took a standardized test. Still, after it was all over, I felt I'd done very well.

As I walked back down the hallway that would take me back to my mother in the waiting area, I saw another kid approaching from the opposite direction. We were the only two people in the hallway, and so as our paths crossed, I prepared to offer up a friendly hello. He didn't offer a hello in return. He had other plans. As we passed each other, his face contorted with anger and he paused just long enough to spit a little hate in my direction. "What are you doing here, nigger?!" And as quickly as he lobbed that verbal and psychic grenade, he went on about his day. Needless to say, I was stunned—but not in the way we might expect. I'd actually been called a nigger before then and more than once. On more than one occasion, when I was five years old, White passengers in a speeding car had screamed the racial epithet at me as I played outside on the street where I lived. This is what I now call, literally, "drive-by racism." It's wrong and hurtful, but it's aimed at Black people in general. This incident was different and hurtful in a deeper way. It was up close, in my face, and the hostility felt personal. And though I never mentioned this incident to my mother until very recently, it clearly resonates for me. It's been thirty years since it occurred, but I remember it as if it were yesterday.

The hostility inherent in this attack was palpable, hurtful, and insulting, but what I find disturbing about the incident to this very day is not so much his use of "nigger"—as much as it is the framework in which he utilized his racial slur. In other words, the logics behind what allowed the White student to state his question as a slur in the first place are what interest me. From the student's perspective, it was a rhetorical question. The question already contained the answer to that which he "asked," "What are you doing here, nigger?!" The only thing this kid knew about me was that I was Black and that I was probably there to take the entrance exam. In all likelihood, he was also there to take the entrance exam or he was already a student at the school. To him I was either a competitor or a potential classmate—or maybe I was just Black, and that was enough. In either instance, he made it clear by the racist condemnation he hurled at me that he felt I did not belong at Keller or in his community just by the virtue of the color of my skin. Over time I have realized that the insult was spat at me, indignantly, as an accusation that I was shamefully out of "my place" in attempting to join this elite educational space. I can now place the incident within an appropriate analytical framework that helps me realize this charged moment was much more complex than a simple, unfortunate, and hurtful racial slur.

First, in considering my narrative arc thus far, we begin to see Black giftedness continuing its attempts to operate as a cause-célèbre sword that creates opportunities. If it were not a sword, a weapon used in efforts to advance, I could not have stepped foot on the grounds of Keller Gifted School to take the test in the first place. But this incident also begins to foreshadow some of the differences that will play themselves out in my young adulthood. In this childhood incident we glimpse how my giftedness functioned within a predominantly Black environment as a call to action for the provision of deeper educational resources that exceeded those available in my home community. With my neighborhood school unable to provide an official gifted learner curriculum much beyond Bennett's patchwork solution, my teacher's identification of me as a gifted student fought for me and carried me into a largely White setting where we could presumably find educational opportunities more in tune with my gifts. In my experience, this is when we begin to see a complication of Black giftedness—how it can function in a predominantly White environment as an innocent co-producer of latent and explicit hostilities towards Black achievement. This is when I began to see how my embodiment of the idea of a Black scholastic elite seeking access to that which had previously remained an exclusive province of the White scholastic elite begins to unsettle some of its White inhabitants.

Ultimately, I would end up crying many inconsolable tears for days and days when I was denied admission to Keller Gifted School. Still, the experience is instructive. In my failed attempt to gain admittance to this elite space, I experienced one of the first foundational moments and clues that, in retrospect, signaled to me that a shift would come—that my Black giftedness would necessarily evolve one day from a metaphorical sword to a metaphorical shield. It would shift from being a cause for educational advocacy in my childhood to, in my adulthood, serving as a barrier of self-protection against the power of White suspicion of Black incompetence in professional settings.

The Evolution Begins: Cast, Caste, and Outcast

BY MY SENIOR YEAR of high school, I had expanded beyond the narrow self-identification of my elementary school years as the smart kid. I was no longer content to be just an academic nerd. After a successful dalliance with my high school's cross-country running team (to prove I could be an athlete if I so desired), I discovered theatre, dance, and writing. I spent most of my time outside of Whitney Young High School's intense classrooms with the other theatre lovers. We called ourselves "The Company." I fused being an academic nerd with being an artistic nerd, and ever since then distinctions between academic and artistic" have always struck me as horribly shallow and false. It was both a strong academic record and an active arts profile that led me, despite my family's inability to afford such things, to participate in various select summer programs. I won scholarships—one in the academic program at the Midwest Talent Search/Center for Talent Development at Northwestern University and at two top-ranked summer collegiate theatre programs at Carnegie Mellon University and Northwestern University through its National High School Institute.

I loved these experiences, and despite some challenges adjusting to the affluent environments at these programs, I did well. As a result, by September of my senior year of high school, I was notified that I was one of five out of the 150 students who attended that summer who was offered early admittance to Carnegie Mellon University (one of the other early admits was my friend Gabriel Macht, better known these days as a talented television star—he plays Harvey Specter on the USA television series *Suits*). But for various reasons, including the fact that I had (and needed) better financial aid offers from other top-ranked university theatre programs, I chose not to attend Carnegie Mellon.

Instead, I began my young adulthood as an undergraduate theatre student in the competitive BFA degree conservatory program at the University of Southern California School of Dramatic Arts. The theatre school was and continues to be a top-ranked undergraduate program, renowned for its rigorous training of stage and film actors. When I first arrived, a Latino student warned me that Black and Latino actors were not cast in main-stage productions with any consistency. But I did well at USC, becoming one of the rare freshmen students (and Black students) at that time to be cast in the school's coveted main-stage productions. This was a bit of a big deal in the small, intense ecosphere of a competitive theatre program, and after being cast in three shows during my first year, including two main-stage productions, I quickly gained a reputation among my teachers and classmates as a smart, formidable actor with great potential.

By the end of my sophomore year, I had racked up excellent grades while performing major roles in six productions, four of them in main-stage productions. At age nineteen, I became one of the youngest performers in the school's history to receive the highest honor the USC Drama School bestowed upon current theatre students. I received the Jack Nicholson Award for Most Outstanding Performer/Student. The award was worth eight thousand dollars. I was thrilled. But, as I later discovered, many of my peers were decidedly not thrilled.

It wasn't long after winning the award that a fellow (White) classmate from Chicago pulled me aside and questioned me about which role of the many I'd played had qualified me to win the Nicholson Award. After I eventually questioned his question, he finally told me that the pervasive rumor around the school was that I had won the award only because I was Black. He suggested that the school was playing politics in selecting me as that year's best actor and student. I was taken aback but shrugged it off. Though I noticed that he didn't say anything about rumors circulating around that year's female recipient of the Nicholson Award (the talented Leigh-Allyn Baker, who would go on to eventually become the recent star of Disney's popular television series *Good Luck, Charlie*). She was my also my age but hadn't done nearly as many productions at that time as I had. She was also White. There certainly were students who were envious of her having received the award, but no one questioned her right to receive the award. While Baker went on to be cast in even larger, more publicly visible main-stage roles during the rest of her tenure at the school, I began to struggle in subsequent years and wouldn't be cast in a visible, main-stage production again until I neared graduation two years later. While there are a myriad of reasons as to why this could have happened, it was hard not to notice that my casting practically ceased after I'd won the Nicholson Award and that my win was not only questioned and resented on general terms but also explicitly linked to race.

I didn't realize it or wouldn't admit it at the time, but the combination of the rumors and then the slowdown in my casting was a blow to my confidence. I wouldn't recover for at least a year. I had felt welcomed and embraced at the school, and while there is always envious sniping that goes along with the casting decisions at top theatre programs, this was the first time such sniping was racialized to the point where I was actually told that my achievements were being dismissed by some of my peers because of the color of my skin. I had optimistically thought that by choosing to educate myself and work in "the world of the imagination" (as I called it at that time) that I was escaping, or least diminishing, the impact of racism on my life. Instead, I began to find the exact opposite to be true. I had failed to consider how deeply Eurocentric American theatre has historically been and remains and that professional theatre, at its highest levels, remains the province of a self-appointed cultural elite. Nor did I have the analytical skills at that time to understand how deeply classed working in culture industries can be. The fact that I—a poor, Black kid from Chicago—won the school's most visible and financially remunerative award based largely on my ability to perform Shakespearean language turned out to be too much cognitive dissonance for some people to accept. In being generously cast in this top school's productions based on a gifted ability to understand and speak classical texts, I had somehow broken through a caste system that students of color consistently complained about and initially warned me existed in the school. In being repeatedly cast in major roles I had broken through this supposed caste system. But in breaking through that caste, I found myself being punished and, for a time, becoming something of an outcast.

My life up to this point and this experience made it very clear to me that my academic and artistic gifts had created educational opportunities. But, in adulthood, as my educational experiences (such as performing in a top theatre program's main stage in Los Angeles) began to resemble professional opportunities, I began to see that there would be resistance and pushback that would implicitly and explicitly be tied unfavorably to the color of my skin. While I thought that embracing an overtly artistic pursuit would shift the rules of engagement for my giftedness, I also eventually learned that my ability to be cast in complex, language-based dramatic literature was as much of an academic gift as it was an artistic one. Thus, the terrain in my young adulthood was not so different from what I encountered in my attempts to gain admittance to Keller School during my elementary school years.

In both instances, my presence was questioned in different but related ways. At Keller Gifted School, a White student questioned my right to exist in an elite environment. As an undergraduate at a top-ranked theatre program, some White students expressed their suspicion that I had not earned my accolades meritoriously and questioned why I was anointed by the faculty as an example of excellence in their elite environment. In both cases, my giftedness was problematized because of my Blackness. The sword, in the form of my abilities and the advocacy of teachers and professors, had continued to justify my presence and clear a path for my advancement. But, in retrospect, as I matured, a shift was clearly afoot. Slowly but surely, the need to wield my giftedness in different ways was becoming evident to me. The ways in which the sword would need to become a shield of self-protection had begun during my college years. It would more fully manifest itself when I entered the professional work force just a few years later.

Black Giftedness as an Adult (The Shield)

A man's gift maketh room for him and
bringeth him before great men.

—*Proverbs 18:16 (KJV)*

AFTER COMPLETING MY UNDERGRADUATE DEGREE, I embarked upon a successful performance career for almost eight years on the New York stage. Many of those years included traveling the world performing in the international hit theatre and percussion show, *Stomp*. After leaving *Stomp*, I began efforts to transition a burgeoning playwriting career into a career as a television writer in the entertainment industry. This was easier said than done, but now, after almost thirteen years in a profession known for very short careers, television is a career that I enjoy working in and pursuing to this day. At the same time, I managed to fulfill my dream of returning to graduate school to attain a doctorate degree.

Soon after finally getting the chance to begin my television career, I was asked to produce an episode of a television drama that I'd written. This was a big deal. This meant that I was the creative steward of the set alongside the director, making sure that the vision of the executive producer of the series is realized as the episode is being filmed. The star of this particular show was known to be difficult and to challenge and even insult the writers and producers on the scripts they had written. But what he did to me, particularly as a relatively new writer in television, was astonishing even to the writers who were used to enduring this actor's outbursts. We were in the midst of filming a scene on a soundstage when he stopped the scene and marched over to me. I was sitting, as is customary, in the episode producer's chair right behind the director and the camera. "You!" He pointed directly at me. "I want to talk to you!" "Sure," I replied, bracing myself for what was coming next. I followed him over to another part of the set. "Explain this to me," he demanded, as he pointed to an emotion-filled speech I'd written where his character reminisced about an old friend. I began to explain my intention and reasons for writing the speech the way that I did and how I envisioned it functioning in the story when he cut me off and yelled, "That's not it!" He then angrily threw his script, the one I had written, clear across the set. Then he stood there, pacing back and forth. I didn't know what to do but thought it best not to interrupt, so I stood there watching him pace. I wasn't sure whether or not he was waiting for me to retrieve the script, but I simply looked at him as he paced, thinking, "I know this man doesn't expect me to pick up that script." Later, I surprised myself as I recounted the incident to my boss, telling her that I refused to pick up the script because "I'm not his slave!" Luckily, after several moments, he seemed to realize I wasn't going after the script. He picked it up but then launched into a loud rant. "See! You writers! You just put anything down here, and I'm supposed to . . . Damn it!" He finally walked away.

Tirades like this continued for the next two days of filming. A typical day working on the set was twelve hours, so these were very long days. The longer the days, the more public were the tirades. At one point the actor ruthlessly berated me at the top of his lungs in front of at least one hundred crew members. Still, I did my best. I stood there, and I took it. During this time I was also subjected to pop quizzes that the star would give me between takes, in the time it would take for the crew to set up his scenes for filming. During the crew's set-ups, he would literally walk up to me out of the blue and just start drilling me with questions about arcane military history. He considered this history to be a relevant part of his character, and he wanted to see if I knew this history. The pop quizzes and tirades went on for two days. At one point, when I did not answer a question quickly enough and to his satisfaction, he bellowed, "That's *two*, Anthony! That's *two*!" The implication was clear. One more answer from me that he didn't approve of and he would attempt to have me fired off the show. He made it clear that he thought I was unqualified to write and produce for his show, and his abusive behavior towards me made this clear to anyone within earshot. The exchanges got so toxic during the filming process that at one point a veteran, respected Black actress who was working as a guest star on the episode came to me between takes and offered encouragement. "It's going to be all right," she said. "You're going to be all right."

Eventually, the actor's son, who worked as his assistant and had become a friend of mine, came to the set and gave his father an earful about his behavior towards me. At that point, the abhorrent treatment turned into a palpable resentment. Finally, my executive producer banned me from the set for a day—not because of my actions but because this actor had made me, a writer who was new to the show, a target of his frustrations and general dislike of his own show.

This was a painful, embarrassing experience. It is also, I would soon learn, just one variation on several other encounters that would play themselves out on several sets, offices, and backstage environments during the course of my television career. Given the intensity of the barrage lobbed at me during this incident, it is a wonder I did not succumb to a public outburst or private tears. Even more so, I was amazed and thankful that, unlike the Nicholson award backlash I endured during my college years, I did not lose my confidence. Despite the circumstances, I was able to fully engage and function with excellence after this encounter. In retrospect, I believe I endured this experience successfully because my giftedness had evolved. It was now a formidable shield that covered and protected me and lent me a necessary resilience. A lifetime reservoir of both good experiences and bad experiences had conspired to build my resiliency up to such a point where race-tinged questions about my competence simply didn't affect my internal sense of self in the same way. By the time I had reached a point where I could be hired by a broadcast network to work in the culturally elite position of a television writer-producer, too many people had nurtured my Black giftedness as a child for me to fall prey easily to attacks on my Black giftedness as an adult. Though privileged spaces, such as this one in the television industry, would continue to test me, I had grown. I didn't realize it at the time, but in my refusal at a crucial moment to bend down and pick up the script that the actor had thrown across the room, I had refused to capitulate to the actor's sense of (White) entitlement, an entitlement that is inextricably entangled with notions of (White) superiority. Thus, I had begun to rely on the evolved, shielding, and protective capacity of Black giftedness, on the fact that I knew I had earned my spot at this elite table as much as anyone else had. I was angry, but I was also a legitimate member of that process and of that space. The identification my Black giftedness as a child was no longer about needing to advance as much as it was about being able to stand still and stand up as an adult.

From Sword to Shield: Notes on the Evolution of Black Giftedness

One ever feels his twoness—an American, a Negro;
two souls, two thoughts, two unreconciled strivings;
two warring ideals in one dark body,
whose strength along keeps it from being torn asunder.

—*W. E. B. Du Bois*

I HAVE A CONFESSION. Privately, I often thought that identification and cultivation as a Black gifted child primarily offered an opportunity to become educated and then attain the material goods and lifestyle associated with the American Dream. In plain terms, I thought it was a chance to live the good life—to acquire individual wealth, to climb the socio-economic ladder, to be able to say one day that I had "arrived." I now regard such narrow, materialistic goals as a much smaller part of my ambition. The gift of being a Black gifted learner and being identified and educated I now consider from a more expansive societal viewpoint. As much as it is a responsibility for the American education system to make sure talented, culturally different students do not fall between the chasms in the system, I now also consider Black giftedness to be as much of a calling and responsibility for the child who endures into adulthood.

I would like to suggest that one of the most valuable utilities of Black giftedness is that it enhances the possibility of the strength of will to not be, in the words of Du Bois, "torn asunder." While I believe in and applaud individual achievement, both my own and others, I do not wish to restrict the impact and purpose of Black giftedness to the realm of individual enrichment. In short, I'm certainly not against the traditional markers of success, but Black giftedness is not necessarily and exclusively about getting paid. It is inevitably entangled with the American notion of progress. Black giftedness might include an upward economic mobility but should not be defined solely by the achievement of such mobility. It hurts me to say that because I felt the sting of working-class struggle at crucial moments when I was a child. I do not romanticize poverty or near poverty as some perverted form of "keeping it real." I do like many nice, stimulating things that life can offer. But it has also hurt even more to discover the trap of spiritual and political impoverishment that is engaged when centering narrow definitions of success as a reward or worse, a validation of Black sentience and Black giftedness. I have come to understand, through my narrative and the study of those similarly situated, that Black giftedness is not so much about me and my progress as much as it is about us and our progress as a family, a nation, and as a people.

I have argued through an articulation and examination of several narrative vignettes that the manifestation, reception, and purpose of giftedness in the Black body shifts over time. The giftedness that often begins as a weapon, as a *raison d'être* for educational advocacy on behalf of a gifted Black child, often transforms into a protective armor for the gifted Black adult once that adult encounters the ambivalence and systemic rage that the embodiment and reality of social progress engenders in significant segments of White society (Sparks, 2009; Coates, 2014; Anderson, 2014). In other words, as an adult, Black giftedness becomes less a cause for celebration and becomes more an imperfect shield against racial suspicion and hostility from those in dominant culture that seek to question the Black presence in so-called elite spaces and thereby reify their own positionalities and privileges by reinvesting in the (false) sense of an essential (White) superiority.

It is not, however—as Nina Simone, Langston Hughes, and so many others have warned us—a shield that predetermines positive outcomes. A Black giftedness that is properly cultivated and educated can create space for opportunities, it creates the capacity for excellence, and it does demand notice. Like a sword, it creates the possibility of cutting through the thicket and matrix of institutional bias. But it cannot guarantee acceptance or control the behavior of any individual. Black giftedness cannot dictate or control the responses of any society deeply invested in maintaining a social order, but it does complicate the society's response to the sentient power of the Black presence. I do not wish to diminish the power and potential of that complication. Indeed, in this case, the complicated response is partially the point, for the complicated response is one that contains fissures, cracks, and inconsistencies. The complicated response that Black giftedness demands may not result in the freedom and equanimity that the human spirit yearns for and often dies in the pursuit of. But as inchoate as it may be with regard to the goals of Black civil rights, educational access, and social justice, the complicated response of White society to the existence of a Black, gifted child that survives and thrives long enough to become a productive Black, gifted adult is a response that contains the possibility of possibility. To the question posed earlier—just who the hell do you think you are?—my giftedness, my identified and nurtured Black giftedness speaks for me, even when I'd rather keep quiet. It answers, simply but self-determinedly, "Who I think I am is up to me. It is not up to you."

References

Anderson, C. (2014, August 29) Opinion: Ferguson isn't about black rage against cops. It's White rage against progress. *Washington Post*. Retrieved from http://www.washingtonpost.com/opinions/ferguson-wasnt-black-rage-against-copsit-was-white-rage-against-progress/2014/08/29/3055e3f4-2d75-11e4-bb9b-97ae96fad33_story.html.

Bennett Jr., L. (1988). *Before the Mayflower: A history of Black America* (6th Ed.). New York, NY: Penguin Books.

Coates, T. (2014, December 22). Blues lives matter. *The Atlantic. com*. Retrieved from http://www.theatlantic.com/politics/

archive/2014/12/blue-lives-matter-nypd-shooting/383977/?s-
ingle_page=true#disqus_thread.

Day-Vines, N., Patton J. M., & Baytops, J. L. (2003). African American
adolescents: The impact of race, culture, and middle class status.
Professional School Counseling, 7(1), 40–51.

Edmunds, A. L., & Edmunds, G. A. (2005) Sensitivity: A double-edged
sword for the pre-adolescent and adolescent gifted child. *Roeper
Review, 27*(2), 69–77.

———. (2014). The sensitivity of precocious child writers: More
evidence of the double-edged sword. *Roeper Review, 36*(3),
178–189.

Ford, D. Y. (2010). Underrepresentation of culturally different students
in gifted education: Reflections about current problems and recommendations for the future. *Gifted Child Today, 33*(3), 31–35.

Ford, D. Y. & Grantham, T. C. (2003). Providing access for culturally
diverse gifted students: From deficit to dynamic thinking.
Theory Into Practice, 42(3), 217–225.

Gilmore, R. W. (2007). *Golden gulag: Prisons, surplus, crisis, and opposition in globalizing California.* Berkeley, CA: University of California Press.

Grantham, T. C. (2004). Multicultural mentoring to increase black
male representation in gifted programs. *The Gifted Child Quarterly,48*(3), 232–245.

Hale, J. (1982). *Black children: Their roots, culture, and learning styles.*
Baltimore, MD: Johns Hopkins University Press.

Henfield, M. (2012). Masculinity identity development and its relevance to supporting talented Black males. *Gifted Child Today, 35*(3), p. 179–186.

Johnson, E. P. (2003). *Appropriating Blackness: Performance and the politics of authenticity.* Durham, NC: Duke University Press.

Lawson-Davis, J. (2010). *Bright, talented, and Black: A guide for families
of African American gifted learners.* Scottsdale, AZ: Great Potential Press.

Lipsitz, G. (1998). *The possessive investment in Whiteness: How White
people profit from identity politics.* Philadelphia: Temple University Press.

Moore III, J. M., Henfield, M. S., & Owens, D. (2008). African American males in special education: Their attitudes and perceptions toward high school counselors and school counseling services. *American Behavioral Scientist, 51,* 907–927.

Neal, M. A. (2005). *New Black man.* New York, NY: Routledge.

Omi, M., & Winant, H. (1994). *Racial formation in the United States: From the 1960s to the 1990s* (2ⁿᵈ Ed). New York, NY: Routledge.

Sparks, A. (2009). Minstrel politics or "he speaks too well:" Rhetoric, race, and resistance in the 2008 presidential campaign. *Argumentation and Advocacy, 46*(1), 21.

Townsend, B., & Patton, J. (1997). Creating inclusive environments for African American children and youth with gifts and talents. *Roeper Review, 20*(1), 13–17. doi:10.1080/02783199709553844.

Whiting, G. (2009). Gifted Black males: Understanding and decreasing barriers to achievement and identity. *Roeper Review, 31*(4), 224–233.

Young, V.A. (2007). *Your average nigga: Performing race, literacy, and masculinity.* Detroit, MI: Wayne State University Press.

CHAPTER 5

Paving the Way for a Career That Makes Room for Your Gifts to Flourish

Tia Shaffer, EdD

Introduction

IT IS MY FUNDAMENTAL BELIEF that each person on earth is gifted in some facet. We all have something to offer this world, something that benefits not only us but others too. But gifts don't develop by themselves. We need opportunities to nurture them, to coax them out into the light. Unfortunately, many of us have not realized such opportunities. Instead, we spend our entire adult lives doing nothing more than earning paychecks. We live our lives committed to things that inhibit the ability to give back. Sadly, never fully realizing one's gifts can be detrimental to the soul, thus inhibiting the ability to blossom and smile.

I am eternally grateful for those who recognized the seeds of my talents. Not only did they acknowledge my giftedness in music and education, but they also gave me a platform to really explore my gifts. Though cognizant of my gifts, I remain challenged when discerning how those gifts can help me navigate my life and career. Contributing to *Running the Long Race in Gifted Education: Narratives and Interviews from Culturally Diverse Gifted Adults* was therapeutic as I embarked upon a retrospective journey that started when I was five years old. But as I wrote this chapter, at first I still did not identify as a gifted individual. My reluctance to being distinguished as gifted was due to a deep sense of humility and fear of being viewed as someone who stands out from the crowd. However, after researching various definitions of giftedness and reflecting upon how I have always stood out among my peers, I now embrace being regarded as gifted. Furthermore, writing this chapter helped me to contemplate and envision a career path that makes room for my gifts to flourish.

There is significance in culling a career in which one can use one's gifts. The ability to utilize gifts in the workplace is constructive, valuable, and essential. According to a 2014 Gallup poll, full-time US employees report working an average of forty-seven hours per week (Saad, 2014). Nearly four in ten of those surveyed report working at least fifty hours per week (Saad, 2014). It is dreadful to imagine gifted individuals spending over a third of their day performing tasks that do not cater to their passions or areas of giftedness. So again, I assert that paving the way for a career that creates space for one's gifts is vital.

I carry the blessing and burden of being a Black woman who is gifted. In the grand scheme of life, I prefer to view my gender, race, and giftedness as manifestations of God's benevolence. God gave me these attributes because I could handle them! This adage is very true in my life: To whom much is given, much is expected. Currently, I am a theatre director and chairperson of Fine Arts in an urban high school in Georgia. As stated earlier, my areas of giftedness include theatre, music, teaching, writing, and leadership. My educational background includes a BA in journalism and film from Georgia State University (Atlanta), Master of Arts in Christian education from the Interdenominational Theological Center's Morehouse School of Religion (Atlanta), K–12 Theatre Educator Certification from Columbus State University (Columbus, Georgia), and EdD in leadership from Liberty University (Lynchburg, Virginia).

In this chapter, I provide a narrative of my experiences as a gifted individual. Specifically, I explore definitions of giftedness and how I discovered my gifts. Next, I discuss how I am currently coping in a work environment that, at times, stifles my gifts and how I am paving the way for a career that makes room for my gifts to flourish. Lastly, I reflect upon how ambassadors for giftedness can help others to discover their areas of giftedness.

Discovering Gifts in Childhood

SINCE THIS ANTHOLOGY OFFERS various perspectives and narratives pertaining to giftedness, it is appropriate that I first focus on key definitions of giftedness, all of which inform my unique perspective on what it means to be gifted.

According to the National Association for Gifted Children (NAGC), "Giftedness, intelligence, and talent are fluid concepts and may look different in different contexts and cultures. Even within schools you will find a range of beliefs about the word 'gifted,' which has become a term with multiple meanings and much nuance" (NAGC, 2010). Additionally, the NAGC (2010) asserts it is necessary to redefine giftedness for the twenty-first century. It argues that gifted individuals demonstrate exceptional aptitudes, competences, or achievement in areas that include math, language, music, painting, dance, sports, etc. (NAGC, 2010). Likewise, the renowned scholar Renzulli contends:

> Gifted behavior occurs when there is an interaction among three basic clusters of human traits: above-average general and/or specific abilities, high levels of task commitment (motivation), and high levels of creativity. Gifted and talented children are those who possess or are capable of developing this composite of traits and applying them to any potentially valuable area of human performance. As noted in the Schoolwide Enrichment Model, gifted behaviors can be found "in certain people (not all people), at certain times (not all the time), and under certain circumstances (not all circumstances)" (1978, p.180).

Francoys Gagne (1985) argues that giftedness is characterized by the possession and use of untrained and spontaneously expressed natural abilities (called aptitudes or gifts) in at least one ability domain to a degree that places a child among the top 10 percent of his or her age peers.

The aforementioned descriptions of giftedness (from the National Association of Gifted Children, Renzulli, and Gagne) are vital because they acknowledge that there is no one-size-fits-all definition of giftedness. Giftedness may apply to multiple fields or disciplines; giftedness is not solely measured by a test score or one's academic performance.

As an elementary and middle school student, I do not remember being tested for a Talented and Gifted (TAG) program. In fact, my grades indicated that I was slightly above average but certainly not gifted according to my school's standards. I vividly recall the students who were labeled as talented and gifted. They took more academically rigorous courses than the general-population students. I always viewed myself as a smart girl, so in the back of my mind, I wondered why I was not labeled gifted. However, I do not remember being particularly bothered by not being a TAG student. I instinctively knew there was something special about me. Furthermore, the adults in my life recognized and nurtured my unique gifts, although those gifts were not discovered via specific aptitude tests. Instead, they witnessed a raw talent and sought to develop it further.

For example, my mother put me in the church choir when I was seven years old. Mrs. Jacobs, my elderly choir director, immediately made me a featured soloist. Freddie Hendricks, my high school theatre teacher, identified my potential for a future in theatre, although I was scared out of my mind and lacked experience. Again, I am thankful for parents, teachers, and church elders who recognized my gifts and acted upon that recognition. I can only imagine how my life would be today if the adults in my life had taken on a limited or one-dimensional perspective on giftedness.

Due to my religious upbringing, I ultimately came to view gifts as more than being extraordinarily good at something. Rather, I saw gifts as supernatural endowments from God. God gives us gifts in order to bless others. When we believe our gifts are from God, we are then convicted to use them to carry out the mission of loving, giving and serving for the sake of kingdom or "queendom" building. There are passages of Scripture in the Bible that speak about spiritual gifts. Romans 12:6–8 (New Revised Standard Version [NRSV]) states, "We have gifts that differ according to the grace given to us: prophecy, in proportion to faith; ministry, in ministering; the teacher, in teaching; the exhorter, in exhortation; the giver, in generosity; the leader, in diligence; the compassionate, in cheerfulness.

I Corinthians 12:4–10 (NRSV) states:

> Now there are varieties of gifts, but the same Spirit; and there are varieties of services, but the same Lord; and there are varieties of activities, but it is the same God who activates all of them in everyone. To each is given the manifestation of the Spirit for the common good. To one is given through the Spirit the utterance of wisdom, and to another the utterance of knowledge according to the same Spirit; to another faith by the same Spirit, to another gifts of healing by the one Spirit; to another the working of miracles, to another prophecy, to another the discernment of spirits, to another various kinds of tongues, to another interpretation of tongues.

The remainder of I Corinthians chapter 12 (NRSV) explains that gifts are interdependent. One cannot exist without the other, for they all make up the members of one body. Each part is needed so that the body may be whole. Therefore, we should not erroneously assume that one gift is superior to another. Here, we see that both secular and sacred texts speak to the importance of validating the various gifts that individuals possess. To limit giftedness to certain areas (e.g., math reasoning or music) is to exclude segments of our student bodies, religious communities, and society from the birthright of realizing their unique gifts.

The discovery of my gifts has been an on-going process. This began when I was about five years old and continues to unfold to this present day. In the next section, I pay special attention to how my talents were discovered, reaffirmed, or both at various stages in my life.

My parents said I used to sing a lot at home. This prompted my mother to put me in the children's choir at church. My choir director was an elderly woman named Eugenia Jacobs. I was her pride and joy. She told me I was special, and she took me under her wing. My first solo was a song titled "A Sunbeam." The words to the song proclaimed: "A sunbeam, a sunbeam. Jesus wants me for a sunbeam. A sunbeam, a sunbeam, I'll be a sunbeam for Him." I learned and delivered the song effortlessly. One Sunday after service was over, my church's sound technician, Mr. Henry told my mother that I had a special talent for singing. He was impressed that I could hear the notes and stay on pitch. Additionally, during a Black History Program at church, Jacobs taught us an old Negro Spiritual titled "Wade in the Water." She also had us narrate the story of how enslaved Africans escaped from Southern plantations to freedom in the North. I was one of the main narrators. After my performance that night, my parents and church elders realized that I also had the gift of speaking.

It was not uncommon for children in our church to be called upon to speak. All of us had our share of speeches, poems, and recitations. However, I was recognized as someone particularly gifted in that area. Thus, at age thirteen, I was selected to represent my church in an oratorical contest sponsored by the Progressive National Baptist Convention in Memphis, Tennessee. Through that oratorical experience I discovered more of my gifts. Sister Ramona Benson, one of the youth ministry volunteers, worked with me on crafting a speech. It was to be based on the Book of Ezekiel 37:1–14, which tells the story of the "Valley of Dry Bones." The process for developing this speech was to read, discuss, and interpret the Scripture. Of course, the last steps included writing the speech and practicing its delivery.

Sister Ramona Benson reported to my mother that she did not have to do much in the process of preparing me for the speech. After she and I talked about the Scripture, I wrote the speech on my own. This act was exceptional and quite unusual. After some practice and preparation, Sister Gloria Hollis, the Youth and Children's ministry director, put me and the other participating students on a chartered bus to Memphis for the convention.

I vividly remember the day of the oratorical contest. Sister Hollis and I were invited to an exclusive luncheon just before the contest. I ate the gourmet chicken and rice, but the butterflies in my stomach would not allow me to contain what I had just consumed, as I regurgitated all of my food in the nearby restroom. Sister Hollis tried to comfort me, but there was not much she could do to console me. Finally, the time for the contest arrived. I remember my opponent, a young, confident girl from another church. When my time came to speak, I recall a room filled with teenagers, all of whom watched me as I approached the podium. Other details after approaching the podium were a blur; it seemed as if I was possessed by the Spirit. It felt that the Spirit used my mouth to speak and then exited when the task of speaking was done! The next moment I remember was standing on the stage as the judges announced that I was the first place winner. The youth from my church spoke in amazement about how boldly I delivered the speech. Sister Hollis could not believe that the same sick, nervous girl from earlier that day had done such a phenomenal job in the contest.

News of my performance at the convention resulted in me being invited to be the keynote youth speaker at the First Lady's Luncheon at my church. I was just as nervous reciting the speech at church as I was at the convention. However, I received a standing ovation, and people were amazed by the sermonic qualities of my speech. Yes, sermonic! Looking back on the experience, I realize that I was writing sermons at age thirteen. Hence, I had suddenly discovered the emergent gift of interpreting Scripture, writing sermons, and even preaching. Please note that this gift of preaching has been indefinitely put on hold since I was thirteen and may be revisited only if God chases me down and forces me to do it.

At age eleven, I joined the youth choir under the tutelage of the late Crystal Michelle Harris, the pastor's daughter. Reflecting back on that time, I remember that she eagerly awaited the year I turned eleven so I could join her choir. Jacobs reluctantly released me from the children's choir, knowing it was time for me to move on. Immediately, Crystal put me to work as a soloist and much-appreciated addition to the soprano section. I must give Crystal credit for exposing me to various genres of music, such as spirituals, traditional gospel, contemporary gospel, and even opera. She herself was a trained opera singer, and under her influence, I became a versatile singer. She recognized my gift, and she was one of the people that supported me in my choir studies throughout my school years.

Church was the first context in which my gifts were nurtured. However, public school teachers and administrators were also instrumental in developing my gifts and talents. As a fifth grader, I joined the chorus at A. Phillip Randolph Elementary School. I was not assigned solos in the choir, but once other adults in the school realized I had the gift of singing, they quickly found ways to feature my talent. Mrs. Gray, my fifth grade teacher, arranged for me to sing at a hotel event. I do not remember what kind of event it was. I simply recall her picking me up from my house early one Saturday morning. My accompanist was a teenager whom I did not know and had never practiced with before the day of the event. I sang "Tomorrow" from the musical *Annie*. As usual, my singing was a hit, and everyone loved it.

Another gift that emerged in elementary school was leadership. During that time, I did not see it as a gift. In spite of that fact, I ran for Student Government Association (SGA) president, and although it was my first year at the school and people doubted I would be popular enough to pull in enough votes, I won! Though I cannot remember if I made any significant impact, I would like to think I made a difference.

At Camp Creek Middle School in Fulton County, Georgia, my musical talents were further nurtured by adults who saw my potential. Some classmates and I formed a singing group called Fusion. Fusion performed at talent shows and special programs around the school. John Elmore, our school's paraprofessional, who was also a talented musician, was instrumental in arranging songs, playing the piano for us, and teaching us harmonies. We were exceptional, because at age twelve, we were singing three- and four-part harmony, a talent that many of our peers did not possess. We also performed at churches and a special program at a shopping mall. This singing hobby soon became serious.

By our eighth grade year, Fusion met with Ms. Marilyn, the aunt of one of the group members. She was a producer and songwriter who wanted our group to sing her music. We had rehearsal sessions at her house and performed at a couple of events. It was only a matter of time before Marilyn noticed that three of five of the group members were not serious. She made changes to Fusion by removing the three unfocused girls and adding a cute little boy. This new, unique group was now called Signature. Marilyn taught us one of her original songs, set up a recording studio session, and introduced us to a management team. It was at this moment that I realized our musical gifts had transcended shopping malls and school concerts. Signature was now crossing over into the professional arena. Ultimately, Signature disbanded when one of the members decided she did not want to pursue a professional singing career. In 1995, Marilyn submitted our studio recording of her song to a songwriting competition and received an award. Although our group was no more, we took pride in knowing our work was appreciated by professionals in the music industry.

During my stint with Signature, I also joined the middle school choir under the direction of Juliet Anderson, a dynamic, classical and opera trained singer. She ran a rigorous choral program in which we learned sight-reading, tone, diction, and an array of vocal techniques. I was one of her favorite students. She once told my mother she wondered how a student could seem like such an angel. Though it sounds as if I am boastful, I am simply telling the truth. This is how life is when you are gifted!

During my eighth grade year, my leadership gifts re-emerged. I ran for SGA president and won again! To be honest, I did not expect to win since the girl I ran against was more popular than I was. As SGA president, I read daily announcements over an intercom, spoke at special programs, and led an initiative to beautify school restrooms. Also, as an eighth grader at Camp Creek Middle School, I was placed on a gifted team. This team integrated gifted students from grades six, seven, and eight. My eighth grade year was the first year the school had implemented this gifted model. I was placed on the team because I had become too different for the general population of my peers. Along with being gifted, well-spoken, and well-mannered, I encountered bullying and terrorization from certain students who felt I was the teachers' pet. My administrators believed that placing me amongst high-achieving students might shield me from the bullying I had experienced in years past. For the most part, the administrators' plan succeeded. Though I still encountered envy because of my talents, the negativity was not accompanied by threats or bodily harm.

During my eighth grade year in middle school, a few people were instrumental in encouraging me to enroll in Tri-Cities High School for the Visual and Performing Arts. My language arts teacher, Mrs. Barksdale, my choral director, Juliet Anderson, and my youth choir director, Crystal Harris, all assisted me in making the decision. There were two options for high school: Westlake, the neighborhood high school that specialized in math and science, and Tri-Cities, the performing arts high school, which was out of my neighborhood district. The choice was a no-brainer for my parents and me. Clearly, I needed to attend a school where my talents could be nurtured.

In the spring of my eighth grade year, I went to Tri-Cities High School to audition for the choral program. For the audition, we had to sight-read and perform a selection. After a successful audition, I was admitted into the choral program. Ninth grade was a year of hard work, but it was remarkably enjoyable. After a placement test, the music department recommended I be placed in an advanced music theory course, which was uncommon for freshman. Though young, I was able to thrive in a class full of juniors and seniors. I was also a member of three choirs: the Tri-Tones Gospel Choir, the Intermediate Mixed Chorus, and the Show Choir. Music program directors, Don Ogletree and Mason Harper, provided a world-class education to me and other music students. I enjoyed the choir, and I had every intention to stay there, but a phenomenal opportunity appeared that I had never anticipated: auditions for the drama program's production of *Dreamgirls*, an exquisite musical by Henry Krieger and Tom Eyen.

In the spring of 1996, everyone in school was excited about auditions for *Dreamgirls*. Since all my friends were auditioning, I decided that I would audition too. To prepare for the audition, my mother let me borrow her authentic fox boa, and I chose a musical selection that would show off my best voice. I walked into the audition room where the drama director, Freddie Hendricks, was seated. Though I was nervous and afraid, I tried to exude confidence as I sang a song, being sure to highlight my ability to hit high notes. After the audition, my mother witnessed Hendricks walk out of the audition room and heard him say, "God damn! Did you hear her hit that high note?"

The moment of truth came when we found out who was selected for the play. I had hoped to see myself listed as an ensemble member. Instead, I was listed as the understudy for one of the principal roles, the character Michelle Morris. This news far exceeded my expectation. Lakeisha Miles, a junior, who later become a member of the popular '90s R & B girl group Xscape, had landed the role of Michelle Morris. According to some witnesses, I was quite the contender and would have possibly gotten the role if I had belted my notes just a little more. Two weeks into the rehearsal process, Lakeisha dropped out of the play, leaving me to take on the role. When my choral teacher, Don Ogletree, found out I was to play this role, he said to me, "Why didn't you tell me you have one of the leading roles? That's great!" At the time, I did not know that being awarded this principal role as a freshman was a major accomplishment.

Auditioning for and performing in *Dreamgirls* changed my life. As a member of the chorus, I was fading into the background and serving as a small member in a large group. However, when I began acting, I was placed in the forefront, and these theatrical roles forced me to grow out of my comfort zone. Being a cast member in a show of *Dreamgirls*'s caliber was not easy. All the other leads were seasoned actors and singers. They understood the nuances of acting, and they were dynamic. I, on the other hand, was a little shy and timid. My voice did not project very well, and I was overwhelmed by the challenging choreography.

We ran the show for two weeks, and each night I improved. The school year ended, and over the summer, we were asked to perform the show for an additional week. Needless to say, I had learned from my past blunders and had a better run the second time. Hendricks and many of my peers were extremely supportive as they saw my potential. Up until then, my discovered gifts included music, writing, and leadership. Now another gift was added to the equation: acting!

After performing *Dreamgirls* in the summer, Hendricks invited me to be a member of his professional theatre company, which was called the Freddie Hendricks Youth Ensemble of Atlanta (YEA). Being a member of this company was a rigorous experience that I enjoyed fully. In the summertime, we rehearsed every day for long hours. Our performance home was Seven Stages Theatre in Atlanta where we performed numerous shows. We also performed at other venues in the Atlanta area, as well as out of town. Being a part of YEA certainly developed my gift for musical theatre. Additionally, YEA nurtured my gift of writing, specifically playwriting, as YEA performed only original shows, which were collaboratively written by Freddie Hendricks (director), Charles Bullock (choreographer), and the ensemble members. As a matter of fact, rehearsal was a sink-or-swim experience for many of the members. If one wanted to shine in a YEA show, he or she had to write the best material, whether it be a line, a monologue, or a song. We also created our own ensemble characters.

During my tenth grade year in high school, I dropped out of the chorus and switched my major to drama. By now, I was fully initiated in the drama program. I had proven that I could contend with the best of the performers in YEA and at Tri-Cities. However, the best experience was yet to come. In the spring of 1997, Hendricks announced that the school musical was *Once on This Island* by Stephen Flaherty and Lynn Ahrens. I auditioned for and landed the leading role of Ti Moune, a beautiful peasant girl who falls in love with a rich man. Hendricks must have had total confidence in me because he did not assign an understudy for my character. Portraying this role encompassed a great deal of pressure. The entire storyline is based on Ti Moune's character. The role requires that I portray feelings of love, happiness, sadness, and despair. There is plenty of singing, and Ti Moune also has a dance solo. At this time, it was well-known that I was not a strong dancer, and some people doubted that I would be able to execute the dancing. However, I was gifted, which meant I could surely polish my dance skills with plenty of practice. Dawn Axam, the dance instructor at Tri-Cities, choreographed the dance. I imagine she probably modified the dance to suit my skills. However, I must give credit to Asantewaa Ricks, one of my peers, who suggested that if I got lower when I did the African dances, my movements would look more authentic. Another cast member, Jahi Kearse, advised me to kick my legs higher during my routine. So between kicking high and getting low, my dancing became a hit. I knew I had done well when Charles Bullock, YEA's fierce choreographer, who had justifiably removed me from many YEA dance numbers, gave me a compliment. So now added to my list of talents was dancing, including moving well enough to dance a solo.

During the summer after my eleventh grade year, I also landed a leading role in YEA's show *Psalm 13*, a production about teen pregnancy. By this time, I knew for certain that I was gifted if Freddie Hendricks entrusted me to play a leading role in his professional acting company. In fact, he did not require me to audition for the role. He created the character specifically with me in mind.

Additional gifts of playwriting and directing emerged while I was in high school. During an after-school session for drama students, we separated into groups and created short plays. I had the idea to write a play called *The Morgue* in which a group visiting a morgue is suddenly chased by a corpse that rises from death's slumber. I cast a boy of tall stature who slightly resembled Frankenstein's monster to play the corpse. After my group presented, I remember the funniest boy in drama telling me that the play was "really good" and funny. My classmates asked who directed it, and I proudly took credit. The gifts of playwriting and directing would not re-emerge until my college years.

While thriving in the performing arts, I also began to thrive academically. In middle school, I had a 3.3 GPA and struggled in math. By high school, I was maintaining a 3.7 GPA and taking honors language arts and social studies courses. Being a music theory student as a freshman (counting beats and measures) seemed to have awakened a new ability for math reasoning. During my senior year, I was appointed editor of the yearbook staff and editor of the school newspaper. My instructors recognized both my writing abilities and my leadership skills. Thanks to their entrusting me with these jobs, I decided to pursue journalism at Georgia State University in the fall of 1999.

The process of discovering my gifts in church, elementary school, middle school, and high school was vital. Each person that identified my gifts and encouraged me to use them transformed my life. Thanks to these people and the opportunities they created, I graduated from Tri-Cities High School of the Visual and Performing Arts ready to conquer the world as a young, gifted African-American woman.

Discovery of Gifts as a Young Adult and in College

As a college student, I was well-established in my gifts as a singer and actor. I continued performing in plays, and as a journalism student, I became a stronger writer each year, creating essays, articles, sitcoms, and scripts for television news. My gift for playwriting and directing reemerged in 2001 when the Black Student Theatre Ensemble at Georgia State University announced a playwright competition for a night of one-act plays on Halloween. I remember sitting down to write a play, which took less than an hour. I submitted the play and received the good news that it was selected. Suddenly, I went from actor, to playwright and director. First, I had to conduct auditions to select a cast. The auditions went well, and I secured some good actors. However, I soon received the news that my main character was dropping out of the show. With this casting obstacle, I decided to change the title and the content of the play. I rewrote the play to fit the personalities of the remaining cast members, and I called it *Second Chance*. *Second Chance* is the story of a pastor with a tainted past that includes dealing drugs, theft, and fathering several illegitimate children. The entire one-act play takes place in a church on a Sunday morning. Before the church members arrive, there is an ethereal dance battle between demons and angels. This dance is symbolic of the spiritual warfare, or the battle, between good and evil. This Sunday morning in the play proves to be different, as some of the church's biggest gossipers have just found out the pastor has a dark past he is hiding from his congregation.

The experience of writing this play took me back to age thirteen when I wrote my first sermon for the oratorical contest. Because this play is based on the life of a pastor, I had to write an original sermon. So once again, I found a passage of Scripture and wrote a heart-wrenching homily. One day in rehearsal, my lead actor was not present, so I delivered a portion of the sermon. Before I knew it, I was entrenched with the Spirit, and onlookers told me that I looked like a real preacher up there on the stage. Even though I had put this gift of preaching indefinitely put on hold when I was thirteen, I now revisited it somewhat at age twenty-one. But as stated before, I will continue to run from this gift unless God forces me to preach!

On Halloween night, the play went over very well with the audience, with many attendees saying they forgot they were at a play because it felt more like an authentic worship experience. I remember a friend of mine becoming teary-eyed because the message of redemption touched his heart. Shirlene Holmes, a faculty advisor at Georgia State University, spoke highly of the play, saying that it reminded her of playwright James Baldwin's *Amen Corner*. With that experience, my playwriting and directing journey had just begun.

The following year, I directed *Second Chance* at my church using members and church clergy as the cast. The next play I wrote and directed at church was called *Proverbs 3*, followed by *Family, Faith, and Love*. Each play was a success, and I felt proud because each one relayed a special message imbued with moral values. Writing plays is about ministering to people, uplifting them, or changing their way of thinking about important issues, all connected to ways I believe I can offer something positive to the world.

Discovery of Gifts as an Educator

MY TEACHING CAREER BEGAN IN 2004 when I became a part-time drama teacher at Westlake, the local high school I was zoned to attend at age fourteen. As a new teacher going into the classroom, there was a lot I did not know, and I made plenty of mistakes. However, my giftedness as a teacher is undeniable. By emulating qualities and strategies of some of my best teachers, I know that I am continuing the legacy of empowering students. Anne Wimberly, a professor at the Interdenominational Theological Center, modeled how to teach purposefully and intentionally. Whenever I feel that I am losing patience or integrity, I remember that students are watching what I do even more than what I say. Her mission has now become my mission: instilling hope in our youth so they might envision themselves living a prosperous future.

Freddie Hendricks taught me how to be creative and how to invite others into the creative process. His mission has also become my mission: to transform lives through theatre arts. Each show that YEA performed had a purpose; we were revolutionaries. He instilled in us the importance of focus, discipline, and striving for nothing short of excellence.

Other gifts besides teaching would soon surface. In 2009, I left one school district to join another closer to home. I was to teach theatre at a middle school. Five weeks into the school year, I received the devastating news that I was being transferred to a school in Johns Creek, which was almost fifty miles from my home. I sulked for days and pleaded with the Human Resources department to consider sending me somewhere closer to home. My request was granted, and I ended up closer to home than I was before. The only stipulation was that I had to teach language arts and not theatre. Though I was certified in language arts, I had never taught it. This move proved to be one of the best of my life. While working at this school, Christopher Harden, one of the administrators, was impressed by my pedagogy and encouraged me to apply for the lead language arts teacher position. He believed I would do well at collaborating with colleagues and sharing resources. I applied and was accepted into this position.

The following year, more success was to come. There was a shift in administration as a new principal came to the school, and I now had to report to a different assistant principal. The new assistant principal saw something special in me and encouraged me to also apply for the grade-level chairperson position. I did and was accepted. However, I never got the opportunity to serve. Over the summer, I was offered a drama teacher position in the Atlanta public school system.

Atlanta Public Schools paid more, and I would get to return to my first love, teaching theatre. My first year was successful. I began building a drama program from scratch and found innovative ways to unify the Fine Arts department. The following school year, my principal appointed me the Fine Arts chairperson, which I have proudly served for two years. Each employer that I worked with recognized my leadership qualities and encouraged me to take the path that used them. The journey continues, and I look forward to the leadership gifts coming full circle along with my other gifts.

Affirmation of Spiritual Gifts

IN 2004, JUST BEFORE ENTERING THE SEMINARY at the Interdenominational Center's Morehouse School of Religion, I took a spiritual-gifts inventory. I would encourage everyone that is on a spiritual journey or looking for his or her purpose in life to take a spiritual-gifts inventory. This requires respondents to choose the qualities from thirty-five on a list that most accurately describe them. The assessment, which may be accessed at www.mintools.com/spiritual-gifts-test.htm, identifies one's strongest spiritual gifts with the most dominant gifts listed first. I recently took another spiritual gifts inventory, and my results are listed below:

- **Exhortation** – To come alongside of someone with words of encouragement, comfort, consolation and to counsel them. These gifts can be used for counseling, teaching, worship, speaking, and staff-support.
- **Leadership** – To provide people with a sense of direction, to have vision and exercise diligence in motivating them to get involved in the accomplishment of goals.
- **Service** – To identify undone tasks, however menial, and use available resources to get the job done. This gift can be used in a variety of ways.
- **Mercy** – To be sensitive toward those who are suffering, whether physically, mentally, or emotionally; to feel genuine sympathy

for their misery, speaking words of compassion, offering deeds of love to help alleviate distress.

- **Teaching** – To instruct others in a logical, systematic ways so as to communicate pertinent information for understanding and growth.
- **Giving** – To be generous to those in need.
- **Prophecy** – To tell of the will of God.

The results of my spiritual-gifts inventory affirm that I am on the right track in the career choices I have made. Long before I knew what my spiritual gifts were, I was using them. At age thirteen, I wrote a teaching sermon that prophesied that if God can bring life to a valley of dry bones and bring sustenance to a barren land, God can restore anyone's life. In the fifth and eighth grades, I was SGA president. At this young age, my leadership qualities had already begun to spring forth. Though I did not view myself as a leader, others saw qualities in me that I did not and appointed me for leadership roles. One of my spiritual gifts is teaching, and I became a teacher where I innately utilize gifts of mercy, giving, and service.

I declare for myself and for you, the reader, that your gifts are a part of you. You cannot run from your gifts, and you cannot suppress them. Your gifts will always be with you, and your life will be more meaningful if you utilize them.

Surviving the Matrix of a Career That Stifles My Creative Gifts

I ASSERT THAT GIFTED INDIVIDUALS live an unfulfilled existence when the ability to freely exercise their gifts is stifled. There is restlessness, a feeling of entrapment that gnaws at our souls when we are stagnant. Fortunately, my gifts have flourished in my current situation as a public school educator. Initially, I chose to be a theatre educator because I felt it would allow me to utilize my gifts of teaching, encouragement, writing, music, and leadership all at once. After reflecting upon my teaching career, I can say I have been able to do all of these gifts. Because some of the theatrical materials and texts available are not culturally relevant or age-appropriate, I write plays specifically for the students I teach. I constantly challenge my students to write their own texts as a means to evoke creativity and a sense of ownership. As an educator of youth,

I aim to impart knowledge that will enhance life skills (i.e., speaking, listening, cooperation, and self-confidence).

However, the current structure of most school systems makes it difficult for arts educators like me. When there are pay cuts, our programs are eliminated. When counselors need to add classes on students' schedules, disinterested students are placed into our classrooms. Add to the equation that unruly behavior, disrespect, and apathy for learning are common themes in many schools, from the richest to the poorest. These elements add to my current quest to realize my gifts and thrive in an environment in which my educational efforts are appreciated.

Creative and passionate individuals hunger to work alongside other creative and passionate individuals who are working toward the same goal. Each year in every school I have taught, I have declared that arts teachers need more support, more funding, and more autonomy in selecting students for our programs. Due to the limitations placed on us, successes are sometimes few and far between. It is difficult to build programs because we do not get the time needed to cultivate students. Typically, we get students for three to six months, and then they are transferred to other electives or core classes. Schools that are serious about building programs create pathways so that students may concentrate on one discipline during all four years of high school, as I did at the high school I attended.

Coming from an accomplished performing arts high school and a professional theatre company, I experienced culture shock when entering the school system as a drama teacher. I had never encountered people who did not care about acting or performers who do not attend rehearsals. As kids, we misbehaved, but my directors and choreographers had the support of our parents to safely do whatever it took to get our respect. In the current educational system, teachers can hardly say anything to students to gain their cooperation, lest we risk having to defend our jobs for disorderly conduct. Someone like me who is passionate about my craft is drained daily. In the midst of dealing with discipline issues, writing lesson plans, and meeting other deadlines, my creative energy gets zapped.

Nonetheless, there are some successes. Each year, I meet students who say theatre gave them confidence. A handful of them become interested in theatre and choose it as a major in college, or they pursue it professionally. Many of my students with learning disabilities also thrive as a result of being in theatre. Through my yearly variety showcases, Black History productions, and talent shows, the school is revived. As one student said, "Having drama brings life to the school." Some students who skip other teachers' classes all day long come to theatre class because they can express themselves and feel successful for once.

Although I am not always aware of the results of my teaching, I do know I am planting seeds, changing lives, and introducing a fine arts culture to a population of students who otherwise would have no exposure. As Fine Arts chairperson, I also take on the responsibility of coordinating cultural field trips for the entire school. These field trips are not limited to band, chorus, and drama students. I extend trips to language arts classes, social studies classes, and any other class that can benefit from the experience. Again, there are successes. However, as with most gifted people, restlessness and disinterest can set in, causing us to contemplate our next move, especially if we are being stifled. Be that as it may, I survive the matrix by looking at the bigger picture. Everything may not be as I want it to be, and as a perfectionist, things will never be as grand as I wish them to be. Nevertheless, God has placed me where I am for an appointed time, and when the assignment is complete, God will take me to the next stop. So as long as I am in my current context, I shall do my best to use my gifts in spite of the challenges.

Paving the Way for a Career That Makes Room for My Gifts to Flourish

HAVING A MULTITUDE OF GIFTS causes admirers to suggest that we (multi-gifted and talented individuals) can do so much because we possess bountiful gifts. However, I posit that having multiple gifts can be challenging and can cause a great deal of confusion. Multi-giftedness can create a dilemma of not knowing what to focus on in life and career choices. My educational background is interdisciplinary because I could not settle on one area to study. For example, a bachelor's degree in journalism allowed me to explore my gift of speaking and writing. A master's in Christian Education awarded me the opportunity to explore my gifts of teaching and exhortation. Finally, a degree in leadership has added skill and credentials to my innate gift of leading others. With all these gifts, is it possible to find one job or career that allows the gifts to work in harmony? I say yes, it is possible.

What I do now is simple. I utilize my gifts in my current situation because I know they will make room for me to go places in my career that I never imagined. Additionally, I consider every job opportunity. I seek the type of jobs whose descriptions require my specific gifts. For example, I am actively pursuing leadership jobs within Atlanta Public Schools. I know that leadership requires writing skills, communication skills, compassion, teaching, mercy, and certainly creativity.

The possibilities are endless. Now that I am a doctor of education, I also have the option of becoming a college professor. In preparation for this, I embrace opportunities to publish as this allows me to share my research with academic communities. When I received the news that my church's youth ministry leader would be resigning at the end of the year, I informed my pastor of my interest in this position, and I look forward to hearing from him in the coming months. Lastly, I have the dream of directing and playwriting in the professional arena. For this reason, I am compiling all the plays I have written in hopes of publishing an anthology, and I have begun working on additional plays.

I do not know what the future holds, but I know my gifts are paving the way for an exceptional future. In due time, I will flourish. That same reality applies to all gifted people as long as we continue exercising our gifts. If we have suppressed gifts, they will continue to emerge until we can no longer contain them. Certainly, we may apply for jobs and map out a plan, but when using our gifts, we do not know where the Creator may choose to take us.

Transcendence: Unleashing the Gifts in Others

How much value do we have if we do not add value to others? I encourage all gifted people to find ways to help others realize their gifts. Helping others might be as simple as giving a compliment to someone you witnessed do well at something. For example, a peer telling me that he liked the play I wrote in high school planted a seed. Viola Turner, the former director of the Visual and Performing Arts program at Tri-Cities High School lovingly encouraged me to pursue acting. When she gave me a compliment, she made me feel as if I could do anything. When I was working on my MA in Christian Education, Lisa Allen, a professor at the Interdenominational Theological Center put a comment in my paper that changed the way I viewed higher education. She told me I was a deep thinker and that I should consider pursuing a PhD one day. Until then, I had not seriously considered going any further in my education.

Within this essay, I recounted the teachers, mentors, and choir directors who took time to identify and hone my gifts. Freddie Hendricks nurtured my potential and worked tirelessly with me until I became a better actor, singer, and performer. Anne Wimberly modeled sound teaching strategies that guide my practice as an educator. All the way back in 1987, Eugenia Jacobs gave me my first solo in church. Christopher Harden at Paul D. West Middle School was the first administrator to give me advice on how to obtain a teacher-leader position. These people worked with me and gave me a platform to display my gifts.

Those of us who have been graced with the discovery of our gifts must remember to pay it forward. A kid gifted at science might need an extra nudge before becoming the first person to cure cancer. The timid, reserved person in your Sunday school class might be a spiritual leader. According to Maslow's hierarchy of needs (1976), the top of the pyramid is transcendence, meaning that one has attained self-actualization and is now on a mission to help others reach their fullest potential. Transcendence is somewhat of a spiritual act because there is no greater deed than helping people realize and confidently embrace their gifts. Envision how society would be impacted if each person tapped into his or her special gifts and used those gifts for the betterment of their communities.

References

Gagné, F. (1985). Giftedness and talent: Reexamining a reexamination of the definitions. *Gifted Child Quarterly, 29*, 103–112.

Maslow, A. H. (1943). A theory of human motivation. *Psychological Review, 50(4)*, 370–96.

Ministry Tools Resource Center (2014). *Spiritual gifts assessment*. Retrieved from http://mintools.com/spiritual-gifts-test.htm.

National Association for Gifted Children. (2014). *Definitions of giftedness*. Retrieved from http://www.nagc.org/resources-publications/resources/definitions-giftedness# sthash.lCYrV8Fs.dpuf

National Association for Gifted Children. (2010). *Redefining giftedness for a new century: Shifting the paradigm*. Retrieved from http://

www.nagc.org/sites/ default/files/Position%20Statement/Rede-fining%20Giftedness%20for%20a%20New%20Century.pdf.

Renzulli, J. (1978). What makes giftedness? Re-examining a definition. *Phi Delta Kappa, 60*, 180–181.

Saad, L. (2014). *The "40-hour" workweek is actually longer—by seven hours.* Retrieved from

http://www.gallup.com/poll/175286/hour-workweek-actually-lon-ger-seven-hours.aspx.

CHAPTER 6

The Proud Conqueror

Asegun Henry, PhD
Recorded telephone interview conducted and edited by Nadirah Angail, MFT

Background

ASEGUN HENRY'S MOTHER nearly died while giving him life. He nearly died, too. It was a frightening and difficult way to enter the world, but it gave him a sense of purpose that serves him to this day. His mother prayed for her son's survival and promised to dedicate herself to his development if the Creator would allow him to thrive. He was given the Yoruba names Asegun ("conqueror") Sekou Famake ("learned leader")..

Though his mother loved her son's name and its meaning, at times she second-guessed her decision. It was not that she was not proud, but she feared the name would be a hardship on her son and a reason for him to be singled out and bullied. Much to her surprise, Asegun loved his name. It was never a bother or a burden. Even when people intentionally mispronounced it, he found strength in the meaning. When other children had common names with uncertain meanings, his stood out and was clearly defined. It was a daily reminder of what he was and what he would become. His name, Asegun Sekou Famake Henry, was chosen specifically for him by the woman who nearly gave her life for his. Certainly, there was no mistake in her choice.

The son of Oare Dozier-Henry and Anthony Henry, proud Black educators who value African culture, Asegun was immersed in a supportive environment that pushed him to excel academically and develop culturally as a self-assured young man. His mother holds a PhD and is an adult education professor at Florida Agricultural & Mechanical University (FAMU). His father holds two master's degrees and is a political scientist, middle school teacher, and adjunct professor at FAMU.

Given his parents credentials, perhaps Asegun had no choice but to succeed. Or maybe his future would have been just as bright with a different set of parents. It is impossible to say, but what he is certain of is the fact that his parents molded him into the confident man he is today. "Confidence is something you're given," he said. He believes that "the extent to which you compliment and encourage young children builds confidence." In Asegun's case, his confidence was given to him by his doting mother—his father too, but it was his mother who was especially fond of "hoopla," her special word for celebrations in honor of accomplishments. She made every effort to advocate for him and recognize his successes. For example, when he graduated from high school, she rented a billboard on a busy Tallahassee street that read, "Congratulations Asegun for graduating high school!" The big bold words stood out against a colorful kente cloth background. The sign publically sang his praises for a whole year. It was annoying to him at the time, but he is ever grateful for her contributions to his self-image.

Early Signs of Giftedness

"School was always easy for me," he said nonchalantly and without hesitation. He never needed to apply much effort to do well academically. Though he succeeded with ease, he never found school interesting—perhaps because it was not challenging enough to pique his interest. But regardless of his level of interest, his mother and father saw in him a potential he was not yet aware of. As observant parents and accomplished educators, they knew there was something in him that needed to be stirred and cultivated. They made it their mission to see to the full development and progression of their miracle son. If school was not challenging him, they would fill his time with other things that would. His father, a lover of numbers, kept him busy with math workbooks and worksheets. Wanting their son to be well-rounded, they also put him in a chess club, which taught him how to think strategically and act with purpose. They also exposed him to various aspects of West African and

African American culture. It was important to them that their son felt connected to his ancestral roots. Even as a young child, he was privy to adult conversation about culture, art, history, philosophy, and politics. He was comfortable in such a stimulating environment.

Asegun's giftedness extends far beyond academics. At age ten, he began to play the djembe (a West African drum) in a local drum group. Though he was the only child there, he quickly became one of the best, and his interest in math gave him an acoustic edge over other drummers. "I could understand the music better than most people. . . . I was able to go deeply and hear certain nuances in what they were playing because I was seeing it mathematically." As a result of his skill and understanding, he was frequently invited to perform at cultural events across the city. It was obvious he was mature beyond his years.

After years of showing undeniable signs of giftedness, Asegun was officially tested at age twelve. He was not informed of his official IQ, but he scored high enough to be accepted into the Exceptional Student Education Program, an educational resource center for gifted children in Tallahassee, Florida. Even after he was accepted into the gifted program, his parents continued to advocate for their son. In eighth grade, Asegun was ready for algebra, a class typically reserved for ninth graders. His mother knew he was more than capable of doing the work, so she approached the school about allowing him to take the class a year early. The school refused, but she did not give up without a fight. She tried many more times to get her son moved up. Despite her best efforts, the school held its ground. He was forced to take pre-algebra twice. However, the following year, his mother was successful in getting him into an advanced twelfth grade philosophy course. He was the only ninth grader in the class. His mother's persistence in getting him into challenging classes further built his confidence and reinforced the idea of his great potential.

Gifted Program Experience and Recommendations for Improvements

"THE GIFTED PROGRAM wasn't really all that," Asegun admitted with a laugh. "Most of us saw it as a way to get out of school." Asegun and his other gifted classmates were bused to the Academic Resource Center to participate in the gifted program for a few hours in the day. The time was unstructured, and they spent much of it doing whatever they wanted.

It probably was not what his parents imagined when they signed him up for the program, but it gave him the exposure that ultimately led to his career choice of engineering. It was in the gifted program that he was first introduced to the Internet, a new and fresh idea in 1993. There, he was given the opportunity and freedom to play with and explore computers years before his classmates. Finally, he was interested in something other than music.

Though Asegun ultimately benefitted from the gifted program, its laissez-faire structure left much to be desired. It could have been conducted and organized in such a way that the participants were prepared to make use of their talents. Asegun said:

> Gifted programs should identify students' particular talents in some respect and provide them with tools to enhance them. . . . They should provide guidance through interaction with an advisor or in a classroom setting. They should guide kids on the way to develop a vision for how they can use their talents, make their talent useful, whether for their own benefit or the benefit of others.

Asegun knows he could have benefitted so much more if the program had not simply introduced him to the Internet. "Someone could have noticed my connection to music and math and could have guided me toward music software. I eventually found that on my own as an adult, but it would have been nice to have had access to that when I was young." The goal of a gifted program should not be to merely group together gifted children. It should be to help them chart a path. "Once that path is charted, it should facilitate activities to help them walk that path." Thankfully, Asegun was able to chart a path without the guidance of his gifted program, but not all gifted students are as resourceful, and not all have fully involved parents.

Social Experiences

As a confident, well-grounded young man, Asegun had no trouble making friends. Neither his unique name nor his intellectual ability inhibited him when it came to socializing with others. In fact, he was so well-known as a gifted drummer that his music ability overshadowed his intelligence. "I don't think anyone thought of me as particularly smart until grad school," he explained. It was not until he was accepted into Massachusetts Institute of Technology (MIT) that others began to notice how truly gifted he was. Before that, his academic prowess took a quiet backseat to the rhythm of his drum.

Asegun became a drummer just as the Tallahassee dance and drum community began to flourish. Unbeknownst to him, he was stepping into a cultural awakening that would put him in social circles far different from those the average preteen would have access to. Between the ages of ten and fourteen, he spent much of his free time with men ten to fifteen years his senior. He spent long nights performing in places he was not even old enough to legally enter. He took impromptu road trips that kept him away from home for days on end. He grew so used to and comfortable around older crowds that he felt they were his peers, his equals. He began to see himself as he saw them: mature, capable.

Being around so many adults in such a natural setting meant that not only did he have a plethora of mentors but also he was able to bond with those mentors and develop lasting friendships that still serve him today. Thinking back on his unique position as a young man among men, he remarked, "It made me very mature at a very young age. That was probably the biggest gift I was given. I don't look at my intellect as anything special, but I think I had enough maturity to capitalize on it."

Having the sense and wisdom to capitalize on one's talent is something Asegun believes all parents of gifted children should encourage. "Parents should stress activities or conversations to help their children develop a maturity in regards to their talent at a young age, so they can take it seriously, be in charge of it, capitalize on it." He feels his early maturity was the linchpin to his success because it enabled him to make critical decisions at a young age. It enabled him to stay focused academically, no matter how busy his social life was.

Though Asegun was mature beyond his years, he knew he could not escape his chronological age. He did not feel he could relate to most other children, but he strategically made friends to ensure he would not be completely out of touch with his age-mates. "I wanted to be well-rounded, so I went out and made two friends my own age. I made deliberate moves to not be a weirdo," he explained. He used this same tactic when it came to finding his first girlfriend. Though he felt comfortable around older women, he knew he could not logically—or legally—pursue a romantic relationship with them. If he wanted to gain any experience with women and dating, he would have to find someone his own age, and that is exactly what he did. His first girlfriend was a nice young woman who was only slightly older than he. Asegun was able to relate to her in a peer-to-peer manner that he could not have gotten from his older female friends. He truly enjoyed and appreciated the experience.

The meticulous way in which Asegun forged relationships shows the acute level of understanding he had at a young age. "I remember being cognizant of my own development," he said. He knew his circumstances, which placed him in such invigorating environments, were priming him for the type of advanced development most children are not exposed to. He took every advantage of this position.

Career Building

DESPITE HIS HIGH INTELLIGENCE, Asegun spent much of high school feeling disconnected from the material. He knew he preferred science and math over reading and writing—to this day, he still hates reading—but that was as far as his interest went. When it came to what he truly loved and was passionate about, he was much more involved in music. If nothing else, he knew he liked computers thanks to his participation in the gifted program, but it was his twelfth grade calculus teacher, Coach Meade, who finally made an academic subject come to life. Coach Meade made math relevant. He gave it context and meaning. He also showed that it can be turned into a career. Though Asegun had been exposed to engineering though summer camps and an earlier mentor, Coach Meade's class was the turning point that made him decide to pursue it as a career.

Even more influential than his calculus teacher was a manhood development program he participated in as a teen. He described it as "the most impactful experience of my entire life. During those years, I learned how to think for myself." The mentors in the program planted the seed that it is okay to question reality. They forced the participants to examine their own thought processes about everything they knew to be true. The program involved critical thinking and sometimes intense physical activity. "If someone in the group didn't live up to the expectations, it caused a problem for the group. Our punishment was exercise to weaken us, put us in a compromised physical space to open our mind."

This military-style training forced Asegun out of his comfort zone and encouraged him to form his own ideas. Rather than listening to others' opinions and conjecture, he began to pursue facts he could string together to make sense of the world. He lost interest in anyone else's version of truth. His newfound pursuit of verifiable truth reinforced his love for science. He gained a whole new understanding of the world based on linkages of facts. He learned to view mathematical equations not as something merely to memorize but as a way of communicating understanding. He sought to truly understand how equations work. Once he understood what they sought to communicate, memorization became unnecessary.

By the time he graduated from high school, he knew what he wanted to pursue. He earned a bachelor of science in mechanical engineering from FAMU. He then went on to earn a PhD in the same field of study from MIT. He learned early on to be resourceful and goal-oriented. Once he set his mind on being a mechanical engineer, he would let nothing get in the way of that.

After completing his studies at MIT, he conducted post-doctoral research at Oak Ridge National Laboratory in Oak Ridge, Tennessee, and at Northwestern University in Evanston, Illinois. He worked on important solar technology developments as a fellow for the US Department of Energy under the Advanced Research Projects Agency–Energy. He is currently an assistant professor at Georgia Tech's school of mechanical engineering. His goal is to get tenure and start a concentrated solar-power company. He aims to save the world by addressing the energy problem.

Academic Challenges and Triumphs

ASEGUN BREEZED THROUGH HIGH SCHOOL and college, but things changed when he stepped on the campus of MIT. The tests there were unlike any he had ever taken before. They did not merely cover the presented material. They were an extrapolation of the material, meaning students had to have a firm-enough understanding of the information to be able to be tested on concepts that were never officially covered in lectures or homework. Students had to take what they had been given and use it to understand new, foreign information. To call it hard would be an understatement. It took three years for Asegun to receive his first A. The time prior to that was a stressful period of trial and error with various study techniques.

To finally struggle in school after years of easy As is hard, too hard for some. He could have given up under the discomfort of academic stress. However, giving up is not befitting of a conqueror. Growing up, his many drummer mentor-friends modeled for him how to be resourceful and resilient. "We would just jump in the car and go. We learned not to let anything stop us," he said, recalling the many adventures they went on with limited funds. "If we wanted to go on a trip, we would figure out how much money we needed and then get it by any means." Usually, that meant pooling their money. Resourcefulness became so ingrained in him that he was later surprised to meet so many people who lacked this skill. He took that same "make it happen" attitude with him to MIT. He knew he could do well in his classes. He just needed to figure out how. Once he better understood the expectations of the tests and how to prepare for them, he was able to succeed again.

But even during these difficult times, there were successes, big successes. In his first year at MIT, Asegun approached his advisor to seek funding for his education. He thought he had a good chance of receiving it, but his request was declined. Undeterred, he kept searching for funding and was able to receive the Lemelson Fellowship award, which paid for his first year. He then received the highly coveted, highly competitive Department of Energy Computational Science Fellowship, which paid for his remaining years. The year he received it, it was awarded to only seven of the five hundred applicants. Since graduating, he has received two postdoctoral fellowships, the United Negro College Fund (UNCF)-Merck Postdoctoral Fellowship and the Ford Foundation Postdoctoral Fellowship.

Race and Culture

For most of Asegun's academic career, racism was foreign to him. He grew up in a loving, cultured community and attended a historically black college and university (HBCU) for undergraduate school. It was not until he started graduate school at MIT that he felt racism's sting.

Asegun grew up with a lot of friends and access to social events. There was never a shortage of people to spend time with or things to do. College was an extension of that experience. He and the other students worked together on assignments and did their studying in a group, but "in graduate school, no one would work with me," he said. MIT was a vastly different environment for him. He went from being a Black student in a sea of Black students to being the only Black student in a graduating class of six hundred. In all his years there, he made only one friend. To be sure, he was lonely, but he did not let the lack of social interaction get in the way of his goal. "I relied on all the training and confidence building that was put into me prior to going." Though he would have preferred the type of active social life he was used to, his goal in attending MIT was not to make friends. It was to gain experience and graduate with a PhD so he could continue on his path toward becoming a tenured professor and business owner. It was this cemented plan and laser focus that kept him from being steered off course.

The Bigger Picture

ASEGUN HAS TRACED HIS DNA TO NIGERIA and connected with a Nigerian family that has accepted him as family. This knowledge and acceptance has repaired a broken connection, anchored him to his past. Now a parent, he and his wife work to share that connection with their son, Adesina Kamau Iyanuoluwa Oladigbolu. They want to impart upon him not only the importance of his past but also the greatness he has grown from. Even if young Adesina is gifted in the traditional sense, Asegun plans to gift his son, who is only three, with the same confidence and encouragement of maturity that has helped him realize his own talents. Being fruitful in life is not about being exceptionally gifted or having a particular IQ. It is about developing your potential and being the best version of yourself possible.

PART III

Navigating Cross-Cultural Access, Survival, and What's Expected of Me

CHAPTER 7

The Pursuit of Intuition: A Narrative of Grit

Neeraj Kulkarni, MBBS, MD, PhD

Introduction

IN THIS CHAPTER, I cover how I successfully navigated being an international graduate student from India earning a doctorate of philosophy degree (PhD) in the United States. In India, I chose to pursue a medical school education, which in itself demands a high level of dedicated and logical study. While pursuing medicine, I was also motivated to seek the scientific principles underlying clinical manifestations of disease and, consequently, not settle for mastering a medical practice. This inner drive slowly piqued my interests in pursuing scientific research in the United States. Yet, it was during a crisis in the course of my doctoral research that I realized for the first time how intellectual giftedness was a unique trait within itself, accompanied by a distinctive and pressing set of emotional needs.

Early on, I had been aware that I was considered by many as intellectually gifted, but I was not aware of the emotional needs that accompanied such a gifted identification. Additionally, there are no special education programs for gifted children in India, which may explain why I never realized my exceptional abilities until much later. My narrative elucidates the journey to embracing all my innate gifted traits.

Science aficionados can readily imagine how they would feel if they suddenly spotted a renowned scientist, such as astrophysicist Neil Tyson, they held in awe, sitting across them. This was how I felt after wading through a crowded train to get to my seat—I found myself sitting face to face with the great Jayant Narlikar. At the age of fourteen, I had already devoured most of his popular science books, but I never imagined I'd be in such close proximity to him. My excitement knew no bounds. Perhaps it was presumptuous of me to talk with a celebrity author/scientist, but I couldn't help myself. I walked up to him and introduced myself. To my amazement and joy, he readily entered into conversation, and we happily discussed various scientific discoveries and questions for quite a while.

At last the talk gravitated to my choice of career. I mentioned that my parents had already planned to enroll me in medical school. Like most Indian students, I had never seriously considered a career as a scientist, even though I liked basic science. Most middle-class Indian families are obsessed with the idea of medical or engineering careers for their offspring and seem to consider these as the only suitable paths, to the exclusion of scientific research, journalism, writing, or art—careers in which they are often not even aware. My answer brought a sudden cloud over his face, which had genially beamed on me until then. "Such a waste of another talented boy," he remarked glumly to his colleague who was sitting nearby. I confess that this response confused and even dismayed me. However, our conversation ended on a friendly note, regardless of this short disruption, and I returned to my seat walking on air. But this brief mentoring had already left its indelible mark on me.

At the time, I didn't understand his disapproval of my career choice—what could possibly be wrong with going into medicine?—but I was elated by his praise. Jayant Narlikar himself thought I was a bright boy. It felt true. I easily scored high on tests like those given by Mensa. The organization even granted me membership into its elite association. In school, I always scored the highest marks with the greatest of ease. Apart from that, I was awarded the highly coveted National Talent Search Scholarship. (This is akin to winning the prestigious Intel Science Talent Search competition in the United States.) Similar to many other intellectually gifted students, I wrote and passed several competitive examinations without the slightest difficulty or feeling of anxiety. Along with this, I was prominent in a host of other activities as well. So when an accomplished scientist acknowledged me as a bright boy, it felt right.

In due time, I sat for my premedical examinations. I passed and received a full scholarship. My path was apparently set. At eighteen, the usual age for entry into medical school in India, I was ready to begin the five-and-a-half-year journey to achieving my dream—the practice of medicine.

My medical school days in India were crammed with study. I was in one of the best medical schools of the region, V. M. Medical College, Solapur, which was recognized by the World Health Organization (WHO) and had a satisfyingly rich curriculum. By all academic measures, I was an excellent student. Yet I was uneasy with the lack of infrastructure for basic science research, or even the encouragement to pursue it, although medicine is based on research. I quenched my thirst for science by staying abreast of various recent developments through the latest publications, but soon my desire outran the satisfaction that the merely passive consumption of medical school could supply. In short, though it took years for me to realize it, my distinguished companion on the train had been right: Medical practice was far from satisfying my innate drive to know and understand the world at a deeper level. More and more, my thoughts turned to scientific research. Unfortunately, India had no regular MD/PhD program at the time, somewhat limiting my options for higher scientific research-based education. But at least I now knew what I really wanted to do.

By the time I was awarded my MBBS degree (the equivalent of an MD elsewhere), my ideas about my future course had become more clear and solid. I realized the strength of my interests in mathematics and physics—fields unrelated to my specialty. This range of interests and diverse competencies were something that many of my colleagues were uncomfortable with. It was much later that I realized this was the hallmark of being intellectually gifted (Fredrickson, 1974; Kerr 1988). It would take something which combined these diverse domains to enable me to feel fulfilled in a career. I took some time out to consider my deepest interests and eventually realized that bioengineering felt like the right fit for me. It not only combined several disciplines that I was interested in, but it was also open to pursuing basic research.

At this point, I started to think about applying for a master's degree in bioengineering in the United States. I passed the GRE and was accepted into the Penn State bioengineering MS program on a full scholarship. It seemed I was on perfect course for a bright and fulfilling career.

Finding Bliss Worth Following

Independent thinking on any given subject is one of the characteristic traits of the intellectually gifted (Heylighen, 2008). I know first-hand that this kind of thinking is the greatest source of joy and bliss for such a person. For example, while engrossed in a scientific experiment, I deeply enjoy the search for a new facet or possibility. This trait has been responsible for many of my achievements, but it has also caused some setbacks. The multiplicity of my life experiences has helped me to understand one undeniable truth: The social assumption that bright people have everything going for them (NAGC, 2014) is erroneous. Life is supposed to be a cakewalk for gifted intellectuals; they can achieve anything they want, says popular wisdom. Until a certain point, my life story seemed like that. It seemed that I had everything figured out. I was following my dreams successfully, and it was just a matter of time until I reached my goals with ease. However, my life took a turn that disproved this assumption. I learned that even though academic achievement is often easy for the intellectually gifted, they too must face failure at some time. It is then that they, too, must develop and show the grit to endure and push on in order to achieve their dreams.

At this point, I experienced a turning point in my life. It occurred during a weekend in the summer of my second year at Penn State. I was taking a summer course related to nanotechnology and cell biology. While I was searching for books in this area that would stimulate my thinking and give me a broader perspective, I came across a book: *Cells, Gels and the Engines of Life*. At that point I was trying to understand the deeper principles of nanotechnology as related to the cell biology interface, and this book whetted my interest in these areas.

Cells, Gels and the Engines of Life is by Gerald Pollack, a distinguished professor at the University of Washington. It summarizes the results of work on cell research by Pollack (Pollack, 2001, 2002), which carries forward earlier findings by Gilbert Ling (Ling 2006, 2014). The book presents a paradigm shift in our present concept of cell structure.

My medical training had already grounded me in the traditional view of the details of cellular organization and structure. However, this astonishing book illuminated a different and alternative view. It was clear that the author was one who thought deeply, critically, and independently. I was thrilled by the immense significance of the book's implications. If they turned out to be true, my intuition told me it could transform science in a great many areas with staggering results. I was excited beyond all reason.

Maybe this has never happened to you yet, but it may one day. You will encounter a book that will change the direction of your life. I could never have imagined the momentous consequences of that simple choice. In hindsight, I recognize that the overpowering excitement that took hold of me while I read through the book was a classic representation of the over-excitabilities that many intellectually gifted people experience in various domains (Heylighen, 2008; Lind, 2001). I quickly added this book to my list of favorites.

As I came to the end of the book, it was as if I experienced an epiphany. Bits of knowledge now seemed to fit together like the pieces of a marvelous jigsaw puzzle. I felt the deep satisfaction of a treasure seeker who becomes a treasure finder. I wanted with all my heart to continue working in this marvelous area linking the disciplines of medicine and engineering without rigid subject boundaries. Something deep within that indicated this was my life's calling.

Following My Passion despite the Obstacles

FROM THAT MOMENT ON, all I did was directed at finding the right path to fulfill this vocation. I felt the desperate need to explore the implications of the ideas presented in Pollack's book through my own research. As a first step, I started corresponding with him. He became an informal mentor to me. Like a creature of instinct, I sought more and more experiences that would let me wallow in the bliss of scientific discovery. Of course, I did not realize then that if you stretch your limits, you create an opening for the possibility of failure. When you push beyond your comfort zone, you are bound to experience the pain of inexperience, of non-achievement. I would later find this out.

To return to my story, the logical course seemed to be to apply for a PhD program at the University of Washington where I could work under Pollack. Having tested out the idea with him, I then applied for the PhD program at his institution. Here, I encountered my first roadblock: I was denied admission.

This was the first challenge I had ever faced in my academic life. However, it wouldn't stop me from pursuing my choice of career. Disappointed, but not defeated, I sent in applications to other carefully selected bioengineering PhD programs offered by other academically challenging universities. Eventually, I was rewarded for my persistent efforts with an acceptance letter from Drexel University. At this point, I honestly thought I could continue my research into my chosen topic of interest, albeit at a different university. It didn't matter so much where I studied as long as I could continue to explore the immense potential in Pollack's work. I felt a compulsion to pursue this research by any means, direct or indirect. This led me to choose to work in a lab that specialized in cellular neurobiology. I loved it; I was finally doing scientific research, and I was doing it in the area that most fascinated me.

Intellectually gifted people often tend to become so absorbed in their work that they have problems with keeping up with required academic grading systems (Kingore, 2003). Fortunately, this was not my experience. My academic performance was up to par at Drexel. I passed my qualifying exam and candidacy, and consistently achieved high grades for my coursework. To be honest, however, my heart was in the lab. My life revolved around my research on cellular structure.

Despite the surface smoothness of my educational course, turbulent undercurrents developed between my academic advisor and me. It may be best expressed by saying that I was not completely obedient to his wishes. I never intended to be obstinate, but I'm sure it seemed that way to him at times. The fact was that the unconscious resistance he felt was the result of my grit and passion to follow my own dream (Winner, 1996). It wasn't that I deliberately chose to defy his wishes. I was just trying to maintain a delicate balance between what I needed to do to fulfill my personal goal and what he wanted me to do toward completing the PhD program requirements.

During my PhD years, I continually tried to figure out how to apply and work on Pollack's paradigm shift theory in my lab work. This took up the first two years of my PhD work. My line of thinking was simple: If I could use certain advanced imaging techniques,

I could gather some convincing data that would correlate with the predictions made by this theory. However, with the limited availability of research funding and the pressure to maintain the direction of research that my advisor wanted me to pursue, I could not design the right experimental construct.

It was during this period that I had the great good luck to meet and be mentored by another pioneer of this line of research, the great Gilbert Ling himself, now in his nineties. He lives in Philadelphia, where my university is based. This seemed to me like a wonderful coincidence. Ling arrived in the United States from China in the 1940s, at a time when there were very few foreigners doing research in the United States. In 1944, he was selected for the prestigious Boxer Indemnity Scholarship. With his PhD in hand, Ling turned to the study of cell structure theory, which became his life's work. One of his students, Raymond Damadian (Damadian, 1971; Kjelle 2002), went on to become the inventor of the first magnetic resonance scanning machine. He was awarded the National Medal of Technology and Innovation in 1988. This is just one example of the brilliance that Ling has helped mold. This humble man is truly a giant in his field. It is an honor to work under his tutelage.

I originally corresponded with Ling via email. When we finally met, his words dropped a live coal into the seething gunpowder that was my state of mind at the time. He explained that even a simple experimental construct could sufficiently develop the implications of any theory, provided the theory was just a bit close to being true. Thus his advice to me was to initiate a few simple experiments to test the truth of the paradigm shift theory. This suggestion inspired me. With his advice and a stroke of creative insight, I felt ready to devise such experiments— or at least that's what I thought.

But the tightrope act I was performing back at the lab finally took its toll on me. I should have known it was only a matter of time until I fell off. My academic advisor, who had steadily been growing more and more frustrated as I pursued this alternate paradigm in spite of its lack of mainstream recognition, at last took the decision to bar me from laboratory access. He had already stopped my official research funding a few months before this. The worst part of it was that it happened just as I was on the verge of getting results in my alternative paradigm experiments. This was the biggest crisis-level emergency I had ever had to face in my academic life. It was almost too much for me.

Research is difficult, at best, even under ideal conditions, but now I had no funding whatsoever and was completely shut out from the lab. To make matters worse, I failed to understand what wrong I had done. A sense of understanding what I had done wrong might have made the shut-out easier to bear since it would have felt like consequences I had brought on myself. But since I did not see it that way, I was completely devastated by the unexpected blow. I had no clue how to get back on my feet.

This was the start of my journey into darkness. I choose to describe it this way because my overwhelming impression of that time is the absolute lack of direction or clarity as to where I was headed. I felt as though my world had collapsed on me. My mind was filled with turmoil, and I lost confidence in myself. I could not figure things out. Even at this painful time, there were many graduate students from various laboratories who tried to be there for me as my friends and my support network. Yet something was lacking because they too could not really fathom the reasons behind my almost insane pursuit of the alternate cell theory and my obstinate behavior.

Eventually though, I emerged from my dark depression. It took me five or six months. There were a few definite turning points on this long journey out of hopelessness and confusion. First and foremost, I wanted to find out why this had happened, what I had done wrong, and what I needed to learn from this situation. In my search for these answers, I came across an online support group called Intellectually Gifted Adults, which seemed to be made for me (https://www.facebook.com/groups/giftedadults). I found that this was the group I could really identify with, and as I interacted with them, I found a measure of solace. Even better, I was able to identify my problem. Simply put, as an intellectually gifted person, I saw the world differently, which inevitably led to clashes with those who did not have the same view.

This group also helped me clarify in my mind who I really was, and the process of participating answered many of my questions. One important question related to my feeling of alienation and being misunderstood by others. My peers in the group helped me realize that this is a common experience in this special group. Since gifted people perceive reality differently, they express different thoughts, they may behave differently, and these differences can easily lead to misunderstanding. Thus intellectual capability is a two-edged weapon, which can both help and wound the possessor.

The take-away point I got out of this whole interaction was that the crisis I was presently experiencing was not necessarily my fault or the result of my inadequacy. It is a predicament that many intellectually gifted people find themselves in, just because of who they are. This new knowledge almost miraculously restored my self-confidence. In addition to this particular group, I searched for and found more information about giftedness via various organizations, such as Supporting the Emotional Needs of the Gifted (SENG).

With the help of these groups and some much-needed introspection, I came to see myself in a new way. I had known for a long time that I possessed high intellectual capabilities, but I did not accept or like some of my personality traits. In fact, I viewed them just as other people did. Thus when others saw my intensity as agitation or hyper-excitability or my dogged determination as obstinacy, I took these messages to heart. I would constantly think that I was at fault in these matters. Now I know that intensity, complexity, and the drive to go forward are all second nature to the intellectually gifted person. Far from being undesirable traits, they have immense positive value in such people. The new insights I gained helped me unlock the mysteries of my emotional nature (Dabrowski, 1972). I always knew I was intellectually gifted, but I was unaware of the emotional aspects of intellectual giftedness (Lovecky, 1986). Once I started to understand them more, I was able to make sense of my emotional needs, intensities, and complexities (Lind, 2005).

The support group I have mentioned above included many well-known psychologists who work with intellectually gifted adults. Their suggestions were a lifeline to me in my unraveled state. I must mention in particular psychologists Sharon Barnes and Edith Johnston who helped me immensely. They, as well as the support groups and my independent reading, guided me to arrive at insights that helped me emerge from darkness.

I came to see that intellectual giftedness promotes independent thinking and an independent attitude to life (Torrance, 1965). Such people often operate on well-founded hunches and intuitions (Heylighen,

2008; Lovecky, 1986). However, they often find themselves unable to explain how they arrived at their conclusions or hypotheses through a carefully presented logical progression of ideas. The sequence of ideas is very clear to them and forms the basis of their leaps of insight, but they are unable to convey the force of their intuition and convince others. This leads to confusion and, eventually, frustration in the minds of the others who are looking on.

Even worse, the ways in which logic supports the gifted thinker's intuitive reasoning imparts a kind of dogged determination to follow a definitive line of thinking that others may interpret as obstinacy. This often brings the individual into conflict with those in authority, as was happening in my laboratory career and why my advisor and I couldn't see eye to eye. It all made sense now (Heylighen, 2008; Kingore, 2003).

The support group became my anchor. I held on to them while I decided my future course. Eventually, I was able to chalk out my plan of action. The very first decision I took was not to fight but to hang loose, just as many of my friends in this group advised. "Hanging loose" is a phrase and gesture associated with the sport of surfing. Surfers say that while no one can stop the waves, anyone can learn to surf them. In exactly the same way, there are many crises and situations in life that we cannot avoid or prevent, but we can learn to navigate them successfully. When faced with huge waves, an experienced surfer never meets them head-on. Instead, he hangs loose and rides them out.

I took this advice to heart and realized that I would be foolish to face my current situation head-on. This would have meant fighting back irrationally, showing anger, or displaying passive-aggressive behavior. Since none of these strategies is ultimately successful, a wiser choice was to take care of myself, remain peaceful, reflect, and rethink the situation. I chose to ride out the storm. Though I was still angry and hurt because I felt I had been wronged, I steered into calm waters and waited for my mind to clear.

Next I started to develop the habit of freewriting, even as I planned my next step. In this unstructured form of writing, one writes continuously for a set period of time. It helps the writer overcome a mental block and silences the inner critic. One simply keeps writing, not even paying attention to grammar, style, or any other restrictions. Freewriting is valuable in helping the writer to understand the thought process and produce a raw pre-draft of one's work. I came across Phinished, an online support group that advocates freewriting as a useful method for PhD students to collect their thoughts. A good book on this subject is *Writing Your Dissertation in Fifteen Minutes a Day: A Guide to Starting, Revising, and Finishing Your Doctoral Thesis* (Bolker, 1998). Freewriting allowed me to reorganize my research work into a good draft, as well as reorganize my thoughts.

As a result of this reflection and recollection phase, I came to see that the best thing under my circumstances would be to transfer to the University of Washington to complete my PhD requirements. This was an unusual step, and it involved moving all the way across the country. However, I was able to convince both Pollack and my thesis committee at Drexel University to approve my plan.

Changing schools was an intimidating step, but I had already been prepared to face it with confidence through another particularly useful insight I had gleaned on my journey. This involves what is known as the "imposter syndrome," which many intellectually gifted students face (Caltech, 2014; Clance & Imes, 1978). The term describes a psychological condition that prevents people from internalizing their competence. They are unable to appreciate the true dimensions and significance of their capability and achievements, despite strong evidence supporting this view. Thus, they feel like frauds who do not deserve their achievements and success. This is especially true for intellectually gifted people from atypical backgrounds (for instance, women, minorities, or international students, to name a few). Their internal critic makes them feel, "I don't deserve success. I wouldn't be surprised to fail." I am familiar with this voice. I used to tell myself that my capacity did not keep pace with my ambition. Through my struggle, I learned that the first battle one must fight is to convince oneself of one's own capability (Caltech, 2014; Clance & Imes, 1978).

Once I realized this, I started to work on formulating a realistic view of myself, my talents, and my gifts. The payoff was immediate— once I regained my self-confidence, I was able to promote my plans and plead my case in a persuasive way, so that others were receptive to me and my plans. I convinced the Drexel thesis committee to allow me to do further research elsewhere and the University of Washington to allow me work under the tutelage of Pollack. It is under this unique arrangement that I have neared the completion of my PhD.

Final Thoughts

Looking back, I marvel at how adversity brought out the victor in me. I worked for a year and a half at the University of Washington and completed my experimental work. At present, I am back in Philadelphia, preparing to submit my thesis. My journey, obstacles and all, reminds me of a beloved quote from Albert Einstein who stated:

> Most teachers waste their time by asking questions which are intended to discover what a pupil does not know, whereas the true art of questioning has for its purpose to discover what the pupil knows or is capable of knowing.

Experience tells me that this captures the essence of how we can support and foster independent thinking among intellectually gifted students. To illustrate from my personal experience, my medical school background trained me thoroughly to understand the traditional paradigm of cell structure. Then I read the alternate paradigm presented in *Cells, Gels and the Engines of Life*. Though few graduate students have this level of in-depth knowledge relating to both alternate and mainstream cell-structure theories, my research advisor never once asked me in depth about the work I was interested in. It would seem as if the assumption had already been made that I was at fault. This prevented him from probing the ideas and thoughts I was incubating, which would have helped him understand their true importance. This was the source of the misunderstanding between us. I would only point out that once I was given the opportunity to think independently and come up with my own solutions in a new laboratory, I was successful in pursuing my research.

I was driven to travel down a different path from most PhD students and had to find a way to mold my varying interests to my surroundings. There were inevitable obstacles on this journey, but I have come to realize that success is rarely found on a straight path. One must endure twists and turns to reach it. We can always face and overcome the highest hurdles by drawing on our own strength and that of other generous and wise souls. True courage and resilience is often just hanging loose, clearing your mind, and giving yourself time and space to make the right decisions.

Interview

THROUGHOUT THE STAGES OF WRITING this narrative, I asked some of my colleagues for their observations and comments on the manuscript. One of them was curious about some facts not covered in this account. The following section is my response to his questions.

What was it like for you growing up in India as a kid? What can you tell us about gifted programs or other academic curricular advances implemented to meet the needs of gifted children in India? Was it easy for you, as a highly gifted child, to fit in with your peers in India?

Being an only child, I may have had a pampered childhood. My parents both had stable government jobs. My mother was a high school physics teacher at the same school I attended from kindergarten through high school. My father was a civil engineer. I had a safe and secure upbringing. We lived in Purna Junction, a small town in central India.

My school in India provided me with an almost ideal academic environment up through high school. This small and unpretending school fostered independent thinking by teaching science thoroughly but rarely assigning rote homework. This left me with a good fundamental science education, as well as ample time to indulge my scientific curiosity.

Some characteristics of my schooling in India do stand out. For one, I had access to the science laboratory, and I made full use of this privilege. I also balanced my academic interests with other extracurricular activities, such as public-speaking competitions, artwork, and Boy Scouts. However, my scores were never affected adversely by my involvement in these interests.

My teachers, too, were always ready to discuss any subject on which I sought clarification or when I just wanted to think aloud on some point of interest. This cooperative spirit spawned a love of learning in me that still flourishes today. These discussions with my teachers stimulated my mind and scientific thinking to the greatest extent, besides to the intellectual broadening afforded by my wide range of reading and laboratory work. Though the concept of special training for gifted children was unknown at the time, my early mentors were doing just that in their own inimitable way. They groomed me to love science and understand it deeply, to think on my own, and to seek answers by their supplying unfailing encouragement and well-thought-out questions. Intellectually gifted people require environments that foster their potential. In the United States, there is a society named SENG, which supports the emotional needs of the gifted, so that they can thrive (http://sengifted.org/). Unwittingly, my teachers provided just such emotional support.

Fitting in was never a problem for me in India. My impression is that in India the prevailing culture does differ from other places by giving the highest respect for knowledge. Thus, fitting in is never a problem for brilliant students. In retrospect, I appreciate the rich inner life that I experienced in India. I did not share it with everybody in totality, but I never felt alienated.

The Take-Away from My Experiences

My long struggle to find a field that would challenge my intellectual capacity has taught me that success is rarely earned on a linear path. Most often, one has to be prepared to face and override all kinds of obstacles and setbacks. Such difficulties eventually provide even more important life lessons. Thus, I have learned that no matter what, you need to stick to your hunch, follow your passion, and learn to deal with failures in a constructive manner.

Sometimes, the specter of total failure can cloud your mind. It's important at such times to just hang loose, clear your mind, and use some time for reflection. This will eventually allow you to make the right decisions and implement them successfully.

Another valuable lesson I learned from my experience is the priceless place of mentors in your life. If you need to work through problems successfully, you will need a mentor. Not only do they act as role models whom you can emulate and seek inspirations from, but also their advice can, quite literally, transform your life. I knew that these men had so much to teach me, and so I sought their advice. Mentorship is one thing that has helped me tremendously along this journey.

My future goal is to continue working to gather data that will help establish the alternate paradigm of cell structure and bring it due recognition. Yes, I do need the intellectual courage to work on an alternate paradigm, as opposed to one already accepted. It is a challenging task. The path ahead is far from certain. However, I perceive a host of potential opportunities. I am seeking opportunities to be involved in industrial research or technological entrepreneurship or to do research in the right kind of academic laboratory where I can fulfill my potential.

References

Bolker, J. (1998). *Writing your dissertation in fifteen minutes a day: A guide to starting, revising, and finishing your doctoral thesis.* New York: Macmillan.

California Technical Institute. (2014). The imposter syndrome. Retrieved from https://counseling.caltech.edu/general/InfoandResources/Impostor.

Clance, P. R., & Imes, S. A. (1978). The imposter phenomenon in high achieving women: Dynamics and therapeutic intervention. *Psychotherapy: Theory, Research & Practice, 15*(3), 241–247.

Dabrowski, K. (1972). *Psychoneurosis is not an illness: Neuroses and psychoneuroses from the perspective of positive disintegration.* London: Gryf Publications.

Damadian, R. (1971). Tumor detection by nuclear magnetic resonance. Science, *171*(3976), 1151–1153.

Fredrickson, R. H. (1974). Multipotential: A concept for career decision making. Proceedings from Annual Convention of the American Personnel and Gidance Association. New Orleans, LA.

Heylighen, F. (2008). Gifted people and their problems. Retrieved from http://talentdevelop.com/articles/GPATP1.html.

Kerr, B. A., & Ghrist-Priebe, S. L. (1988). Intervention for Multipotentiality: Effects of a Career Counseling Laboratory for Gifted High School Students. *Journal of Counseling and Development, 66*(8), 366–369.

Kingore, B. (2003). High achiever, gifted learner, creative thinker. *Understanding our gifted, 15*(3), 3–5.

Kjelle, M. M. (2002). *Raymond Damadian and the development of MRI: Unlocking the secrets of science.* Hockessin, DE: Mitchell Lane Publishers.

Lind, S. (2001). Overexcitability and the gifted. *The SENG Newsletter, 1*(1), 3–6.

———. (2005). Fostering adult giftedness: Acknowleding and addressing affective needs of gifted adults. Retrieved from https://sengifted.org/archives/articles/fostering-adult-giftedness-acknowledging-and-addressing-affective-needs-of-gifted-adults.

Ling, G. (2014). Gilbert Ling homepage. Retrieved from http://www.gilbertling.org/.

Ling, G. N. (2006). A convergence of experimental and theoretical breakthroughs affirms the PM theory of dynamically structured cell water on the theory's 40th birthday. In Pollack, G. H., Cameron, I. L., & Wheatley, D. N. (Eds.), *Water and the Cell* (1–52). Dordrecht, The Netherlands: Springer.

Lovecky, D. V. (1986). "Can you hear the flowers sing? Issues for gifted adults." *Journal of Counseling and Development, 64*(9), 572–575.

National Asssociation of Gifted Children (2014). Myths about gifted students. Retrieved from http://www.nagc.org/resources-publications/resources/myths-about-gifted- students.

Pollack, G. H. (2001). *Cells, gels and the engines of life: A new, unifying approach to cell function.* Seattle, WA: Ebner & Sons.

———. (2002). The cell as a biomaterial. *Journal of Materials Science: Materials in Medicine, 13*(9), 811–821.

Torrance, E. P. (1965). *Gifted children in the classroom.* New York: Collier-Macmillan.

Winner, E. (1996). The rage to master: The decisive case for talent in the visual arts. In K. A. Ericsson (Ed.), *The road to excellence: The acquisition of expert performance in the arts and sciences, sports and games* (271–301). Hillsdale, NJ: Erlbaum.

CHAPTER 8

British, Gifted, and Disabled: A Personal Narrative of Discovery and Acceptance

Jennifer Quamina, MPhil

The Early Years

I HARDLY REMEMBER MY DAYS in nursery school. It's pretty much a big blur, but I do remember, quite vividly, how I felt. I was a very shy and thoughtful child. I was serious, curious, and wanted to understand the world around me. At the same time, I was extremely sensitive and struggled to get on with my peers. I felt odd compared to other children my age. I don't know how to explain it other than to say I just didn't fit in. I wanted friends. I wanted a best friend with whom I could play, share secrets, and be silly. But the process of building those friendships proved difficult. I couldn't put a finger on why, but I felt like a loner.

Struggling to Fit In

I WAS BORN IN WEST LONDON (Hammersmith) to Trinidadian parents who migrated to the United Kingdom in the 1970s. We lived in a council flat until I was five years old, and my nursery and primary school was located in a prestigious part of London (North Kensington). It was a local authority school that had a number of ethnic minority children in attendance. The majority of the children's parents came to Britain as immigrants in the 1950s and 1960s, looking for a better life. It was a safe, racially diverse environment. I should have felt comfortable, but I didn't.

The primary school I attended was called Avondale Primary School. The standard of teaching was excellent, and the school had good leadership. The headmistress was Mrs. Mamaroo, a Trinidadian-born academic whose goal was to give children from all backgrounds a sound education. She took schooling seriously, so our classes were fairly structured: writing and comprehension in the morning, math and play in the afternoon. It was a safe and nurturing environment, but my sensitivity made it hard for me to be as happy as the other children.

For example, I remember really liking a boy in my class and wanting to be his friend. We used to hold hands and play during break time. One day, another girl grabbed his hand and took him away, shouting, "He is my boyfriend!" I was mortified, and what's worse, he didn't even bother to protest. He left with her. This might seem like a petty playground incident, but I was deeply hurt and unhappy. I remember crying and the teacher trying to comfort me. I imagine any other child would have gotten over it quickly, but I was devastated for a while.

Excelling at Reading and Comprehension

In such an uncomfortable environment, books were my refuge. They absolutely fascinated me, and I absorbed the words, reading each book from cover to cover. I often read books geared toward seven- to ten-year-olds when I was only five. During our school reading and comprehension hour, the teacher would put up sentences and intentionally muddle the words. It was our job to arrange them into a logical sentence. My classmates often struggled at this task, but I found it easy. I couldn't explain how I got the sentence structure correct, but I somehow felt that certain words had to be put in a certain order. It all just flowed in my head. I can only assume my voracious appetite for reading made this possible.

When I was six years old, my family moved from West to East London. The primary schools were different and, according to my mother, the standard of teaching wasn't as good. She noticed that many of the children were not reading yet. Concerned that this less challenging environment would hold my sister and me back, my parents bought supplementary materials for us to use at home.

Trouble in School

AT TWELVE YEARS OLD, I attended a comprehensive school. Although I enjoyed school and worked hard to gain my GCSE (General Certificate of Secondary Education) qualifications, I did not excel in math the same way I did in reading. In fact, I wasn't even performing on an average level. My math teacher was patient with me, but no matter how hard I tried, I could only earn Ds on final exams.

My teachers were good overall, but there were some I didn't get on with. According to them, I had a problem with authority. I remember one teacher in particular, Mr. Atley, refused to have me in his class as I questioned his method of teaching. He said I was rude and had me transferred to a lower class. Looking back, I think he might have felt a little intimidated by me because I asked so many questions he couldn't answer.

My school reports always showed me to be a very hard-working pupil who was willing to learn; however, when it came to taking my final exams, I didn't do well. The problem was that I didn't know how to answer test questions properly. Most of my answers went off on tangents, offering up multiple possibilities as answers. Unfortunately, that wasn't what the external examiners wanted. I left school that year with four Cs, two Ds, and one F. I was disappointed in myself, especially since my sister had received seven Bs. I felt like a failure. I tried harder to get my grades up in school, but I was never successful. I was disorganized, absent-minded, and had trouble accepting the validity of the information being taught. My reading level was still well above average, but that fact was not reflected in my overall performance. It was frustrating to say the least.

After finishing compulsory school, I got my very first job, working as a bank clerk. It didn't last long, though. My anxiety and poor math and organizational skills got in the way. I was asked to leave after a year. I went on to find a retail job and worked as a sales assistant for two years, after which I spent ten years working as a laboratory technician at Queen Mary University of London.

Giftedness? What's That?

I love learning and am always looking for ways to improve myself, especially my communication skills. In my quest for self-improvement, I found an excellent course on interpersonal communication. It was a year-long diploma class held in the evenings. I was intrigued, so I took a chance and enrolled. The course turned out to be amazing, run by two psychologists (Jonathan Smith and Laura Dain) and a life coach (Catherine M. Shaw). It awakened my awareness of the importance of communication. Catherine had an incredible impact on me. It was through her life coaching that I finally accepted my giftedness, but it was a long, arduous journey. Let me tell you the story.

One day after a class on assertiveness, I chatted with Catherine about why I enrolled in the course. I told her about my ongoing problems with communication, and she said she didn't think I had a problem there. She felt my issue was that I was a chronic overthinker, always terrified that if I said something, it would ultimately be wrong and people would disapprove of me. She felt my overthinking was the probable cause of my anxiety.

After several months of class and receiving frequent emails from Catherine, I was offered a coaching session with her to explore my self-esteem issues. Catherine had an extraordinary way of connecting with me. She spoke and communicated in a language that really made me feel understood. At the time, Catherine was writing a book chapter about counseling gifted children. I hadn't heard the term "gifted" before and assumed it meant an individual who was some kind of genius. Catherine went on to explain that a gifted individual is not necessarily an academically bright person (Szabos, 1989). She gave me a leaflet to read about the differences.

Differences between a Bright Child and a Gifted Child

As I read the list in the leaflet, it slowly dawned on me that I displayed some of the characteristics of a gifted person, but I was in denial. My mind immediately went back to secondary school, where I was surrounded by bright, intelligent children who always got questions right—while I always struggled and got things wrong. I, gifted? Impossible. I shook the laughable idea from my head. There was no way it could be true. I learned and thought differently from my peers. I never took what the teacher said at face value, especially in subjects such as science, history, or English. I wanted to know how teachers came to their conclusions and why they believed what they were teaching. All my questions needed in-depth answers. I even questioned the information in the reference books my teachers taught from. I questioned the authors and whether they were correct in what they wrote, or whether they had biases in their literature. Looking back, it must have driven my teachers crazy. That was not my intention, but I read widely and came up with my own conclusions, which led to more questions.

After reading the leaflet, I discussed with Catherine my feelings about education and my difficulty with learning. She had already observed during the diploma class that I was different from my fellow classmates. When I asked how, she said my comments and questions were different: more intense, more abstract, more curious, more probing—all classic characteristics of a gifted adult. That's when she dropped the bombshell: "Jennifer, I believe you are gifted."

I was shocked and didn't know what to say. After a long pause, I told her I couldn't be gifted. I definitely didn't feel intelligent. I was absolutely rubbish at exams. I wasn't an A student like so many others I went to school with, and my study habits were all over the place. Catherine knew these things and still felt I was gifted. She gave me an article by Deirdre Lovecky (1986) called "Can You Hear the Flowers Sing? Issues for Gifted Adults." It was an eye opener. Everything I read in it totally resonated with me and mirrored how I felt. For the first time, I felt understood.

Battling Depression and Self-Doubt in College

ONE OF THE CHAPTERS IN "Can You Hear the Flowers Sing? Issues for Gifted Adults" that struck me most was on the issue of existential depression and anxiety, a trait that nearly all gifted adults have to deal with. My problems with depression started while studying for my first degree and being unable to cope. I was working part-time, struggling to pay university fees, and attempting to complete class homework assignments. I tried to get help with my depressive feelings and anxiety by making an appointment with the university counselor. As I poured out my heart, she could see I was very distressed and asked my permission to write my doctor for further assistance. My doctor wanted to put me on a low dose of antidepressants and arranged for me to see a cognitive behavioral therapist (CBT), but the waiting list was long.

I continued to correspond with Catherine. She sent me extremely encouraging emails that really lifted my spirit. They were written in a language that I understood. I eventually went on to make an appointment with her, and we talked about my depression and anxiety. One of the things I loved about Catherine is that she was an active listener. It was profound the way she understood me. At the end of the coaching session, I felt really good. Over a number of sessions, clarity and eventual self-acceptance of my giftedness manifested. I have a firm belief that people come into our lives for a reason, not by chance. I am ever grateful to Catherine Shaw for opening my eyes to the beautiful, creative world of giftedness.

I get very restless when I'm not doing something to stimulate my mind. My curiosity grows so strong that I get a buzzing feeling in my head if I'm not feeding my mind with exciting ideas, particularly those related to self-development, psychology, or science. One of the many jobs I had during my search for a meaningful career was working as a laboratory technician at Queen Mary University of London. I worked in the biochemistry department, which was connected to the Royal London School of Medicine and Dentistry. My job involved measuring creatinine levels of dentists who utilized amalgam (a mercury-based tooth filling given to patients). I also occasionally helped with laboratory demonstrations with medical and dental students. This is where my love of science really emerged.

After a number of years, I met the university's career development officer, David Pank. He told me about part-time courses for laboratory technicians and suggested that I do a day-release course at the City of Westminster College, London. Impressed with me, David wrote a letter to my head of department and convinced the department to pay the fees. He agreed and I enrolled. The course was excellent. I learned so many skills to enhance my job performance. My study habits weren't the best, but I worked hard and passed my exams with distinction. David was extremely pleased with my exam results, so he convinced my department, yet again, to pay for my certification. I passed with excellent results.

Unfortunately for me, David retired two years later. Due to university job cuts, his position wasn't renewed. This was a very sad day for me, as I knew I'd lost a mentor and career advocate. Before David left, he encouraged me to finish my studies by completing an undergraduate degree at an evening university. Hoping my university would be willing to help me one last time, I asked my head of department if the department would sponsor me. I knew the head of department didn't like me (for reasons I didn't know), so I should not have been surprised by his response, but I was. He abruptly asked why I needed a degree. I thought it an odd question to ask of a person working at a university. Most of the people there wanted to learn and succeed academically. Why would I be any different? Disappointed, I accepted that he wasn't going to support me. I left the university after a year and ended up working in children's social services as a part-time administrator.

Still, with a strong desire to finish my degree, I got a student loan to pay my tuition fees. I worked diligently but struggled to balance my part-time job and my university assignments. Nevertheless, with sheer hard work, I completed my BSc in applied biology in two years.

Struggling to Establish a Career

AFTER COMPLETING THE DEGREE, I felt inspired to delve further into the scientific academic world. I left my part-time job and worked full-time as an editorial assistant for the Society of Chemical Industry. It was a blessing working there as I had access to the latest scientific journals and papers. This spurred me on. I felt I had truly found my calling. I searched for an evening university where I could earn a master's degree. Fortunately, I found the ideal university, Birkbeck, University of London.

I applied to Birkbeck for an MSc in applied biology. I loved the program and had absolutely brilliant classmates who supported each other by holding study groups during exam times or going out socially as a group. The first year of study I did very well, even on exams. I was awarded a full scholarship to complete my second year and was very grateful.

One particular lecturer, Professor Monique Simmonds, especially inspired me. She was a truly gifted teacher who could turn difficult biology subjects into incredible learning experiences. I vowed that if I ever made it into the world of scientific research, I would be just like her. As part of the degree requirements, I had to do a project dissertation. I knew straightaway where I wanted to do my dissertation: at the world-famous Kew Botanical Gardens with Professor Simmonds.

My dissertation involved investigating the medicinal properties of Trinidadian/West Indian herbal plants. Doing laboratory research at Kew Gardens was so satisfying. I loved walking through Kew's paradisiac grounds during my lunch breaks. It was such an inspirational place to work and helped me solidify my career aspirations. During that time more than ever, I knew I wanted a career in science. After completing my master's degree, I searched for avenues to raise money to fund a PhD. I was particularly interested in investigating anticancer drugs.

I contacted one of the lecturers in Birkbeck's biology department to inquire about a fascinating project he was undertaking around anticancer research. A couple of months later, I received a life-changing email informing me that I'd been awarded a full-time, three-year scholarship to complete a PhD investigating the anticancer drug azinomycin B. I was both ecstatic and nervous at the same time. I certainly wanted to take advantage of the opportunity, but it would mean leaving a well-paid full-time job to become a full-time student. It seemed a bit risky, but I went for it.

So, my research life began. I walked into the laboratory feeling happy and ready to work, but just that fast, disaster struck. My second supervisor, who was a biology lecturer, left the university to take another job. I was nervous because I was six months into my studies and reliant on him to teach me biology laboratory techniques, something my first supervisor, an organic chemist, couldn't do. I needed to know those techniques to become an independent scientific researcher.

From there, things only got worse. First, I found out a university in China was researching the same topic as my PhD proposal, and worse still, they were producing tangible results that answered my PhD hypothesis. I was distraught. I had discussions with my first supervisor about how we should move forward. As previously mentioned, my supervisor's scientific background was chemistry, so he wanted me to conduct experiments that had a chemistry slant. I wasn't happy about that. I had spent over ten years studying biology; chemistry is a completely different discipline.

The few biology experiments I did carry out were inconclusive, but some of the results were promising. Nevertheless, my supervisor dismissed my research results, stating that they weren't correct according to the standards of current research papers. I tried to explain that results in biology aren't always set in stone. They are not like chemistry experiments, where you mix chemical formulae and get a definitive chemical product. I discussed with him a particularly promising experiment I was carrying out using a polymerase chain reaction (PCR) protocol, which revealed a definitive deoxyribonucleic acid (DNA) product. I presented him the result, but again he dismissed it, saying I was conducting the experiments incorrectly (even though I repeated the very same experiment very carefully four times). Behind my back, he instructed a postdoctoral researcher to carry out the PCR experiment I originally conducted. He even used the same protocol. Lo and behold, the postdoctoral researcher presented the exact same results. I felt not only betrayed but also undermined by my supervisor, the person who was supposed to be supporting me. From that day forward, my relationship with my supervisor declined.

Though I attempted to carry out basic chemistry experiments at my supervisor's request, my personal problems got in the way. All he asked me to do was calculate simple chemistry solutions using basic math, but I couldn't do it. I'd always had problems with math. But up to that point, I never had to address it directly. I could always find a way to skate around it. Now, I was stuck. I remember sitting on the lab bench, crying with frustration. I didn't know where to start.

After an hour, my supervisor entered the laboratory and asked why I hadn't started the calculations. I had to tell the truth. I told him I had a problem with math. He looked at me incredulously as if to say, "How dare you not know basic math at your age?" I told him I thought I had some sort of math dyslexia known as dyscalculia. He said he'd never heard of it. He pointed out that chemistry uses a lot of math and suggested I practice on my own time. I was very discouraged and felt even more depressed.

Discovering My Disabilities

DYSCALCULIA IS A CONDITION that affects the ability to acquire arithmetical skills. Dyscalculic learners have difficulty understanding simple number concepts, lack an intuitive grasp of numbers, and have problems learning numbers, facts, and procedures. Even if they produce a correct answer or use a correct method, they may do so mechanically and without confidence (Capelletti, Freeman, & Butterworth, 2011). I had not been officially diagnosed, but the description seemed to fit me perfectly.

Research suggests that, like many specific learning disabilities, dyscalculia has varying levels of severity and can affect different areas of mathematical calculations. These difficulties can have an adverse effect on many day-to-day activities, such as dealing with finances, following directions, managing a diary, and keeping track of time (Butterworth, 1999).

Over the next couple of weeks, I became more and more frustrated with my poor organizational skills and math ability. I couldn't go on any longer without addressing the problem. I consulted the Internet to look for anything concerning dyscalculia. Fortunately, I stumbled across the name of a leading international expert, Professor Brian Butterworth, and contacted him. He informed me that he had retired from research and referred me to his colleague, Marinella Capelletti, a cognitive neuroscientist at University College London (UCL). Capelletti is the only scientist in the United Kingdom who investigates the causes of dyscalculia in adults. She invited me to UCL to be tested for dyscalculia using a series of cognitive and neurological tests. The tests were conclusive and confirmed that I did in fact have a severe form of dyscalculia; she was extremely surprised that I was able to earn two science degrees in my condition. Capelletti wanted to do some follow-up studies, so she invited me to participate in a number of cognitive research projects she was working on. I agreed.

Armed with my documented dyscalculia diagnosis, I explained the findings to my supervisor. I was happy to finally be able to prove to him that I had an actual, verified condition. Unfortunately, my late diagnosis couldn't save me. In order to receive a PhD in a UK university, you need to have an oral examination to upgrade from MPhil status to PhD level. I never had the opportunity to upgrade, as I didn't have enough viable research results. Plus, the university academic committee wasn't transparent and honest with me about my ability to graduate on time. I later found out my PhD project hypothesis was impossible to complete within three years. It would have required a whole team of researchers. No one told me this upfront.

Seeking Support for My Dyscalculia

IN ORDER TO SAVE FACE, my supervisor forced me to conduct and undertake chemistry experiments to get results for my MPhil thesis. Apparently, he hadn't fully grasped how very basic my chemistry knowledge was. If I were to apply for an MPhil thesis oral examination, I would be examined by a chemistry external examiner. I was in no way prepared for that.

I decided to make a formal complaint to the school board and examination committee that I was at a disadvantage. I asked my supervisor if I could be transferred to a biology supervisor so I could at least work in my field of choice. He wouldn't allow it. Panic started to set in as I realized I would fail and leave the university with nothing. I had to do something, so without my supervisor's knowledge, I stayed behind in the laboratory for a few months and worked late at night with another biology supervisor. I gained some incredible results on chemotherapeutics for fatal neonatal bacteria that cause meningitis in newborns. With much hesitation, I told my first supervisor what I was doing. I asked if I could include my groundbreaking results in my final thesis. He said no.

At that point, I knew my academic career was over. I sought legal help to support me with my complaint, but the university refused to talk to my legal counsel, citing that it was an "internal university matter." I discussed my case with a fellow PhD student who saw the unfairness of the situation. He suggested I approach the disability office and student union to get support with my dyscalculia. (I later found out that it was my supervisor's job to refer me the disability office when he found out about my condition.) In order to receive student support, the disability office sent me to be assessed by a state-registered educational psychologist.

Learning of a New Disorder: Dyspraxia

MY CONDITION WAS CONFIRMED, again, by the state psychologist, but I also learned about a second learning disability, dyspraxia. Dyspraxia is a form of developmental coordination disorder (DCD) that affects the fine and/or gross motor coordination in children and adults. It is caused by an immaturity in the way the brain processes information, which results in messages not being properly or fully transmitted. It is thought to affect up to 10 percent of the population, with males four times more likely to be affected than females. Although dyspraxia may occur in isolation, it frequently coexists with other conditions, such as attention deficit hyperactive disorder (ADHD), dyslexia, dyscalculia, language disorders, and social, emotional, and behavioral impairments (Gibbs, Appleton, & Appleton, 2007).

Thanks to the disability office, I received educational support in the form of a learning mentor, a math tutor, equipment to help me write my thesis, and extra time to write my MPhil thesis dissertation. All these things were helpful, but I continued to feel very bitter and depressed. A career in academic scientific research was still beyond my reach. When I completed my dissertation, I wasn't even invited to my university graduation, nor was I given any career advice or support. I felt discriminated against by the university and let down by my entire university experience. I left the university with an MPhil degree. Many of the lecturers at the university didn't even think I would complete the thesis. Some were surprised and others were very impressed that I had the stamina to finish.

The Coexistence of Disability and Giftedness

My dual diagnosis of both dyspraxia and dyscalculia came as a relief. The more I read, the more things began to make sense. I understood why I couldn't read music notes but could easily play a tune on the guitar by ear. I understood why I struggled to retain short-term information but had an excellent long-term memory. I understood why I am so disorganized and messy but still able to find what I need in the mess. I understood why I was anxious and suffered from depression so frequently. The fog I had been living in my whole life finally began to clear.

I was diagnosed with both dyscalculia and dyspraxia at the age of thirty-eight. I knew I had had problems with my working memory and organizational skills since secondary school, but I had no idea what exactly was wrong. I can only thank my fellow PhD student friend for insisting that I contact the disability office at my university.

Now that I understand my condition, it is easier to handle. I have coping mechanisms that help me conquer challenges. For example, to help with my working memory, I make to-do lists to keep me on track. One of the major challenges I still face every day is understanding instructions. It can impact the quality of my work, which has caused many problems in my career over the years. At one point, I was very reluctant to tell my line manager that I had dyspraxia and dyscalculia. I was working in publishing, and my job required a high level of attention to detail and organizational skills. I didn't want to risk being fired, so I kept my diagnoses to myself. But time and time again, I failed to live up to my work standards. My line manager had to put in emergency measures to get my work up to par. That was the lowest point in my career, but it was also a good thing because it forced me to take responsibility and get help.

I found a government program called Access to Work, which is tailored for individuals with dyspraxia. It provides employment coaching, computer equipment to help me work efficiently, relaxation exercises to calm me down if I feel stressed, and awareness classes for my work colleagues to help them understand what dyspraxia is and how to handle it. It took a lot of effort to ask for help, but it was worth it. I now feel confident in my ability to produce excellent work. Now that I know how to handle my disorders, I have no trouble accepting my giftedness. I understand that giftedness presents differently from person to person, and my co-occurring disorders give mine a particularly unique presentation. Understanding these facts has helped me tremendously.

It took a long time to get here, but I now take great pride in all things I do. I'm very tenacious, and though I didn't get my PhD, I recognize my accomplishment in working hard enough to write my MPhil thesis with very little help from my (unsupportive) supervisor.

Gratitude Opens Doors

I'M NO LONGER BITTER about what happened with my university. In fact, I am eternally grateful for everything, as it has made me the person I am today. In 2012, I was at my lowest point and bitterly angry with my university. This bitterness spilled over to my job as I was suffering from depression and anxiety. This impacted my health. I developed a number of anxiety-related illnesses. I was a nightmare to be with, and my family was worried. I felt like a failure, as if my dream of becoming a scientist had been taken away. My doctor once again put me on antidepressants, which I hated as they made me feel like a zombie. He also made another referral for CBT. At my lowest point, I frequently phoned the Samaritans, a 24-hour helpline for people in distress. I felt so low, I didn't want to go to work or even be near other people.

I spent a lot of time on the Internet trying to find answers to how to manage my depression. I stumbled across an old email from a friend referring me to a human behavioral specialist named John Demartini. Attached to the email was a YouTube video explaining what Demartini understood to be the causes of depression:

> Whenever you have a fantasy about how you think your life should be, instead of being grateful for how it is, you split yourself in two. The fantasy appears to be more positive than negative, and as a result, you compare your reality to it. You then become sad and depressed whenever you perceive that your life doesn't match the unrealistic ideal in your mind.

I'd never heard of depression being explained like this. I had always believed it was caused by a chemical imbalance in the brain. Studies on the cause of depression have been going on for decades and are still being conducted. Of course, it is in the interest of pharmaceutical companies to maintain the notion that depression has a physiological, if not neurological, basis. Maybe it does, but I was ready to try something different.

I decided to take an alternative approach to my anxiety and depression. I felt antidepressants were only masking the problem, and I didn't want to be on them for the rest of my life. I contacted a friend who'd attended one of Demartini's workshops called "Breakthrough Experience." She suggested I read his book called *The Breakthrough Experience: A Revolutionary New Approach to Personal Transformation* (Demartini, 2002). She also told me to contact Gal Stiglitz, one of Demartini's students.

My first meeting with Gal was strange. I had been reading self-help books, going to therapy, and taking antidepressants for years, so I was skeptical to say the least. I remember looking Gal straight in the eye and asking whether the Demartini Method, which it is officially called, would help relieve my symptoms. He reassured me it would. "Yes, 100 percent," were his exact words. I was still skeptical, so I asked for more details. He said it was a systematic, predetermined series of mental questions directed toward the objective of assisting an individual to feel present, certain, and grateful. The method neutralizes, he claimed, emotional charges, balances mental and physical reactions, and is a continuous thinking and writing process, repeated over a course of time, that results in the resolution of disequilibrated perceptions.

I was intrigued and booked another session with Gal. The Demartini Method was very challenging to work through. I was holding onto so much—feelings about my past, my family, my work colleagues, people I resented, people who hurt me. I had an emotional treasure trove of stuff to unpack. But sure enough, as I was going through the process and slowly coming to a place of gratitude for everything I'd been through, it began to work. I had a breakthrough! The Demartini Method isn't about helping people to live positively; it's about helping people live in a balanced, realistic way so they can see challenges as chances to learn important life lessons. It teaches how to reflect on positive and challenging situations so both can help you grow as a person.

My sessions with Gal were profound and totally changed my perception of life and all the things that have happened. I now look at my experience with my university and supervisor as a blessing that has served me and taught me humility. I learned that some things are simply not meant to be and that my not receiving a PhD wasn't a mark of failure. Instead, it was a learning process that taught me several lessons, namely that I have disabilities and need to ask for help in overcoming them and achieving.

I learned to surround myself with supportive people who help me reach my goals and appreciate my highest values. I learned that challenging situations and people are good for me as they help me reflect on how to change my approach to dealing with difficult situations. I learned that I needed to work on truly loving myself and looking after myself as I had a tendency to be a passive-aggressive people-pleaser and rescuer. All these things were linked to my anxiety and low self-esteem.

Unleashing My Full Potential as a Gifted Adult with Disabilities

IT TOOK MANY MORE DEMARTINI METHOD SESSIONS to totally clear my self-limiting beliefs and perceptions. I learned so much about myself, especially my strengths. I learned that I am creative, laser focused, and an excellent problem solver and hard worker, particularly if I'm working on something I truly enjoy.

Gal invited me to join the Foundation Program, a six-month personal development course that helps individuals map out the type of life they would like to live. The program was life changing. It gave me the confidence to start my beaded jewelry business, as well as pursue a career in art therapy. One of the requirements of the program was to create a vision board, which has been extremely useful in helping me stay focused on building my business and training as a therapist.

As I write and look back on all that has happened in my life, I feel the future is bright. I look forward to going back to university to get my MSc in art therapy. I also plan to get a PhD in the study of gratitude and the Demartini Method as treatment for symptoms of anxiety and depression in children and adults. I'm profoundly grateful to have met and worked with some amazing people who have shaped and touched my life. I look forward to meeting more in the future.

After all I've been through in the search of happiness, confidence, self-fulfillment, and achievement, I can honestly say I believe gratitude is the key to all life's ills. I am a great advocate for sharing this concept to help people bring their lives into balance. I would like to reach out to authoritative figures in the self-care and education sector to collaborate on how to better assist neurodiverse individuals living in a non-neurodiverse world.

My disorders make certain things more difficult, but they also offer certain advantages. Dyspraxics are highly intelligent people whose cognitive thinking, creativity, and problem-solving skills are different from other individuals. Though we learn significantly slower than non-neurodiverse individuals, our strengths often attract academic institutions to employ us because we are extremely hard working and will always finish a project, no matter what. As long as dyspraxics receive clear, detailed instructions on a task and are allowed to master it through repetitive study, we can achieve the impossible and produce work in the realms of genius.

As a gifted adult with disabilities, I need ample time to learn and work things out in my own way. I understand that my giftedness is not at all diminished by my disabilities. It is only shaped and personalized. My mind works differently, and I have learned to see that as an asset.

Nontraditional thinkers hold the key to producing superior work because of our unique worldviews and unconventional solutions. As one educator illustrated, the dyspraxic brain runs like a state-of-the-art car that is stuck in first gear. It needs a little extra help to reach its full potential.

References

Butterworth, B. (1999). *The mathematical brain*. London: Macmillan.

Capelletti, M., Freeman, E. D., & Butterworth, B. L. (2011). Time processing in dyscalculia. *Frontiers in Psychology, 2*(364). doi:10.3389/fpsyg.2011.00364.

Demartini, J. F. (2002). *The breakthrough experience: A revolutionary new approach to personal transformation*. London: Hay House.

Gibbs, J., Appleton, J., & Appleton, R. (2007). Dyspraxia or developmental coordination disorder? Unravelling the enigma. *Archives of Diseases in Childhood. 92*(6), 534–539. 10.1136/adc.2005.088054.

Kingore, B. (2004). *Differentiation: Simplified, realistic, and effective*. Austin, TX: Professional Associates Publishing.

Lovecky, D. V. (1986). Can you hear the flowers sing? *Journal of Counselling & Development, (64)*9, 572–575.

Szabos, J. (1989). Bright child, gifted learner. *Challenge Magazine*, 34.

CHAPTER 9

Crossing Spaniard-American Cultural Lines: How Being Gifted Helped Me Find Home

Sara del Moral, MA

My UPBRINGING AS A GIFTED CHILD led me to unexpected places. No one—not even my parents, teachers, or classmates—expected me to turn away from a professional career to explore the world in my own way. However, my insatiable curiosity and desire to understand the world led me to do just that. Along the way, I found out who I was, connected with my family roots, and became a bicultural citizen of the world. Based on my experiences, I offer lessons for those who educate today's gifted youth.

Born to Be Gifted

BEFORE I WAS BORN, the path was cleared that I would be raised as a gifted child. My Spanish grandfather, Armando, a prominent journalist in Los Angeles, overcame many obstacles as an immigrant to become successful. My father worked his way through college, earning a PhD by age twenty-four and a professor position immediately after. My mother was also educated and intelligent, first specializing as a librarian and later earning a master's in engineering while I was in elementary school.

Growing up in a tranquil North Seattle neighborhood, the importance of learning and education was a given. It was never discussed explicitly. Rather, books were always present. My parents prioritized my education, and I quickly developed a love for reading. I was reading books unassisted by age four, the age at which I also began reading music and taking piano lessons. None of this seemed exceptional at the time. It was all I had known, normal.

I was comfortable learning independently, so the Montessori preschool I attended proved a great fit. In this environment, I was allowed to work through learning materials at my own pace. That meant I was free to learn reading, writing, and basic arithmetic at four years old.

By the time I finished preschool, I had worked through all the available kindergarten materials. That meant I was able to skip kindergarten and move directly into a class with first through third graders. This is when I first became aware that I was learning faster than other children, but I did not think much of it. The new arrangement worked well from my perspective. The age difference was not enough to make me feel uncomfortable, and I was able to continue learning at a pace that suited me.

The Gifted Program

Toward the end of my "kindergarten" year, I took my first standardized test, a requirement for acceptance into any gifted program in the Seattle Public Schools. While the thought of attending a new school in a far-off neighborhood intimidated me, I found the test easy and fun. I was accepted to the program, which accepted only the top 1 percent of testers.

In the gifted program, the students were placed in different groups for math, reading, and spelling. This meant we worked with different students depending on our level in an individual subject. We would rotate to different stations to sit with others in our learning groups, but much of our time was spent working independently with our textbooks. This arrangement worked well for me because the subject matter came easily, and I was naturally motivated.

It was after my first grade year that I also began making summer visits to my Spanish grandparents, Armando and Amelia, in Los Angeles. My grandmother would spoil me with movies, candy, and shopping, while my grandfather would tell funny stories and perform songs to get a laugh. While both could speak English, among themselves and with the many friends who visited, Spanish was the preferred language. My burning curiosity had found another target. I wondered, what were they saying? I had to learn more. My first Spanish words were some of my grandmother's favorite phrases, such as "¡Mira!," "¡Ándale!," and "¡*Cierra el pico!*"

I didn't spend enough time with my grandparents to learn more, but I had intermittent opportunities in school. In kindergarten, I learned basics, like colors and numbers, from a Spanish class with an Argentinean teacher. At the gifted program, I took after-school classes with a Guatemalan teacher for at least several quarters. I was not fluent, but I had a modest foundation.

In my five years in the gifted program, I earned high grades and praise from teachers. I also had no trouble fitting in with my peers, who were all similarly talented. At home, I continued my learning as well. I read voraciously—mostly any sort of novel I could get my hands on, including those written for adults. By my fifth grade year, I was working at the eighth grade level in reading, math, and spelling.

During my grade school years, I became aware that I had been labeled "gifted." Attending the gifted program made that fact plain. But because I mainly socialized with my gifted classmates, the label did not play a strong role in my identity.

High Expectations Matter

MY GIFTED EDUCATION ENDED AT FIFTH GRADE. At this point, my mother transferred me to a parochial school in our neighborhood. Thanks to the dedication of a single educator, this phase of my education has played a major role in my success to this day.

The school principal, Sister Dolores Crosby, took a special interest in me and went out of her way to support my development. For my sixth grade year, she arranged that I would study reading and math with a group of accelerated seventh graders. This provided a sufficient level of challenge, and I became friends with the advanced students, as well as others in my own grade.

Sister Dolores had high expectations, which, as a shy and slightly introverted child, stressed me out. Throughout primary school, I dreaded presentations. Whenever it came time to present a book report, science project, or story I had written, I felt anguish at the thought of standing in front of my class to speak. Piano recitals made me equally nervous. Not only did my new school emphasize public speaking for all students, but also it competed in interscholastic speech tournaments.

Though I abhorred public speaking, Sister Dolores saw potential in me. Technically, competing in speech tournaments was optional, an extracurricular activity, but Sister Dolores did not present it as such. And so my timidity and desire to please resulted in my competing in speech tournaments annually for each of my junior high years. As it turned out, Sister Dolores was right—I had a talent for it. I took home numerous trophies, but more important, I gained confidence in my ability to speak before others, a skill I have applied many times in my life since.

The summer after seventh grade, my mother suggested I study Spanish. She gave me her old college textbook, and I used it to formally begin learning. Building on the smattering of Spanish I had picked up through annual summer visits with my grandparents, I worked through much of the book over the summer. I read words aloud, wrote vocabulary lists, and learned verb conjugations. I even took my book on camping trips and vacation. I was determined.

Because of my prior exposure, the language felt intuitive to me. As I learned new grammar and verb forms, things just began to sound right. I felt greatly motivated to learn the language, as not being able to understand my grandparents piqued my curiosity. More than wanting to know a new language, I wanted to understand them.

My excitement for learning Spanish serves as an example of my general attitude toward learning. I have always been intrinsically motivated to learn nearly any subject. I find that deepening my understanding of the world, analyzing, or improving my skills gives me great satisfaction. I was equally motivated with my schoolwork in junior high. I earned all As as a result.

An Elite Learning Community

For ninth grade, I enrolled in one of Seattle's most academically challenging high schools, an all-girls Catholic school called Holy Names Academy. The school expected top performance of students and offered a robust selection of honors and AP classes. Courses were so challenging that many of my classmates transferred out after freshman year. But those of us who continued valued academic success, and doing well at school was no reason for social difficulty.

While the environment differed from the small parochial school I had come from, I found the transition easy. This is probably due to the fact that the school allowed me to continue studying at a level that challenged me. Teachers held all students to a high standard, and we were encouraged to excel in the sciences and math.

I found the introductory biology course fascinating my freshman year, so when AP biology was offered my junior year, I enrolled. However, I quickly realized our class was not on track to work through the one-thousand-page textbook in time for the AP exam. As it was my goal to pass the exam and earn college credit, I set up my own plan to work through the book. I determined that reading forty pages a night would allow me to cover the whole book on schedule, and that is what I did. This kept me up very late some nights. After a full day at school, two hours of cross-country practice, chores, dinner, and hours of homework, I would pore over the material until I had completed the necessary amount. I survived on an average of five hours of sleep during that time, but it did not matter. I was determined to meet my goal.

Throughout high school, I took every advanced placement course I could. That gave me a total of nine AP exams over my last two years. Because of my unusual talents, the school allowed me to study independently, so I studied AP Spanish 4 and AP Calculus 2 on my own in my senior year, earning college credit for both.

In high school, I had numerous motivations that all resulted in my success. First and foremost, I intrinsically enjoyed learning most topics. To this day, nothing pleases me more than when I am engaged in learning, particularly if it involves solving problems or analyzing complex information. Second, my goal was to attend a private out-of-state college. Having spent all my life in Seattle, I wanted to see more of the world, and moving away for college seemed the perfect plan. I knew I would need a scholarship to do this, so I sought to earn all As and take as many AP and honors classes as possible.

I was also motivated on a personal level to learn Spanish. My burning desire to connect with my grandparents through language led me to study diligently. When the Spanish class moved too slowly and did not get through the entire textbook, I used class time to study ahead.

Over each summer, I finished studying the remaining course materials. I knew speaking was the most important thing, so I took every opportunity to speak the language out loud. I spoke grammar exercises and chatted with everyone I could. By age sixteen, I was conversational. As well as with my grandparents, I used my growing skills to communicate with kitchen staff at my restaurant job. I wrote letters to my family in Barcelona. This gave me great satisfaction.

My senior year felt like a whirlwind. I took all AP classes, and the workload felt brutal. In particular, as it came time to apply for colleges, life felt incredibly busy. Completing nine college applications while simultaneously doing five AP exams and writing a lengthy term paper was very stressful. I continued to get less than the recommended amount of sleep each night. However, I continued my efforts and graduated valedictorian of my class. The only blip on my record was a B in gym class.

The school principal told me that, because of my many talents, I could be anything I wanted. Yet, I am amazed at how little consideration I put into my choice of majors. Because of my quantitative skills, someone suggested I think about engineering. Because I also loved biology, I determined that biomedical engineering would somehow be a perfect combination of these fields. It all sounded good, but I actually had only a vague notion of what biomedical engineers do. Despite the wealth of academic resources available to me, I do not recall ever discussing my possible career choices with any advisor or mentor in any focused manner.

Based on my choice of majors, my next step was to find colleges. Ignoring the reams of mail from college recruiters all over the United States, I reviewed a listing of the top-rated schools for biomedical engineering. Of these choices, I applied to eight out-of-state schools and the University of Washington. From these, I received several attractive scholarship offers, including full-ride offers from three universities. In the end, I selected Tulane University in New Orleans. Again, I sought out little support as I made this life-altering decision. I decided on my own with only limited discussion with others.

During my high school years, I did not think of myself as gifted because the word was not often used in my presence. I knew I was a high achiever, though, because I consistently received considerable praise from teachers and peers on my success in schooling and extracurricular activities. I was known as one of the smartest students in my elite college preparatory high school. Naturally, my identity and self-worth centered on the way others viewed me.

An Engineering Student in New Orleans

IN AUGUST 1992, I PACKED MY BAGS, got on a plane, and flew five hours to the water-bound city of New Orleans. I moved into the dorms and began classes shortly after. As an engineering student, little time was allowed for humanities courses. Nearly all my classes were in math, physics, and computer programming. The first year felt much easier than high school. For the first time in a long time, I found I had time to sleep a full eight hours. Although I had earned over a year's worth of college credit while in high school, I was required to take courses that repeated material I had already studied. Repeating material, coupled with the impersonal lecture-based approach of the professors, diminished my sense of engagement. I found I preferred to study independently from the course books, so I avoided attending many classes.

Despite my boredom, I was determined to tough it out. I had selected engineering as a major, and I assumed it would become more interesting as time went on. Meanwhile, I set about widening my horizons beyond the campus. I had come to New Orleans to see more of the world, beyond my insular upbringing. As I had developed an interest in independent music, I joined the college radio station, which was run by a small clique of indie rockers and activist punks. They seemed to be the only weirdos on campus, and among them, I found new friends. This new crowd introduced me to all sorts of music. The activists also exposed me to their progressive views and activities, which included running a grassroots soup kitchen, bicycle parades, veganism, and advocating against racism, homophobia, and other sorts of prejudice.

These activists' relentless questioning of the status quo, in the context of an intriguing arts community, attracted me to collaborate in their efforts. I helped organize the soup kitchen and organized shows for local and touring underground bands. I moved off campus to live in a racially and economically diverse neighborhood. I went vegan and rode my bike all over the city with the stray dog I had adopted.

Meanwhile, I continued my engineering studies, even though I was becoming less and less engaged. I began to detest my classes and most of my classmates, who were primarily sexist, homophobic ROTC men. The sterile world of engineering studies held no attraction, especially in comparison to the new and diverse world I had found. Finally, it occurred to me that I should drop out of school, but I refused to give up my full-ride scholarship. I had worked too hard. I decided to finish my bachelor's degree, but I saw no clear target beyond that. To make matters worse, I received no guidance from potential mentors. Academic advising consisted only of helping me select courses for subsequent semesters.

Things came to a head the summer after my junior year. Upon moving from the dorms to a shotgun shack shared with several other young people, I began an internship with the city's sewer department. The job turned out to be one of the most mind-numbing experiences of my life. I appeared at work daily to review city sewer maps and compare them with corresponding charts to ensure their reliability. The job seemed easy enough to be administrative. It certainly did not apply my three years of engineering studies. I staved off misery by listening to X, the Los Angeles punk band, on repeat while reconciling maps eight hours a day.

After one week of this, I came to a crisis point. I had waded through three years of engineering studies, waiting for something to captivate my interest. My first job should have been it, but instead it solidified my discontent. I could not tolerate the thought of spending an entire summer reconciling sewer maps. So, on Monday morning, the beginning of what was to be my second week on the job, I called the office and quit. I was determined to switch majors.

Upon returning to school in the fall, I changed my major to ecology, evolution, and organismal biology. This felt right, as it would build on the interest I'd had ever since taking introductory biology in ninth grade. But switching majors so late in my studies meant I had to overload if I was to finish within four years.

Although I still couldn't see what my career objective would be upon graduation, I continued on with my goal of completing my degree in four years. I worked very hard my final year, taking upper-level biology courses and organic chemistry. I learned voraciously and my grades improved. However, unlike in high school, I did not earn all As. I was stretched too thin to achieve this.

I was most enthused about the big-picture, systems-oriented thinking required in the ecology and evolution courses. One professor, Thomas Sherry, soon became my favorite. I respected and appreciated his teaching and assessment methods and found his classes intriguing. I was able to excel on his assignments and exams, which required applying complex concepts to novel problems. While my classmates complained the tests were too difficult, I found them a welcomed and diverting challenge.

Sherry recognized me as talented. During our lab sections, we would engage in small group discussions and answer questions about the material. I spoke at length during these discussions because, like the exams, his questions required us to apply concepts and solve problems. It was obvious I was different from my classmates—I actually enjoyed the work and spoke up voluntarily.

While I had a friendly relationship with Sherry and other biology professors, I still did not experience any sort of career-oriented advising. I had selected my coursework so as to graduate and felt exhausted by a lifetime of schooling. Since ninth grade, I had continually dedicated great effort to studies and extracurricular activities that felt constricting. I wanted freedom and to discover the world, which I knew expanded far beyond the protective world of academia and the educated class.

EXPANSION OF WORLDVIEW

THROUGHOUT MY YEARS IN NEW ORLEANS, I met many traveling musicians and activists from around the United States. I often helped host them at my house and assisted in organizing their concerts and events. As I built friendships with others from around the country, I developed the desire to travel, to see their homes, meet others, and learn more about the greater world. I cared little about my own personal wealth. I even desired to hold an unskilled, low-wage job, which I believed would allow me freedom to relocate or take time off as needed.

Not long after finishing my degree, and to my parents' chagrin, I departed Seattle in a 1975 Ford van, along with my dog and a friend, for no final destination in particular. After meandering down I-5, stopping off to see friends in various West Coast cities, we made our way east on I-10. After an interminable drive across Texas, we stopped for a break in Austin. We knew no one there, but after some phone calls, we located friends of friends who offered a place to stay.

The city and its community were pleasant and fascinating. Austin harbored a progressive community, as well as a vibrant arts and music scene. What's more, the city's strong Latino character helped me feel right at home. I delighted in using Spanish in my daily life. After a few weeks, my travelling companion and I decided to stay in Austin.

My time there allowed me to explore the greater world as I had longed to do. Early on, I collaborated with a grassroots activist newspaper, *Voces de la Frontera* (*Voices from the Border*), assisting them with Spanish-English translations. I also accompanied them to cross the border and interview anti-*maquiladora* activists in Matamoros. My experience in hearing firsthand stories of struggles for justice impressed me greatly.

Over the three years I spent in Austin, I did not achieve in the way my parents and others who knew me as a youth would have expected. Rather, I rejected the idea that I needed to achieve formally. These were years of exploration. I read voraciously—fiction, history, politics, nutrition—and continued to study Spanish. To improve my literacy and expand my vocabulary, I read classic Spanish novels and kept written vocabulary lists for practice. All the while, I spoke Spanish on the street and developed a distinct Mexican accent.

As I developed my identity as a young adult, my giftedness carried less and less weight. Outside of an academic environment, my talents were less noticeable. Still, I had a great sense of self-confidence because of my upbringing and earlier successes. The belief that I could do anything was intact. It was during this time that I was first able to learn, explore, and understand the world on my own terms.

Independent Thinking and Following My Heart

After three years in Austin, I needed a change. I wanted a challenge and a more serious career. I also wanted to see Barcelona, my grandfather's hometown, the place where I had cousins, aunts, and uncles. I had taught Spanish in Austin, so I decided to build on this experience by becoming an ESL teacher. I flew to Barcelona and took a one-month certification course while staying with my cousin Josep Maria.

From day one, I adored the city. Barcelona is impressively charming, beautiful, and vibrant. What's more, the challenge of integrating myself in a new culture drew me in. Beginning with my first meal with my cousin and his girlfriend, my burning curiosity impelled me to learn Catalan. The language was puzzling, but I did not find it difficult.

According to plan, I returned to the United States after the certification course. However, as my airplane hit the tarmac, I knew in my heart I had made a grave error in leaving Barcelona. I felt an enormous pull to return to the city. I needed to make my life there. Immediately, I began planning and saving. In a few months, I set off once again for my grandfather's childhood home.

Upon arriving in Barcelona, my first task was to find housing. Through a series of acquaintances, I found my way to a newly opened grassroots community center that also served as a collective house. About twenty environmental activists had established the project shortly before my arrival, so the place was brimming with possibility. The goal was to renovate a long-abandoned mountainside property at the outer edge of the city, to create community gardens and meeting spaces, and to set a model of community living that rejected conventional notions of consumerism.

I fell in love with the project. The location was fantastically beautiful; the people were inspiring; and it offered me housing, a community, and a meaningful project beyond the economically necessary goal of teaching English. I dove into the effort by organizing the community gardens, serving as media spokesperson, helping rebuild the roof, cooking, and doing other chores.

My drive to learn and grow was satisfied by my daily existence in this environment. I was fascinated by learning Catalan and becoming integrated in the culture. During my first year, I actively built my Catalan skills, mainly by reading newspapers, listening, and conversing with friends who were patient with me. Within a year, I had sufficient conversational fluency; I could speak with anyone on the street. My fluency astounded Catalans, most of whom had never met a foreigner who spoke their language.

Learning the language allowed me to feel I was fully connected with my newfound home. It also enabled me to access a world of information not available in Spanish or English. Over time, I sought out the classics of Barcelonan literature, written in both Spanish and Catalan, and also learned as much as possible about the local history and politics. With my family's history centered in Barcelona, I felt drawn to the culture. Understanding the past was an important part of my becoming connected to the city.

Returning Home

AS THE YEARS PASSED, I became very comfortable in Barcelona, perhaps too comfortable because daily life and my ongoing studies became less stimulating. I began to wonder if I had truly chosen a permanent new home. I grew concerned that leaving my nuclear family so far behind was not right. I finally considered this notion after being told as much by many Barcelona natives with their strong family values. After a year of considering my next step, I relocated to Olympia, Washington, and enrolled at Evergreen State College to pursue a master's in environmental studies.

After many years outside academia, I worried I would no longer exhibit the same talent as before. Thankfully, I was mistaken. While my studies were at times demanding, I felt capable of completing the highest quality work. As a result, many professors recognized me, both in private and publicly, for excelling.

While this recognition pleased me, I needed more than praise to reach my full potential. To this day, I most appreciate Anita Lenges for encouraging me as a writer. While I entered the program as a strong writer, she saw ways to improve my writing. Her detailed comments and conversations helped me see how I could do more. I appreciated that she expected me to excel and further develop my competencies. Her support led me to improve my approach to writing so as to better synthesize my thoughts and communicate more effectively. Thanks to her efforts, my writing skills continue to distinguish me professionally. They were crucial to landing my first job after graduate school, and colleagues at my current job recognize my writing skills.

As a student, I focused my studies on environmental policy. I had never stopped wanting to make a difference in society. Given that environmental problems naturally demand government action, I felt my most important contribution could be in the realm of policy. Based on this focus, along with my strong skills in analysis and writing, I landed my first job after my studies as a budget analyst with the Washington State Legislature.

Since then, I have transitioned to a different state agency. In my current position, I act as a project lead for long-term research projects aimed at improving state programs. I find my work incredibly fulfilling, as I am able to apply much of my diverse skill set. My role requires rapidly mastering technical and complex subject matter, performing both qualitative and quantitative analyses, strong oral and written communication skills, and strong project management skills. The diversity of expectations and unique nature of each project means I always feel challenged to excel. In addition to all of that, my ability to think outside of the box and approach problems with a can-do attitude has helped me achieve. I feel quite fortunate to have this type of work because it provides an outlet for many of my talents. I truly enjoy what I do.

My job satisfaction stems from the fact that much of what I am expected to do is aligned with my natural inclinations. I am impelled to explore unfamiliar topics that spark my interest, and I think critically about new information—testing it to evaluate its validity. I am a compulsive organizer and planner, but I balance that with recognition of the need for flexibility. My innate desire to think, create, and grow is, to a large extent, satisfied by my daily endeavors.

My Identity Today

EVER SINCE BEGINNING WORK with the state legislature, I've been fortunate to work with highly intelligent people, most of whom hold advanced degrees. Within this peer group, I have not felt as exceptional as I sometimes did during school, but that is a good thing. While being recognized for success is pleasant, I prefer to be surrounded by others of similar or greater abilities. These types of environments push me harder; therefore, I am more comfortable being myself.

Today, if you asked me to explain my identity, I would tell you I am both Spanish and American—a progressive, highly educated, professional, White female in her forties. I would not mention gifted, though I realize I am a critical thinker and rapid learner. I also recognize that many others excel in areas where I have no special ability, so I don't allow myself to feel superior in any way.

While my identity does not center on a sense of giftedness, my upbringing as a gifted individual paved the way for my unorthodox path as a young adult and my current successful career. Based on my experiences growing up, I have always believed I could succeed at almost anything if I set my mind to it. In my twenties, my inclination to think outside the box and explore new possibilities impelled me to take "the road less travelled" and reject the notion of a conventional career. As I moved into my thirties, I focused my desire to learn, explore, and connect with Barcelona and Spain. My talent for rapid learning facilitated my connections with others, resulting in a wildly rewarding experience. And of course, my gifted abilities enabled me to experience immediate success in my graduate studies and my subsequent career.

In connection with my lifelong studies and travels, my giftedness has facilitated a sense of connectedness with my family's past and allowed me to develop my current identity as a Spaniard and an American. My burning curiosity drove me to pore through Spanish textbooks every summer of my teenage years. My drive to learn the language in the absence of an immersion experience resulted in conversational fluency while I was still in high school. The ability to speak with my grandparents, as well as numerous others, in their native tongues has opened up a whole new world and allowed me to connect with my family roots.

As a result of my giftedness, I had near-native-level fluency in Spanish the day I moved to Barcelona, and I was able to focus my efforts on learning about my family, the city, and the local history. I was able to communicate readily with everyone, and this meant I was able to assimilate quickly. I have now spoken, written, and thought in fluent Spanish for over half my life, and on good days, I have spoken Catalan well enough to pass for a native.

My adeptness with languages has allowed me to traverse cultural boundaries with ease. It has helped me feel connected with many others, even while half a world away. In particular, my fluency in Spanish has helped me blend across cultural lines, both in the United States and abroad. Regardless of their national origins, I feel strong kinship with other Spanish speakers because the shared language, culture, and history unify us without obscuring the beautiful diversity among people identified as Latino or Latina.

What I Learned

I feel intensely grateful for the life I have led. I was born into a comfortable life and had every material need met. As a young adult, I had a type of freedom that, even today, so many women around the world do not have. I was able to select my studies, plan my career, and deviate from the expectations everyone had set for me. I recognize that I have been very privileged.

Based on my experience, I would offer a few words of advice to teachers and mentors of gifted youth. First, allow them the freedom to explore and direct their own learning, but make certain to challenge them at the appropriate level. Second, teachers must challenge gifted children beyond their comfort zones. In my case, the school principal who pushed me to compete as a public speaker was instrumental in my development.

Third, no matter how gifted children are, it shouldn't be assumed they are able to make wise career choices as teenagers. They need guidance because their intellect cannot replace the value and wisdom of those with real-world experience. Lastly, mentors should encourage interested youth to consider getting off the career treadmill for a period. Less structured opportunities, like service-oriented programs, help individuals develop a much fuller understanding of the world beyond the sheltered upbringings experienced by many middle-class Americans.

Due to my personal lack of guidance, I encountered two significant consequences. First, I devoted a great amount of resources to applying myself to studies that I do not make use of in my current work. Second, the lack of guidance left me uninspired, with no vision for a post-university career. Instead, I rebelled against expectations to find a different path. While I feel rewarded by the path I ultimately took, I wish I had been aware of exciting career opportunities upon completing college. Such an awareness would have allowed me to make a more informed choice about my future.

On a final note, effective learning opportunities can be developed for every gifted child, even in the absence of a gifted program. During my education, I spent only five years in gifted education. Yet, I experienced rewarding, stimulating education for all those years. The teachers and mentors who got things right truly made the difference. Today, I would like to thank so many teachers and mentors, especially those who recognized my ability to learn independently and allowed me the freedom to do so. To those who did not settle for my easily won successes but pushed me to achieve in areas I found uncomfortable, to those who developed special challenges in areas where I had a latent yet fervent interest, I am thankful. Their belief in my abilities has supported my growth to become the well-rounded, satisfied, multicultural woman I am today.

PART IV

NAVIGATING FAMILIES

CHAPTER 10

Deliberate Choices: How Gifted Education Knowledge and Experiences Dictated a Family's Lifestyle towards the Embrace of Cultural Pluralism

Joy M. Scott-Carrol, PhD

FOR MORE THAN THIRTY YEARS, I have pondered the question, "Just how should parents, teachers, and other adults responsible for the education, upbringing, and character development of children respond to youth who are actually smarter than those adults?"

Before I plunged into writing a first draft of this narrative, I took a trip to our family's public storage in search of supporting documents sequestered in an antique footlocker, specifically interested in collections from my gifted adult child's educational background. Approximately fifteen minutes into sorting through numerous family photos, school report cards, certificates, awards, transcripts, and much more for nice reminders of the past, I eventually came across the handwritten note my daughter's middle school history teacher sent home with her for parental intervention. Years ago I promised myself that I would frame the note (as a reminder of poor teaching), but there it was, still in the footlocker. I unfolded and read: "If Sasha does not behave herself in class, she will be moved to a classroom for behaviorally disturbed children." Even to this day, that short, direct sentence has as much visceral heft as the first day I read it. It represents a grave disconnect—not only between my child and her teacher—but between other gifted children and teachers as well.

This chapter's focus is on observed parent-child and teacher-child interactions in relation to the conscientious, deliberate decisions I made to support enrichment opportunities, inside and outside the classroom, over intense gifted and talented curricula. I chronicle various occurrences that spurred the development of my personalized philosophy on parenting, schooling, education in general, and giftedness in particular. Despite being a scholar and practitioner in the gifted and talented field, both nationally and internationally, my personal narrative of raising, guiding, and advocating for my gifted child does not fit a cookie-cutter schema or model. Rather, it is written non-linearly and may not satisfy readers searching for prescriptive formulae. However, readers with the willingness to test formulated hypotheses or, perhaps, develop their own theories about giftedness, parenting, and cultural pluralism may very well find an alternative way of viewing giftedness in relation to parental goals, desires, and objectives.

Upon reading the teacher's foreboding note all those years ago, I immediately recognized that there was too much she did not know about my daughter. She was clearly oblivious to Sasha's abilities, achievements, and consistently high (ninetieth percentile) stanine achievement test scores. On a grander scale, there was no doubt the school staff needed to implement a more effectual means of communication about addressing the unique needs of gifted children, particularly those of culturally diverse children, who are under-represented in gifted programs or identified as gifted, compared to mainstream children. I understood all of this.

I was so engaged in responsibility—working full-time and creating other ways to supplement my salary, such as teaching private piano lessons to young children—that I did not apply lessons learned earlier, specifically, not to expect school officials to respond *in loco parentis* and value my child's worth and academic ability. I knew better than to expect every teacher to nurture my daughter's gifts and talents as I would as a caring parent, but I at least expected that my child would receive enough specialized attention to be able to perform at an advanced level in school. I could accept the fact that the teacher had not studied my child's test scores or discovered from school records that, at age five, she was accepted into Mensa, the noted high IQ society that only admits individuals who score in the top 2 percent. What I could not accept was a classroom teacher lacking even a basic understanding of the fundamental characteristics of gifted children. If teachers are trained to identify a potentially challenged child who is not performing on level, should they not also be trained to recognize a gifted child who is performing above level?

Children Should Be Seen and Heard, Shouldn't They?

WHEN I WAS GROWING UP, Black children in the 1950s and 1960s received very clear messages from church and home that children should be seen rather than heard. This was a general expected behavior for the time, but it was particularly pronounced in the South, which meant my Alabama- and Kentucky-born parents had little tolerance for my opinions and self-expression. They drilled staunch submission and obedience into my mind in a way that made me yearn for something liberating and personally validating. When I became a parent, I seized the opportunity to create for my child the type of unrestricted environment I had longed for. Of course, I taught her to be respectful (no profanity, no yelling at or talking back to adults), but I also taught her to stand her ground when making a factual claim, particularly one she could back up with reputable sources. I wanted her to have the confidence and finesse to be able to speak her mind at any age and in any setting.

Unfortunately, her confidence was not always well-received in school. When Sasha questioned what seemed to be shaky facts presented in her middle school history class, the teacher perceived it as being indecorous, unruly, and out of control—hence the handwritten note. Apparently, the teacher who is also of our ethnicity and a Black female, thought Sasha had a downward educational trajectory, which was not the case. She had already demonstrated a proclivity toward high academic achievement and precociousness. Her reading aptitude was several grade levels above average, and she had taken a particular liking to historical facts. She read history books ravenously and was able to contextualize her readings by discussing them with her parents, family, and friends.

In addition to the voracious appetite for reading books, Sasha participated in numerous extracurricular activities. Our family vacations consisted of visiting historical sites—the White House and the State Capitol; Colonial Williamsburg, Jamestown, and Yorktown in Virginia; Old Quebec City in Montreal—and we took trips that educated her in ways a competitive classroom setting could not. While these exposures and experiences did not make her an authority on history, they afforded her enough insight and understanding to notice and question historical inaccuracies. I imagine it is not often that middle school students are astute enough to catch a teacher's errors, so I can understand the teacher's surprise and embarrassment. However, there is a marked difference between a behaviorally disturbed child and one who knows enough to correct a teacher.

Since the mid-nineteen sixties and until present day, education scholars cite the research of Rosenthal and Jacobson, who found high correlations between teacher expectations and self-fulfilling prophecy. Children with teachers who have low expectations of their performance tend to achieve at lower levels (Jussim, Eccles, & Madon, 1996). This may be particularly true for Black students (Ford, 2013). To both scholars and laypersons, this should come as no surprise. When children are treated as if they can do well, they usually do. When they are treated as if they are destined to fail, they usually do. When it comes to children who appear to be misbehaving, teachers and other authority figures should not rush to judgment. There are often layers of their own biases and expectations that influence educators' perception of the problematic behavior (Jussim, Eccles, & Madon, 1996).

Irrespective of Sasha's familial support system, she possessed the ability to channel her high intelligence and excel academically within an environment of low teacher expectations. "Expectations may lead to *perceptual biases*: perceivers may interpret, remember, and/or explain targets' behaviors in ways consistent with their expectations. This type of expectancy confirmation exists in the mind of the perceiver rather than in the behavior of the target" (Jussim, Eccles, & Madon, 1996, 286). I am certain the teacher's perceptual bias prevented her from acknowledging Sasha's intellect and equally sure the woman was trying to help.

When teachers are not equipped with the appropriate knowledge and skill to encourage achievement in students who are culturally different—because they are most familiar with high achieving mainstream children—those who fall outside the teachers' scope of understanding and training suffer. In such cases, the teachers' focus may fall predominantly on the students they find easiest to teach or relate to (who, coincidentally, are the ones the teachers tend to have the highest expectations for). The other children—the inquisitive ones, the "rebellious" ones, the "out of control" ones—are labeled, disregarded, and shuffled off to another classroom to become someone else's problem. These types of teachers set a classroom norm that makes their jobs easier but at the same time stymies the growth of gifted students with unique learning needs. In order to serve all students, it is imperative that teachers learn to appropriately recognize and manage academic and behavioral challenges presented by gifted children of all racial, ethnic, and culturally different backgrounds (Ford, 2013; Taylor, 2004).

In our case, Sasha had the advantages of both coming from a background with highly educated parents and having educators in her extended family, many of whom have a long history as school teachers. My daughter's educational support system was stronger than many, so she was protected from the negative circumstances that can, unfortunately, befall misunderstood students, particularly those considered culturally different. Notwithstanding the constant of a nurturing and supportive family background, there was no chance Sasha would end up in a classroom for behaviorally disturbed (BD) children. The imprint of a long family history that valued obtaining advanced degrees and credentials saw to that. But I wondered, what about other children? I knew I had no say-so in the educational path of anyone else's child, but I could not resist a grave concern about other gifted or high-potential children who had been tragically piped into BD classrooms.

When I began to observe school operations specifically and educational systems more generally, I was confronted with the fact that children from certain backgrounds are more likely to be fast-tracked to failure, and this held especially true for children who represent one or more of the following social structures: (1) lower socioeconomic status, (2) reared by parents who are not educators, (3) reared by a single mother, particularly if she parented more than one child, or (4) reared by parents working two jobs. To be clear, parents from these backgrounds can and do rear children who successfully traverse their education landscapes. As a working mother, I was proof of that, but many parents from the above mentioned backgrounds are less likely to understand the ins and outs of arbitrary classroom placement, especially if there is not an accompanied crisis such as school expulsion.

The Emergence of a Gifted Child

From infancy, it was obvious that Sasha was exceptionally bright. At seven months old, she would sit up in her crib and turn the pages of her soft-cloth fabric books, slowly following along the familiar story as if she herself was reading the storyline using whole language or perhaps phonics. At two years old, she could accurately subtract numbers in her head, and her vocabulary was exceptional for her age. It was an everyday occurrence to hear her correctly and appropriately use words like "splendid" and "enchanted" in full sentences. I know firsthand, as some researchers empirically and observationally conclude, parents are the first to recognize exceptional ability in their children (Klein, 2007).

But what I knew about childrearing did not come to me based on observation alone. I first learned from my family of origin and home exposures (parents, maternal and paternal grandparents, home library consisting of *World Book Encyclopedia*, the Made Simple Series in mathematics, science, and geography), and I learned from an introduction to psychology textbook from the 1970s how affluent families with gifted children nurture their children's talents and abilities at home. So from birth, my daughter was exposed to numerous children's books and popular bedtime stories. She played with high-end, expensive Mensan-level educational toys and, in fact, mastered these toys so quickly that at times our family budget could not support purchasing new educational toys. To keep her challenged, I often had to turn to adult conversation and made-up games, and in Sasha's early years, watching television was an occasional treat. I eventually learned that nurturing a child's gifts and talents at home mattered more than what amounts to four to five hours of highly intense classroom instruction. My social life consisted of frequenting bookstores and libraries and selecting and consulting numerous child-rearing resources. When financially feasible, I purchased books and invested in opportunities that offered my daughter invaluable challenging experiences.

Before Sasha entered the toddler stage, I made it a point to expose her to other children whose parents valued education without pushing elite schooling. I rarely tolerated comments from parents who bragged—"My child will attend Harvard University"—but such comments were quite common in Hyde Park's University of Chicago community, populated by second- and third-generation college graduates. Likewise, I exposed my daughter to families with whom there would be a mutual exchange of knowledge, experiences, and ideas. It was my philosophy at the time and remains so today that true education is received informally and organically. I never wanted my daughter to get stuck on what school or university she attended. Rather, I wanted her to focus on learning, how she made sense of acquired information, and how she accepted, rejected, or applied knowledge in her life.

Because my early self-selected socialization would include a lifestyle of non-conformity, a term tossed around in the 1970s, which essentially means to follow your intuition, your beliefs, your values, and so forth, to the extent possible school and community choice became a welcomed and perhaps much needed obsession. I began to adhere to a mindset about education that stressed being an educated individual or, as I correctly note, "education over schooling" being the general rule. Though Sasha went on to graduate cum laude with a degree in African diaspora studies from Tulane University, this was never the end goal. Education would be for oneself and not to live up to parental expectations only. The ultimate aim was to massage and develop the positive qualities that already existed within my daughter—to facilitate the blossoming of her intellect and the growth of a self-respecting, socially astute, well-rounded, caring, non-judgmental young woman. Elite schools and degrees mean nothing if the information does not edify.

Since Sasha demonstrated an exceptional aptitude for language arts (e.g., an extensive vocabulary, impressive verbal expression skills, and above-average comprehension), I went out of my way to nurture these abilities. I enrolled her in a bilingual school, La Escuelita Pre-School, in Seattle. This school exposed and introduced children and their families to what it is like to live, study, and work within communities where cultural differences are celebrated, irrespective of language barriers, socio-economic status, parental education, and more. The school's environment of racial/ethnic, cultural, socioeconomic, and religious diversity exposed young children to the many advantages of living among various cultures and acquiring knowledge from multiple perspectives. Given this stimulating environment, Sasha's voracious appetite for books, and our many educational trips, she quickly acquired a love for culture and diversity. Her self-expression, problem solving ability, and critical-thinking skills surpassed those of her age-mates, and she seemed to naturally apply new knowledge and language acuity without much coaching or effort.

I cannot recall the exact source, but I do remember hearing or reading that there is no benefit to children knowing their IQ scores, and in a protective sort of way this made sense. If children are nurtured and intellectually stimulated, they will naturally rise to their full potential. There is no need to attach to their budding self-image a number that may interfere with their social or emotional growth. Just knowing my child required a challenging curriculum and specialized instruction was enough. It was not until her dad, who is a Mensan himself, suggested I have our daughter tested that I even considered it. Swayed by the prospects of her qualifying for challenging gifted education classes, programs, and scholarships, I arranged for IQ testing at the University of Washington. Records retrieved from the above-mentioned footlocker indicate that she was tested at three and a half years old.

It did not matter to me if Sasha qualified for Mensa. I loved observing her affable nature and fascinating mind. I knew in my heart and intellect I could not go wrong nurturing both. A Mensa qualifying test score would not change that. At any rate, Sasha's IQ surely was within the gifted range for her age. Besides validating that my child was indeed gifted, the primary purpose of the assessment was to place her in academic milieus that nurtured, challenged, and supported her highest potentials. For the most part, this was achieved by either changing schools or changing environments.

The standardized Stanford-Binet IQ test was not normed across racial groups. It was not (and still is not) considered a culturally sensitive testing instrument, meaning it does not take into account cultural differences that may serve as advantages or disadvantages for certain test takers (Padilla, 2008). I assert this fact specifically to quiet the critics who assume certain IQ tests are purposefully made less challenging for racial, ethnic, and other culturally diverse groups. In fact, IQ and other screening test of intelligence that account for cultural differences have nothing to do with level of difficulty. Rather, the purpose is to create tests that can accurately gauge ability without penalizing students for their cultural differences (Padilla, 2008). Nonetheless, the Stanford-Binet Test of Intelligence the University of Washington used to test my daughter's intellectual ability was no different from the test a White child would take. Imagine my surprise when another parent tried to explain away my daughter's IQ score by saying her top 1 percent score meant something different and less remarkable. This was not an isolated incident. Though we were not mired in attitudes that bordered racism, there had been other instances where mother and daughter were made to feel the weight of their Blackness.

Confronting Racial and Ethnic Socialization

AT THE TIME, WE HAD been practicing Catholics and active members of our parish's religious community. Considering our active participation, it was a given that my daughter would begin kindergarten at the adjacent church school. We enjoyed a few friendships with other young families who were, for the most part, racially White and traditional for the times. This meant the norm was one or more of the following: two-parent families—households headed by a divorcee, separated parents, or single mothers would be out of the ordinary; the typical family vehicle was an SUV or station wagon; nearly every family owned their home; the average income was middle to upper income; and most parents were educated and/or employed in professional careers. As scary as it was to find myself navigating life as a single parent, in my heart I knew that every future decision I made would be grounded in a desire to protect and guide the most precious gift God had entrusted to me. Despite my educational status (a traditionally earned master of science degree), church involvement, Sasha's second grade preparation to receive first communion, and my volunteering as a Sunday school teacher, a second grade incident at this school we had otherwise come to love led me to seek gifted program placement in the public school system.

When tested for public school placement in gifted education, Sasha qualified for the highest program offered, the Individual Progress Program (IPP). For gifted verification, I submitted her standardized achievement test scores taken at the Catholic school and the Stanford-Binet IQ results from the University of Washington. Shortly after qualifying for IPP and with the proud acceptance letter in hand, I withdrew my daughter from the Catholic school and officially enrolled her in the prestigious (testing at the top 1 percent) public school program, IPP.

My decision to leave the Catholic school and church community came as a surprise to the school principal, teachers, and many parents, but to me it felt like a natural and necessary progression, especially after the spelling bee incident. But more on that later. Besides a young family from India and a White family with adopted multiracial children, we were the only Blacks in the school and church community. The school, located in the Ravenna area and not too far from the University of Washington, might be classified as a predominantly White institution (PWI), which would automatically present a certain set of challenges for a Black child. Gray-Little and Carels conclude that "schools where a student's racial group comprises less than 20 percent of the student body are 'racially dissonant'" (Stevenson & Arrington, 2012, 78). Black students in racially dissonant contexts—environments that rarely reflect their image and/or culture but nonetheless provide the benefits that typically come along with PWIs (e.g., increased resources and opportunity)—present a false sense of individualized security. However, according to Arrington, Hall, & Stevenson (2003), "PWIS [predominantly White, independent schools] are similar to all school contexts in that they do not escape the trappings of institutional racism, the denial that accompanies it, and the interpersonal interactions that can thwart the psychological well-being." For our well-being, I chose to withdraw my daughter from the parochial school.

Recently and some thirty years later, Sasha shared with me that she still remembers the exact word she, a first grader, spelled correctly over a fourth grader in a kindergarten-through-fourth grade spelling bee. I, on the other hand, had searched the farthest recesses of my mind and had yet to remember the word that should have earned my daughter first place. I must have subconsciously suppressed it—that along with other details of that unjust incident. Exactly how the school principal managed to rationalize and explain away circumstances leading up to my child's deference to another child remains fuzzy yet heartbreaking to this day. What will never escape my memory is that another child was awarded first place when Sasha was the last speller standing.

What hurt perhaps even more than the initial injustice was the fact that the administration made no effort to offer a corrective solution. In their dismissal of the situation, the response was that Sasha's mother was insignificant, her concerns invalid, and her child unworthy. I am not one who can easily forget injustices, and when it comes to my daughter, such memories are painfully imprinted. Stevenson and Arrington (2012) explain this not-so-uncommon phenomenon perfectly: "the trauma of confronting racism as a Black person and talking about racial matters with one's children appears to affect the emotions of Black parents" (74). Yet, in my case carrying the obvious anecdotal or even ancestry gene of "the strong Black woman" proved to be real.

Though I vowed never to let race dictate my decisions (and I believe I did a good job at that), as an educator and mother of a Black child, I knew the importance of racial/ethnic socialization (R/ES), particularly if I wanted Sasha to maintain a solid sense of self in an environment that lacked the diversity she had become accustomed to in her youth. R/ES research seeks to examine how children are taught, directly and indirectly, to conceptualize race and ethnicity (Johnson, Spicer, & Hughes, 2009; Neblett et al., 2009)

Like other parents of Black children in PWIs, I knew I had to equip Sasha with the knowledge, understanding, confidence, and emotional wherewithal to "survive and thrive against the dynamics of racism" (Stevenson & Arrington, 2012, 70). Aside from teaching her about Black history and establishing an atmosphere of self-love and racial pride in our home, I nurtured her in every way I knew to ensure that she never felt alone and outnumbered. I also had to practice self-care as I struggled to manage the "race-based inequities unconsciously perpetrated by well-intentioned authority figures such as teachers, and shamefully other school administrative staff" (Stevenson & Arrington, 2012, 66).

To add to an already stressful situation, it did not help that I was not a homemaker like so many of the other moms at the Catholic school. As a working mother, there was only so much I could do in the way of parent involvement: walking or driving my daughter to and from school, being at the school door at the beginning and end of the school day, attending parent-teacher conferences, knowing who her friends were, and listening to all the details about teachers, other children, and interactions with parents. I knew these were important tasks that showed my love and dedication, but it pained me that I could not be the type of visibly involved parent who regularly attended school functions that occurred during working hours. However, what I lacked in physical availability, I made up for in deliberate action. Everything I did was part of my goal to offer my daughter the best.

Apartheid in a Public School . . . How Can That Be?

THE LOCAL PUBLIC SCHOOL SYSTEM's IPP was housed in a totally separate location within the public school building in Seattle's Madrona neighborhood. From a distance the gifted children in IPP could see other children, but interaction with them rarely happened. With the exception of playground recess time, IPP children were apart from the other children—an apartheid of sorts. This bothered me because, though most children in the building were Black, Sasha and the one-other Black child in IPP did not have many opportunities to interact with them. Being around so many White children was never an issue (Sasha had no racial preference when it came to making friends), but it did mean she was, yet again, in a racially dissonant environment that offered little diversity. Despite this fact, I still felt it was an academically challenging environment that would benefit her, so I continued to make the daily twenty-minute drive to Madrona from our home in the Sandpoint-Matthews Beach community in Seattle.

As the school year progressed, I began to see just how challenging the IPP curriculum was. Second graders learned high school algebra, and homework was so rigorous and challenging that, in my opinion, it bordered the unmerciful. My daughter was an exceptional child. There was no doubt in my mind she could do the work, but I was concerned that the heavy workload and highly competitive atmosphere interfered with her childhood. I wanted her to be appropriately challenged, not forced into a harsh and sterile environment of relentless homework, never-ending studying, and excessive competition. As far as I could observe, cooperative learning and teamwork were not written into the curriculum, and opportunities to nurture developing friendships with classmates were not encouraged by teachers or other parents within the school day. There was no question in my mind as to what the outcome might be: an unhappy, hypercompetitive child.

Aside from the stress of the academic rigors, Madrona's IPP program was a poor fit in other ways, too. For example, at first glance the school appeared to be quite culturally diverse: at the end of the school day one could easily observe Black, White, Asian, Hispanic, disabled, male, female, and possibly other categories of culturally diverse children leaving the building for home or to participate in some after-school activity. Yet, upon closer inspection, it became clear that the separation of the students created a bellicose mentality between those in IPP and those not, hence a deliberate us-versus-them dynamic in school. It was Sasha who brought this observation to my attention. One evening she mentioned hurtful feelings of being isolated from other Black children and never having an opportunity to interact with children who looked like her. She also disliked how snobbish some IPP students were toward students who were not participants in the gifted program.

One Black teacher, a very kind woman but not an IPP instructor, recognized Sasha's high ability and impressive self-expression skills. (It must have been during recess or lunchtime.) She decided Sasha would be the perfect student to recite an inspirational poem in an upcoming school assembly. Sasha practiced with me and her teacher until the poem was committed to memory, all within a few days. On assembly day, her recitation of "Don't Quit" was without error. Though I was proud of my little second grader's accomplishment, I immediately recognized that she was displeased. Looking out onto the assembly audience filled to capacity mostly by Black students reminded her of what she had been missing all school year. It upset my daughter that she had been isolated from them. She hated that she felt so detached, and it was obvious the audience primarily comprised of Black children who felt the same detachment. They just stared at her instead of applauding in support. I could see how anxious Sasha was to leave. She sprinted to our car, desperate to get home, where there was love, appreciation, and no competition. The sadness I recognized on her face had become all too familiar. It was a regular part of her experience at Madrona.

This school assembly scenario might not have been a ground-breaker for other parents, and Sasha's reaction to the racial unfairness could have been less intensive had she not been highly gifted. Gifted children have a heightened awareness of their environment (Mendaglio, 2003). They sort and interpret societal inequities and injustices in ways other children do not. This is especially true for children who attend segregated schools and are one or few from their racial/ethnic backgrounds present. They develop a protective racial awareness that provides insights that may not be apparent to their White counterparts (Stevenson & Arrington, 2011). Thanks to gifted children's elevated metacognitive processing, their interpretation of events is keener and, in many cases, based not necessarily on what is known firsthand but on what they have been able to gather from reading and interacting with those more informed (Lovecky, 1994). Because Sasha had already been somewhat exposed to my stories of institutional racism, she had an awareness of injustice well beyond her years. Though she was very young, I chose to preemptively share my experiences of triumph over adversity to instill strength and racial pride (Stevenson & Arrington, 2011). Given her intense awareness, I imagine she never felt as if she belonged in the IPP program.

When I was a child, the kitchen table was always where our family assembled to listen to my father's lectures about everything, from how my sisters and I were to conduct ourselves in public to his micro-managing our peer relationships. Our kitchen table became a symbol of serious conversation. I carried that symbol into my own home, and so, one day, after enjoying breakfast (our favorite mealtime), I relayed that the IPP program was wrong for our family. The program was highly competitive and did not encourage cooperation or espouse a philosophy of learning that complemented my overall educational objectives as a parent. It mattered to me that my daughter was happy. It matter that she liked school. It mattered that she was able to enjoy our family time.

Finding the Perfect Independent School

THE THOUGHT OF CHANGING SCHOOLS, which I knew could mean changing where we lived, was not a huge issue for our family. I have always taken a "whatever is best for the family" stance, and separation from her dad worked in my favor in that I made major family decisions independently. Sasha completed the first semester of second grade at Madrona, but whenever I had the urge to take her during school hours to the Pacific Science Center, the Elliott Bay Bookstore, or to browse libraries, I would. I sent notes to the teacher the day prior to say that my daughter would be absent the next day. Since she always performed two or three levels above her age and grade level, I did not see the harm in taking a few days away from school to expose her to a healthy balance of academic competition and school-related enrichment activities, especially since, in my mind I was simply homeschooling.

Starting in the second semester of second grade, Sasha transferred to another Catholic school, St. Joseph's in Seattle's Capitol Hill neighborhood. St. Joseph's Catholic Church and school were about the same distance as Madrona was from where we lived in Seattle. Thankfully, Seattle's diverse population is expansive enough that most people can find a community to suit their individual lifestyle. I desired the comfort of a suburban environment and the cultural range of an urban living, so we always took up residence in single-family homes in the city. After the spelling bee experience at the first Catholic school and the rigidity of Madrona's IPP program, it was clear to me that selecting the right community mattered as much as selecting the right school. Since we already attended St. Joseph's Church and the surrounding community there was somewhat diverse, the adjustment for Sasha and me offered a certain comfort.

Despite the lack of diversity among teaching staff and student body, the Catholic schools offered a curriculum that included character development, which appealed to me. Besides high standards in general education the character education curriculum emphasized family values, politeness, responsibility, persistence, dedication, and the golden rule. These qualities were just as important to me as reading, writing, and arithmetic.

As is common with independent and private schools, the class sizes at St. Joseph's were small. There were also many co-parenting opportunities. Stay-at-home moms were often available to keep others' children after school, and because Sasha was so socially astute, gregarious, friendly, polite, and linguistically dexterous, parents were always delighted to have their children spend time with her.

The Importance of Culturally Responsive Teaching and Pluralism

Every year in elementary school, Sasha scored in the ninetieth percentile or higher on all subjects tested. But from the start, it was obvious where her heart lay. She would devour books and excelled in academic areas that included vocabulary, writing, poetry, geography, history, and new languages. Mathematics was never an area of high interest for her. It did not have the same magnetic pull as other subjects, but still she performed well. It mattered a great deal to me that Sasha was well-rounded, so I wanted her to at least appreciate mathematics and understand its importance. I explained that math is a universal language that helps us organize and contextualize the world, but I accepted that she would revel in its numeric folds the way she immersed herself in language and writing. As a parent, it made more sense to nurture potential where potential matched performance and interests. So I followed her lead and gently guided. This is the foundation of culturally responsive teaching (CRT).

CRT values respect and connectedness, choice and personal relevance, challenge and engagement, and authenticity in and effectiveness at what students value (Ginsberg & Wlodkowski, 2000). Rather than taking a one-size-fits-all approach to teaching, where all children are expected to learn the same thing in the same way, CRT takes into consideration factors such as language, ethnicity, social sophistication, race, nationality, socioeconomic status, religion, and educational advantages or disadvantages. This additional depth allows lessons to be much more dynamic and interactive. It also allows children to connect to the information on their own terms, thus making it relevant and more interesting.

CRT is particularly useful with gifted children. It is often assumed they will automatically excel in all areas. This is not necessarily so. Of course, gifted children must be challenged in all subject matters, but they should be especially challenged in the areas that interest them most. Beyond that, they should be challenged in ways that resonate with who they are and what they value. All children, gifted or otherwise, should be encouraged to pursue and explore the subjects they genuinely enjoy. Given that children have unique interests that will, no doubt, differ from their peers', teachers should be skilled in implementing classroom differentiation methodologies to ensure all students can thrive (Tomlinson, 2001). Sadly, most are not.

Gifted and talented programs, too, should recognize and accept that students may excel more in their particular areas of interests. There are some programs that do not admit children if their across-the-board subject area achievement scores are not at the eighty-fifth or ninetieth percentile. In other words, a student who scores in the appropriate percentile in all areas but one will not be admitted. Such a standard suggests gifted children should be monolithic and noncomplex. Reality refutes that model. Just as Sasha displayed a love for words and a slight disinterest in mathematics, other gifted children, too, feel drawn toward and away from certain subjects.

Not only did I want CRT methods practiced in Sasha's classrooms, but also I wanted them to be a staple in our home. I wanted to be sure I was stimulating her mind in a way that was most fitting for her, not necessarily for me. That meant I allowed her to choose her own path, rather than force her down a prescribed one I had chosen based on my life. Many parents do live vicariously through their children. I could not become such a parent. All parents want the best for their children, so I can understand why some insist on their children going to elite schools or entering certain professions, but attempting to plan out their children's life without their input removes what should be their ability to choose.

As much as I could, I gave Sasha the chance to make her own decisions. That meant allowing her to quit piano lessons when she no longer wanted to play. My mother, an accomplished pianist, had given me the freedom to make the same choice. Like mother, like daughter I suppose. To this day, I enjoy playing classical music on my baby grand piano, if only for personal enjoyment. I chose to nurture and encourage Sasha's love for reading, history, civics, and critical thinking. I cheered her on as she read books that were grade levels above her chronological age. I admired how she naturally expressed a genuine interest in reading and interpreting the world around her. From the many books she read, she acquired a worldview that valued individualism, family, social activism, and citizenry. She learned to appreciate worlds beyond her immediate environment. An appreciation of these skills activates the sparkle and twinkle I had observed in Sasha since her infancy.

In keeping with my emphasis on valuing diversity, I taught Sasha the importance of cultural pluralism and how an appreciation for other cultures does not have to obfuscate her attachment to her own. I taught her to consider the multiple perspectives of persons from diverse cultures, ethnic backgrounds, races, socioeconomic statuses, educational backgrounds, religions, and lifestyle choices. It mattered to me that she would grow up knowing without a doubt who she was in relation to all the aforementioned operational variables.

So what did cultural pluralism look like in our home? Sasha was exposed to Latin, Spanish, and French. She traveled extensively across the United States, to Europe, and in Canada. She took part in multicultural activities at school and within the community. She celebrated Martin Luther King's birthday every year with a cake we baked together, and even at the tender age of five, she engaged with me in meaningful discussions about the research on Kenneth and Mamie Clark's doll study (Clark & Clark, 1939). Knowing so many young Black children are overtly and covertly taught self-loathing, I used the study as an inroad to teach self-esteem and love of her skin color. I did not want my daughter to be socialized to associate negative qualities with Black dolls or Blackness as a whole, so I consistently reinforced her value in every way I knew. I am her first culturally responsive teacher.

Debunking the Myth of the Socially Awkward Intellectual

In addition to her high intellectual ability, Sasha found herself rested at the apogee of popularity. Her social prowess belied stereotypes that place smart children in the socially awkward category. Though there are certainly gifted and other children who do not take well to social environments (I was one such child), there is no reason to assume that high intelligence necessitates an inability to form attachments with others. I recognized and acknowledged that my daughter's true inclination was naturally social and needed no orchestrating on my part. Because I had fit the "bright and somewhat socially awkward" stereotype as a child, I quickly recognized that Sasha certainly would not be her mother's clone. The ease with which she was able to immediately communicate and connect with others was a welcomed joy. A true social butterfly, she demonstrated a high aspiration toward establishing long-term friendships, a penchant for cultural diversity, and a fearless craving for cross-cultural experiences—she appreciated sushi and managed the art of using chopsticks long before I ever did.

On a grander scale, popularity among friends bears little weight, as it does not necessarily say much about an individual's value or self-worth. We can all think of people who were popular in school despite their immense lack of positive qualities. Sasha's popularity was different. It did not exist in spite of her personal characteristics; it existed because of them. As the mother of an only child, I encouraged and supported the mere notion of long-lasting and meaningful friendships. As a close observer of my daughter's development and radiance, I loved that she was able to build a give-and-take balance, which allowed her to share joy, happiness, empathy, and caring with and for others. Witnessing the phenomenon of this exchange still brings me delight to this day.

Something else that stood out about Sasha's social nature is that it was able to flourish despite any artificially imposed barriers that could have inhibited her growth as a young, Black, gifted girl. She had already acquiesced to high self-worth, self-esteem, and self-value. She had already come to appreciate and desire diversity, so lacking confidence would have been as unfamiliar as anything else foreign. No matter where Sasha went or whom she was around, she never allowed internal dynamics of race, class, or gender determine her place. She chose her place, and it was always at the top, among the best affiliations and the brightest of friends. Her ability to make friends across racial and cultural lines is indicative of one who does not limit herself to one culture, one race, one ethnicity, one language, or even one country.

All-In Parenting

I ENROLLED IN GRADUATE SCHOOL when Sasha was just fourteen months old, and I either studied or worked in college and university environments all her early childhood, adolescent years, and young adult life. She quickly grew accustomed to town-and-gown communities, also known as college/university cities. Some have even referred to children like Sasha as "academic babies." So when we moved from the Pacific Northwest to Evanston, Illinois, when Sasha was nine years old to be closer to my family, the adjustment was not as complicated as one would imagine. In general, when it came to being flexible, idealistic, or even realistic, I was neither hesitant nor shy about exercising my right to choose. No matter where we lived, I was determined that Sasha enjoy the benefits of a balanced, fulfilled life, including being properly challenged in school. This meant creating an environment in which my caring, extroverted child could grow socially and emotionally and thrive academically. I still firmly believe it was not a mistake that God blessed me with a child who could benefit from my willingness to adapt her environment to spare her the indignities of societal "isms."

The position I took to be wholly supportive of my child's development is most likely what all parents desire. But the particular realities faced by Blacks (i.e., racism, colorism) made my deliberate choices unpopular to some. Despite this unpopularity, I made decisions I thought were best. I refused to accept artificial, race-based boundaries that attempt to dictate where a Black child can and cannot go. My parents taught me long ago education is the one thing "they" can't take from you. Yet, who "they" happened to be was never explained. From my parents' perspective, there was no need to discuss race relations in the home. The message was received, and eventually life had its own way of revealing truths.

As a new resident in Evanston, my immediate priority was to find a good school. I did not want to risk underachievement by enrolling my intellectually gifted daughter in a school where she would not be academically challenged (Reis, 1998). I first enrolled her in a public school, thinking she could benefit from the diversity. I did not want her to go on feeling isolated from other Black children. Unfortunately, an incident on the middle school playground led me to change my mind.

I was summoned to the school because at recess time my usually pleasant and gregarious child had punched a little White kid, who just so happened to be one of the few White children at the school. The child had yelled and directed the N word not at my daughter but at another Black girl. Sasha did not have a close relationship with the girl she was defending, so it was clear her reaction was based on principle alone. Although she was only a fifth grader, she knew all about racism and injustice. She knew it was ugly. Also, I am certain it was no coincidence that this playground incident happened just days after watching the PBS miniseries *Roots*, based on Alex Haley's novel. We had meaningful discussions during and after the miniseries, but I think it lit a spark in her that was later intensified that day during recess time. My little fifth grader simply could not bear the idea of standing idle while racism occurred in such close proximity.

After speaking at length with the school principal, a Black woman, I realized she had no intention of disciplining Sasha. In fact, she had only called me as a formality, a standard part of administrative protocol. Outside of the children's earshot, she whispered, "Good for Sasha! She is not in trouble. Handle the matter in any way you wish." Those words left an impression on me. They made me ponder, would Sasha have escaped being disciplined and received private praise had the incident occurred at a PWI?

It was perplexing to know that Sasha felt hitting was the proper way to handle the situation. I never once modeled that type of behavior in our home. I neither spanked nor spoiled. I prided myself on being balanced and progressive in my parenting style, so how did we get here? I recognized that my daughter had every right to be upset, and it pleased me to know that empathy and social awareness compelled her to stand up for someone else. Yet, I was obliged to communicate that her decision to hit, though well-intentioned, was wrong. I used the incident as a teachable moment to discuss how to use words and appropriate actions to successfully traverse the rocky terrain of prejudices, daily indignities, injustices, blatant stereotypes, and discrimination.

After weighing all the pros and cons of public and private middle schools, I chose National Louis University's Baker Demonstration School, another North Shore PWI, for the small class sizes and one-on-one attention given to students at PWIs.

Across the country, Black children are underrepresented in gifted and talented programs. Various studies have shown that Black children are not being identified and included in gifted and talented classrooms and programs (Singleton et al., 2008). At the time and years prior to selecting the field of gifted and talented as a focus of post-graduate interests, I was unaware of the statistics and facts on Black children's underrepresentation in school districts' gifted programs.

More often than not, Sasha was the only Black child in most of her early childhood classes. Once after school and during our usual mother-daughter chats, I asked if she enjoyed writing for the Smith College essay competition. With sadness in her voice, Sasha explained that she and only one other Black student were in a large study hall filled with other student competitors. For Sasha, being the only one or even one of two Black children in a classroom or entering a competition or sharing a space, was never met with jubilance. To this day I believe my daughter would agree that, in reference to being the "only one," the expression "that's nothing to brag about" was a household staple. I believe she eventually understood that other intelligent Black children simply had not been advocated for in the same way as she had been.

On Embracing Differences

At times, Sasha's exceptional abilities set her apart from other children her age. This was not always met with favor. After all, what child would choose to be different from her peers? I never had a predilection for rearing a child who had no desire to learn from and become friends with people who are culturally different. My desire had been that the whole world would be Sasha's stage to enjoy, love, explore, test, and embrace from a culturally pluralistic perspective. All the culture and art I exposed her to, all the languages, all the international travel were part of my vision of nurturing a limitless child. As much as I wanted her to love and appreciate her heritage as a Black female, I never wanted her to feel limited to loving and appreciating her obvious heritage to the exclusion of others. I learned back in my college days how stifling it was to restrict my exposure exclusively to those with whom I could identify by skin color.

As a Black college student in the mid-1970s—a time of Black militancy and unapologetic pride—I felt some ambivalence about my place on campus. I shared in the pride of the "I'm Black, and I'm Proud" movement, but at times there were small differences that I now know are unimportant but nonetheless got in the way of friendships with the few Black students on campus. As a child and a young adult, my life revolved around religion, and my family did not discuss racial politics. Though I spent a great deal of time with my parents and grandparents, we never discussed Martin Luther King, Malcolm X, Huey Newton, or any other relevant Black leaders of the time. Given that my parents and grandparents hailed from the South during a racially turbulent era, perhaps it was just easier to detach. So, by the time I entered college, I felt somewhat disconnected from the intelligentsia of my culture as a Black conscientious objector, a potentially Black civil rights leader, or a follower of civil disobedience. It did not help that there were only a handful of Blacks on campus, which meant that I did not have much to choose from when it came to obtaining close friendships with other Black students.

During an office visit with Professor Murphy, my major advisor and department chair at Creighton University, a discussion ensued concerning feelings of not fitting in among other Black students. Professor Murphy outlined a simple yet profound idea that led to a change in perspective and a new worldview, a paradigm shift. He articulated the idea of racial complexities, noting that there are intragroup as well as intergroup variances that must be respected and not separate people. He went on to say that there is no one particular way to "be Black," and so I should never feel constrained by differences that are, in actuality, a mark of diversity. No student at this Jesuit University should feel prohibited from making connections with students who do not belong to the same racial, ethnic, or cultural group. Blackness is not eroded by an engagement in cross-cultural friendships. That half-hour office visit, one many students avoid because of shyness to meet with a professor, prompted a desire to investigate possibilities of forging relationships with interesting people from all over the world—the Middle East, West and East Africa, Southeast Asia (India), Europe, Jewish culture, etc. I joined the international student organization and met other students and some faculty/staff who welcomed my presence and Black frame of reference.

When I became a parent, it was important that everything I learned and gained through intercultural friendships be imparted upon my daughter. Despite what others may have expected of me as a Black woman and parent, I deliberately went out of my way to expose my gifted child to the broader world. I chose certain schools, neighborhoods, churches, and friendships based on what they could contribute to my being a well-rounded woman and my child a well-rounded, sophisticated, young lady.

That differences should be accepted and celebrated was a large part of my personal ethos, but looking back, I realize I was a bit naïve to assume others would embrace this position. My hopefulness and optimism were sometimes lost on those chained to dogmatic thinking and racial stereotypes. I was forced to face this fact as a Black American mother in predominantly White, affluent settings. The spelling bee incident is a perfect example of the disrespect I received at a PWI, which is why I changed schools. I enrolled my daughter at a public school, the same public school with the teacher who sent the note home about transferring her to a classroom for behaviorally disturbed children.

As previously stated, I was a bit naïve in my thinking, so when I saw that Sasha had a Black female teacher, I automatically assumed my daughter would be safe in her classroom. I expected that a Black woman would take the time to get to know my child's needs and nurture her development as a gifted child. A face-to-face meeting with the teacher revealed that she was old school, the type of teacher who believed children should not challenge adults on any topic. Clearly, she had not even a modicum of understanding about differential giftedness. Perennial inquiry is what characterizes gifted children, not out of disrespect but out of sheer thirst for information.

My position is that all aspiring teachers, especially those interested in specializing, should understand and become familiar with characteristics of gifted children, if only for the purpose of steering the child into appropriate classrooms or to facilitate communications with parents. If a school does not offer specialized enrichment programs, pull-out classrooms, opportunities for acceleration, or classroom differentiation, teachers and administrators should at least be educated on the basics of giftedness.

Being a parent of a highly verbal, gifted child is quite a challenge, so I can partially understand the teacher's frustration when confronted. Gifted children often express themselves with a great deal of intensity. They may verbally back adults into a corner with no way out, but this is not to be mean. Rather, it is to be heard. When teachers are open to dialogue, they can learn from parents how to relax and not feel threatened in these situations. Besides parents and other responsible guardians, the teacher is the next adult a child looks up to as role model. Several studies have noted that most teachers who enter the teaching profession are indeed intrinsically motivated to teach. Studies on teacher motivations for entering the profession have indicated that the number one reason for becoming a teacher is the love of children (Ornstein et al., 2013). That love coupled with proper education should enable teachers to recognize and manage gifted children and other children with unique educational needs. Ideally, parents and teachers should be partners, working together in the best interest of the child. This cannot happen if teacher education programs and the accompanying curriculum do not address the characteristics of giftedness and how to best meet the child's social, emotional, and intellectual needs.

A Career in Gifted Education

I VIVIDLY RECALL MY FIRST EXPOSURE to the concept of gifted education. It was in an educational psychology course. Two pages into reading the required textbook, I felt my life had changed. The idea of a particular type of education that caters specifically to the needs of highly intelligent individuals struck me, perhaps because I was quite intelligent as a child and could have benefited from such a sector. I did not have a priori knowledge concerning the full extent to which I would commit to the study and practice of gifted education.

Many empirical studies have elucidated reasons why people choose to enter one profession over another. Sometimes people choose their career paths based on parent occupations. Others are motivated by a precipitating event that puts them on a particular career path. Additionally, I have worked with educators who claim their motivation to enter special education, gifted education, or teacher education in general had been to better understand the nuances of the profession. In my case, I felt compelled to enter gifted education, first and foremost, because of my gifted child and, second, because of a desire to make a difference in the lives of underrepresented gifted children, irrespective of race, culture, or other differences.

When Sasha was in middle school, I was hired by the Center for Talent Development (CTD) at Northwestern University (NU) to direct NU-Horizons, a counseling program designed for economically disadvantaged, gifted, and talented college-bound high school sophomores. The purpose of the three-year, grant-funded program was to offer young students an opportunity to prepare for college admissions.

This position helped me retain my interest in and commitment to gifted education. My career took off while employed at Northwestern University, where I worked under the tutelage of the center's director, Paula Olszewski-Kubilius. Olszewski-Kubilius nurtured and mentored me through my growth. As an employee of the university, I was afforded the opportunity to enroll Sasha in gifted classes at the university. These classes were costly, and we would not have otherwise had room in our family budget for her to attend. I also had the opportunity to work closely with and present at the National Association of Gifted Children (NAGC) with Olszewski-Kubilius (Olszewski-Kubilius & Scott, 1992). Working with such a well-known and accomplished scholar provided the impetus to matriculate toward my doctorate. For my doctoral dissertation, I chose to study the undergraduate experiences of Black students identified as gifted prior to enrolling in college.

From Olszewski-Kubilius, I learned to adopt a philosophy that children do not stop being gifted once they reach adulthood. That notion, that giftedness lasts a lifetime, drove my desire to persist in the field and provided the impetus for the fundamental question, "Does participation in gifted programs or being identified as gifted make a difference?" Embedded in this question is the hypothesis that gifted education has the power to change the trajectory of the lives of those who are exposed to it early in life.

As a gifted education professorial educator, I believe my desire and ability to commit fully to my gifted child's development was heightened. Given my level of understanding and dedication, I was able to easily and lovingly make decisions that might have seemed onerous or excessive to others (e.g., changing schools repeatedly until I found the right fit or going out of my way to expose my child to various forms of cultural and intellectual stimuli). From my perspective, there was no burden in helping my daughter become the best version of herself. As a mother and as an educator, it was a joy to watch. I am thankful for the opportunity to take part in my daughter's development.

Enrichment Opportunities as Prescription for Success

Gifted children are exceptional learners. Through self-initiated projects and independent reading, they naturally take advantage of informal learning opportunities that present themselves outside the classroom (Olszewski-Kubilius, 2012). Through enrichment programs, gifted children are exposed to added content that is not typically covered and/or may be more abstract than what is taught in school. These outside-of-class learning opportunities allow the child to indulge and further explore his or her interests while receiving real-world experience. In contrast to acceleration, enrichment seeks to meet the educational needs of gifted students by the addition of content rather than adjustments to the pacing of instruction (Southern, Jones, & Stanley, 1993). Intuitively and academically, I knew Sasha would benefit greatly from enrichment programs and opportunities, both formal and informal, so I encouraged a less restrictive definition of education by setting a culture of learning in the home and beyond the walls of classroom buildings (Olszewski-Kubilius, 2012).

Though I never underestimated the learning that took place in the classroom, I knew there would not be an adequate focus on the individual child, not when teachers are clamoring to keep their jobs by fixating on standardized test results for whole classrooms. As school policies require teachers to prove their worth through students' test scores, the curriculum becomes stiff and formulaic, and there is little opportunity for educational discovery and exploration. All children need an element of freedom in their learning, but this is particularly true of gifted children. According to Wai et al. (2010), students who are exposed to supplementary educational opportunities are more likely to go on to make meaningful and innovative contributions in their career fields. If nothing else, I wanted my daughter to live a life of meaning.

Because of my emphasis on developing the whole person, Sasha was involved in a number of enrichment programs through her childhood and young adult years. She began ballet lessons in second grade and continued through high school. (Looking back, I believe ballet contributed to her very focused and disciplined personality.) She participated in Saturday enrichment classes at the Center for Talent Development. Before high school and at the CTD, she enrolled in a financial enrichment course that taught young people how to buy and sell stocks. It was a delight to see her pick up the newspaper and turn to pages I had never learned to appreciate. In middle school, she and other children co-founded and organized "Brain Juice," a North Shore children's group for young Mensans. I kept her busy with an eclectic mix of activities: swimming, Girl Scouts, Campfire Girls, sleep-away summer camps, piano, flute, modern dancing, private voice lessons, horse camp, and preparation courses for the Scholastic Aptitude Test (SAT).

Sasha felt about her high school experience the same way I felt about mine: It was a complete waste of time. In fact, she could have easily skipped it. The stale, non-challenging curriculum at Evanston

Township High School was a disappointment to us both. My perspective today, as a gifted education scholar and parent, is that the lack of a
critical mass of culturally diverse students enrolled in honors and gifted
classes in a school building where such students are enrolled in large
numbers is, again, an apartheid of sorts operating in public schools.
Thankfully, centers like the Center for Talent Development and the
Johns Hopkins Center for Talented Youth offer enrichment programs
to meet the needs of culturally diverse gifted learners. Typically, I would
have simply changed schools, but things were different in Evanston.
Logistically, there was only one high school, but more important, my
family was nearby, my career was taking off, and I had begun my doctoral studies at Loyola University-Chicago. I was anchored in a way
that made moving unrealistic, and as a child, I learned the importance
of stability. My parents purchased our family home before I was born,
and I had the privilege of living there until I left for college. We were
comfortable and lived within our means. I understood stability better
than many. The pressure was on to remain stable and adhere to long
family (both paternal and maternal) traditions of home ownership and
stability. From middle school years on through high school years, Sasha's
life was quite predictable and stable.

I already knew out-of-school learning was vital for children whose
school environments were not challenging (Olszewski-Kuiblius, 2012),
so we intensified my daughter's activity involvement. She became involved in the city of Evanston's youth government program sponsored
by the YWCA, where she was elected student representative city alder-
man in her sophomore year and student mayor in her junior year, shad-
owing the city's mayor and having a voice on important city ordinances.

Sasha's ability to easily recall and explain facts led to an after-school
youth volunteer position with the Red Cross as an HIV/AIDS instructor. We used every presented opportunity to enrich her education, and
I shunned the idea that learning takes place exclusively in a classroom.
The takeaway message was that education can be gained through exploration of the world, interactions with people, and self-discovery.

I realized by Sasha's junior high years that I had accomplished my
goal as a parent of a gifted child. I watched her grow into a balanced
and confident young woman, and I was certain she had internalized
the virtues of cultural pluralism, hard work, dedication, kindness, and

empathy about others. It mattered to me that Sasha could think for herself and make good decisions that kept her safe, healthy, and happy. It mattered to me that she was kind, honest, and respectable and that she lived a life that would make her mother proud—and she indeed has made me proud. It mattered to me that she embraced different cultures and valued family and friends. All this she has accomplished by the age of fourteen. Because graduating from high school was a natural given, my only other requirement was that she go on to earn a bachelor's degree at a respectable university, which she did, Tulane University; and enter a career that would challenge her intellect. I had no lofty plan for her to become a rocket scientist. My educational goals did not revolve around tangible accomplishments. In sum, I am indeed proud that my daughter entered a career that challenges her more advanced cognitive skills, as she is presently employed as a specialized computer science profession-al at a leading American corporation with national and international recognition. I am a happy mother of a gifted adult daughter, who is herself a wonderful mother and wife and no doubt passing along many life experiences and lessons learned to my two adorable grandchildren.

Giftedness Is a Lifelong Journey

GIFTEDNESS IS A NATURAL GIFT that must be continuously tended and engaged from birth through adulthood, which explains why this chapter is included in a book chronicling narratives on the journeys of cultur-ally diverse gifted adults. From a parent's perspective, I believe children exhibiting gifted characteristics should be identified to ensure they are challenged adequately. Parents owe it to their children to provide stim-ulating home environments and excellent schools. We must insist on culturally responsive teaching and a diverse curriculum if we want our children to develop to their fullest potential. When schools fail children by not providing culturally responsive curriculum, the proactive parent seeks out other ways to accomplish the same end result.

All paths toward becoming an educated person begin in the home. When we turn our children over to schools as overseers of their edu-cation, we must not give up our responsibilities as their first teachers. There are many gifted children who have fallen through the cracks of a one-size-fits-all education system. More often than not, no one knows a child's proclivities better than the parent. We should never relinquish the top spot as our children's biggest advocate—at least not until they are old enough to advocate for themselves.

References

Arrington, E. G., Hall, D. M., & Stevenson, H. C. (Summer, 2003). The success of African-American students in independent schools. *Independent School Magazine, 62*, 10-21.

Clark, K. B., & Clark, M. P. (1939). The development of consciousness of self and the emergence of racial identification in Negro pre-school children. *Journal of Social Psychology, 10*, 591–599.

Ford, D. Y. (2013). Recruiting and retaining culturally different students in gifted education. Waco, TX: Prufrock Press.

Ginsberg, M. B., & Wlodkowski, R.J. (2000). *Creating highly motivating classrooms for all students: A schoolwide approach to powerful teaching with diverse learners.* San Francisco, CA: Jossey-Bass.

Hinnant, B., O'Brien, M., Ghazarian, S. (2009). The longitudinal relations of teacher expectations to achievement in the early school years. *Journal of Educational Psychology, 101*(3), 662–670.

Jussim, L., Eccles, J., & Madon, S. (1996). Social perception, social stereotypes, and teacher expectations: Accuracy and the quest for the powerful self-fulfilling prophesy. In M. P. Zanna (Ed.), *Advances in experimental social psychology* (281–388). San Diego, CA: Academic.

Klein, B. (2007). *Raising gifted kids: Everything you need to know to help your exceptional child thrive.* New York: AMACOM

Landis, R., Reschly, A. (2013). Reexamining gifted underachievement and dropout through the lens of student engagement. *Journal for the Education of the Gifted, 36*(2), 220–249. doi: 10.1177/0162353213480864.

Lovecky, D. (1994). Exceptionally gifted children: Different minds. *Roeper Review, 17*(2).

Mendaglio, S, (2003). Heightened multifaceted sensitivity in gifted children: Implications for counseling. *Journal of Secondary Gifted Education, 14*(2), 72–82.

Olszewski-Kubilius, P. (2012). The importance of learning outside of school for gifted children. *Parenting for High Potential, 2*(3), 2–3.

Olszewski-Kubilius, P. M., & Scott, J. M. (1992). An investigation of the college and career counseling needs of economically disadvantaged, minority gifted students. *The Roeper Review, 14*(3), 141–148.

Ornstein, A., Levine, D. U., Gutek, G., & Vocke, D. (2013). *Foundations of education.* (12th ed,). Cengage Learning: Belmont, CA.

Padilla, A. M., & Borsato, G. N. (2008). Issues in culturally appropriate psychoeducational assessment. In L. A. Suzuki, J. G. Ponterotto (Eds.), *Handbook of Multicultural Assessment: Clinical, Psychological, and Educational Applications* (5–21). San Francisco, CA: Jossey-Bass.

Rosenthal, R., Jacobson, L. (1968). *Pygmalion in the classroom: Teacher expectations and student intellectual development.* New York: Holt, Rinehart, and Winston.

Singleton, D. M., Livingston, J., Hines, D., & Jones, H. (2008). Under-representation of African American students in gifted education programs: Implications for sustainability in gifted classes. *Perspectives, 10*(1) 11–21.

Southern, W. T., Jones, E. D., & Stanley, J. C. (1993). Acceleration and enrichment: The context and development of program options. In K. A. Heller, F. J. Mönks, & A. H. Passow (Eds.), *International handbook of research and development of giftedness and talent* (387–405). New York: Pergamon.

Stevenson, H. C. & Arrington, E. G. (2012). There is a subliminal attitude: African American parental perspectives on independent schooling. In D. T. Slaughter-Defoe, H. C. Stevenson, E. G. Arrington, & D. J. Johnson (Eds.), *Black Educational choice: Assessing the private and public alternatives to traditional K-12 public schools.* Santa Barbara, CA: Praeger.

Taylor, G. (2004). *Causes associated with classroom management and discipline problems.* Lanham, MD: University Press of America.

Tomlinson, C. (2001). *How to differentiate instruction in mixed-ability classrooms.*

(2nd *ed.*). Alexandria, VA: Association for Supervision and Curriculum Development.
Wai, J., Lubinski, D., Benbow, C. P., & Steiger, J. H. (2010). Accomplishment in science,
technology, and mathematics (STEM) and its relation to STEM educational dose: A 25-year longitudinal study. *Journal of Educational Psychology, 102*, 860–871.

CHAPTER 11

The Conversation: A Mother and Daughter Discovering Their Shared Experiences as Gifted Black Women

Shawn Arango Ricks, PhD
Nia Ricks, BFA

Introduction

THIS IS A SHARED STORY, an attempt by a mother (Shawn) and daughter (Nia) to interrogate our experiences as gifted Black women from two separate generations. We have engaged in a critical reflection of our experiences as gifted Black women and how this giftedness has affected our worldviews. We share our personal narratives in an attempt to better understand ourselves, our worlds, and each other, as well as to share our stories with the goal of providing guidance for others who may be on a similar path. As such, this piece is written in a format that we hope is highly accessible to a wide variety of readers.

The goal in this chapter is to explore shared experiences as gifted Black women, despite drastically different childhood circumstances (socioeconomic status, geographical location, educational access, and parental support). This chapter is also designed to provide insights and support to other Black parents of gifted children. As such, the following section will provide background information from my perspective as a parent to help situate the reader and provide a better foundation for understanding the reflections that will be presented later in the chapter.

I, Shawn, am the parent of three wonderful children: Imani (Kiswahili for "faith") who is twenty-five years old, Nia (Kiswahili for "purpose") who is twenty years old, and Nathan (Hebrew for "gift from God") who is fifteen years old. As a family we have lived in Arizona, Colorado, Pennsylvania, and North Carolina. These geographical locations are important to note, as they contributed to our worldviews. I have been married for twenty-two years to my college sweetheart. As we moved around the country, I worked in a variety of jobs and, at times, worked as a stay-at-home mom.

Nia is my middle child. Her "purpose" is to be a companion to her big sister and a protector of her little brother. Nia is just beginning to find the words for some of her life experiences and recognize that some of them are not isolated events but, rather, shared standpoints.

I sought out Nia as a co-author for this chapter in part because of her increasing vocalization regarding her experiences. She had always been the most openly reflective and critically engaged of my children. I was also curious to see if my good parental intentions had been effective. When I had children, I wanted them to have the best of everything. The most important thing I thought I could do as a mother of Black children was to provide them with the educational foundation they would need to be competitive. Although I had grown up with a variety of educational experiences and had some basic understanding of how these experiences leave their imprint on one's soul, I knew that I had to make an important, foundational choice for my children and that this choice would involve a trade-off: education versus environment.

I knew this trade-off well having attended ten schools in the thirteen years of my K–12 education. I was *that* inner-city kid—one of the relatively few who had seen a tennis racquet, played golf, taken swim lessons, and played field hockey. These (dis)advantages shaped me so deeply to my core that they had no choice but to affect my parenting skills. When it came to examining this educational trade-off for my children, I conveniently utilized my coping skills to allow myself to believe that our upwardly mobile, middle-class socio-economic status would somehow provide a normalizing buffer. I wanted to believe that we were no different from our White neighbors and would be viewed as such.

The more Nia and I talked, the more I understood the need for social support for Black mothers who may be dealing with an additional layer of stress regarding the tough choices they have made for their children. Choices regarding preschool, neighborhood, playgroups, and after-school activities are heavily weighed decisions for most mothers. For Black mothers, however, these decisions are additionally layered with concern regarding the psychological well-being of their children. Hill Collins (1990) discusses the unique role of Black mothers as it relates to raising their daughters when she notes, "Black mothers of daughters face a troubling dilemma . . . to ensure their daughters' physical survival, mothers must teach them to fit into systems of oppression" (123).

Beverly Daniel Tatum (1987) has examined the tough choice of housing in her landmark book, *Assimilation Blues: Black Families in White Communities, Who Succeeds and Why*. Black mothers who choose to live in White neighborhoods (primarily for safety and quality of schools) must deal with the trade-off of a potential lack of cultural rootedness and the fallout of assimilation. Tatum (1987) discusses this price of assimilation for Black families noting that many Blacks struggle with the concept of biculturalism daily, adjusting or assimilating to both worlds in which they must function. She asserts, "Black parents have to guide their children through conflicting developmental tasks during which the child must internalize the dominant views of our society and at the same time learn to recognize and reach his own potentialities" (14). In short, Black parents (most often Black mothers), have the tasks of "providing for the child's basic needs . . . but in addition Black mothers are almost always involved in socializing their girls and boys to cope with the reality of racism . . . particularly if they are raising children in predominantly non-Black areas" (Tatum, 1987, 10).

Part of my coping skills and attempts at motherly protection involved choosing not to share my own childhood experiences or my concerns for my children with my children. The critical conversation we had in writing this chapter officially began a long overdue dialogue that was illuminating but also, ultimately, cathartic for both my daughter and me. Before sharing what we discovered through discussing our critical self-reflections with each other, it is important to contextualize this narrative chapter with an introduction to our individual backgrounds. As Beverly Tatum asks regarding the costs to a Black family residing in a predominantly White neighborhood, I have begun to wonder what the access to an academically gifted status and education, this crossing over to the "other side," really cost in terms of psychosocial well-being. Although education has been touted as a panacea to racism, as a way to get ahead, I am pretty certain both my daughter and I paid an unexpected but substantial price for our giftedness, one that may never be fully understood and can never be fully recovered.

Our Stories

Shawn (Mother)

I GREW UP IN POVERTY in a large northern city. I was born to a teenage mother, and in a sense, my mother and I grew up together. She was adventurous and fun-loving, but she knew that education was the way up and out for me. It was, in part, because of this firm belief that she insisted I attend the best schools in the city and take my education seriously. My mother truly believed in the power of education as a tool for liberation. As a teenage single mother, she worked hard to find ways to expose me to every opportunity—yet these exposures did not come without a psychosocial price. In some ways the very path that was supposed to liberate me was choking me, the multi-dimensional me, with over-determined, limiting terms such as "minority," "underprivileged," and "scholarship." These words began to possess a negative connotation that was translatable to "unequal." And in some sense, I began to believe it.

In fourth grade, I attended a Montessori school in Philadelphia, Pennsylvania. This was my first cross-cultural experience. I was surrounded my teachers and students from the majority culture. I learned a lot about myself there and began to notice lots of cultural differences. For instance, the teachers wanted to be called by their first names. Students could wear almost anything they wanted. Lunches and snacks were different; they contained less processed foods and more fresh fruits and vegetables. After my experience at the Montessori school, my exposure deepened when my mother secured a scholarship for me through the A Better Chance (ABC) foundation. This foundation was developed to allow underprivileged children to get a better education. My first experience with ABC took me to the Springside School, located right outside Philadelphia.

Springside was the beginning of my experience in isolation. My giftedness had bought me a sense of aloneness and desperation so deep that I did not even recognize it for decades. After Springside, I attended the Baldwin School for Girls in Bryn Mawr, Pennsylvania. Again, I attended on a scholarship. Again, I stood out. It is both hard and painful to describe the feeling of being an outsider. Academically, I did fine. But socially I was slowly dying. I returned to Baldwin for the first half of my ninth grade year, and by that age, I could more easily discern the differences. To get to school I left at about six in the morning to catch a public transportation bus to the elevated train (El) station. I took the El to Thirtieth Street Station, where I took an Amtrak train to the Bryn Mawr stop. Then it was just a seven-minute walk to the school. I went home the same way. I rode the train with a couple of other "underprivileged" girls who had received scholarships. I was friendly with them, but we weren't really friends. For me, that was really a year of no friends. My academics suffered a little as well. Although giftedness could expose to me to a different socioeconomic class, it couldn't provide me with the cultural capital found in those living within the upper-class socioeconomic world. I went home every day to my Black neighborhood, painfully aware that my visa to that upper-class world was conditional and carried a nightly expiration time.

In retrospect, I realize now that I was beginning to feel the effects of being the "other." Audre Lorde (2007) defines the "other" as "the outsider whose experience and tradition [are] too 'alien' to comprehend" (117). In addition, Michelle Wallace (2004) claims women of color have an additional layer of marginalization by being historically labeled and viewed as outsiders from all men, as well as from White women. This has left women of color as "the other of the other." Although I did not know how to name it, I was struggling with my existence on the periphery. I was accepted, but it was an acceptance that felt more like a curiosity then a genuine acceptance. It was during these formative years that I am sure I began to develop my psychological armor. Bell and Nkomo (2003) posit that Black women and girls have developed an armor they wear as a "strategy for self-protection and psychological resistance that provides a way to diminish the threat of racism and sexism" (410).

As a parent, I wanted to give my children the childhood I had fantasized about. This included a two-parent household, a single-family home, and even the benefits of having a stay-at-home mom for a while. I was determined to protect them from the feelings of isolation and alienation I felt. It was not until years later that I realized I could not shield them from the world. No matter how much money we earned, what car I drove, or how many degrees I obtained, race mattered.

Nia (Daughter)

I went to a predominately White elementary school. I remember knowing only two other Black kids that also attended the school. I grew up in the suburbs and had a happy, easy childhood. Yet, in retrospect, my childhood was still lacking in some important aspects. Of course I never felt as though I had missed out on anything until I got older. My parents gave me everything a little girl could dream of. We lived in a suburban neighborhood in a great school district. My dad coached basketball, and my mom started a Girl Scouts troop. In a sense, my childhood was ideal, but there was always something missing. Despite my mother's best effort, I had very little experience with other cultures. I was told about African, African American, and Black cultures, but I never really saw or experienced it first-hand. Black culture was completely separate from my sheltered world, which was mainly due to my higher socioeconomic class and my giftedness.

Growing up, I definitely had issues defining what it meant to be Black. I felt so separate and different from the few Black peers I did have. But when I got to middle school, it was a whole other deal. There was a greater amount of diversity, but I had no idea how to navigate it. I did not know how to communicate with people who talked or acted differently, and I did not really understand the Black community or the role I should play within it. Also, most of my friends in my neighborhood and at school were White, and I had very few ties to the Black community. This was partially due to the fact that I am gifted and tended to focus on academics. I was uncomfortable with social interactions in general. So, in middle school, instead of facing or overcoming uncomfortable situations, I would usually just retreat further into myself, my comfort zone, and focus on schoolwork. In other words, my upbringing left me at a disadvantage with regard to communication with those from different backgrounds. But my personality and fear of extending myself socially only perpetuated my lack of ability to develop friends and social skills in the Black community.

So, basically, I have lived most of my life on the outskirts of the Black community. I have always been surrounded by a majority of White peers. It would seem logical that I would fit in with my fellow gifted students (White and Black) perfectly, but this was not the case. While I have lived most of my life on the outskirts of the Black community, I have also been alienated by the larger, White gifted community at almost every turn because of my Blackness.

Throughout my life, I have always felt relegated to the position of the dreaded, token Black friend. In social gatherings, I usually end up surrounded by White "friends" and acquaintances where these friends take it upon themselves to point out that I am different from the rest of them. This is typically done through sly comments, questions directed towards me about Black people as a whole, or racist jokes that are meant to be ironically funny but are instead alienating and hurtful. I can never just be a gifted person within a group of gifted people. I am the gifted Black woman in a group of gifted people. This is a distinction I recognize, accept, and I admit, have occasionally taken pride in—but others have a way of making this distinction alienating. In middle school and high school, I was called an "Oreo" (Black on the outside, White on the inside). This highlights many of the issues I have faced within the White community. People seem to have trouble wrapping their head around the idea of a gifted, fully Black woman, so they qualify me with the description of White on the inside; therefore, I am never thought of as really a "Black" Black.

As a gifted Black woman, I have been alienated by the two groups I should belong to. I was physically separated from my Black peers because my classes excluded most Black students (Academically Gifted, or AG, in grade school and Advanced Placement, or AP, in high school). My extracurricular activities (theatre, art clubs, tennis) also suffered from a lack of Black participation. My socioeconomic class and neighborhood are predominantly White, but what separated me from my gifted, White peers was my skin color. Though I have reached a higher level of awareness, I am not sure I can ever fully bridge the gap between myself and these two groups. I communicate well with my Black peers now, but I still suffer from a cultural disconnect. And as long as ignorance around race continues to exist, it seems I will be forcibly alienated by my non-Black gifted peers.

Mother and Daughter: Coming Together

Although our upbringings were drastically different, one similarity we noted was the recurrent feelings of alienation throughout our lives. This alienation oftentimes presents itself in subtle forms, yet it has demanded that we pay a psychosocial price for our giftedness—being socially neither "here" nor "there," neither fully accepted in the gifted community nor in the Black community. Giftedness has become an additional challenge we must navigate as Black women.

By communicating and coming together to discuss our lives as gifted Black women, we discovered upon reflection that, despite our different upbringings, our experiences were, at their core, still surprisingly similar. In particular, the challenges we face are eerily similar. Communication is a huge tool for resiliency. By getting the chance to discuss these issues with each other, we have come to a higher place of awareness and have a better chance of understanding our situations and coping mechanisms.

The Conversation

One afternoon, in preparation for this chapter, we decided to sit down and share our thoughts regarding how being gifted, Black women impacted our experiences. The informal discussion was recorded and lasted about thirty minutes. We sat on our living room couch and just allowed the conversation to flow naturally. We had no prewritten questions and no expectations. The result of the conversation was cathartic for both of us. We learned more about our perspectives and perceptions in that thirty minutes than in our twenty years together. We have presented below what we think are the most salient themes from the conversation. These include socioeconomic status, awareness, coping and resiliency, and code-switching. To assist with the reader's understanding, we will use "Shawn" and "Nia" during the transcribed portions of the conversation, and "S" for Shawn and "N" for Nia when we are narrating.

Socioeconomic Status

S: As mentioned previously, my hope for my children was to provide them with a carefree upbringing. I attempted to do this by securing a stable job and a decent income. I had not thoroughly interrogated my understanding of class, and it was not until I read bell hooks's *Where We Stand: Class Matters* (2000) that I first began to understand and expand my definition of class. Previously I had associated this term only as it correlated to income. The more money you made, the higher economic class you were in. Although this is accurate, I fell short of understanding "that class was more than just a question of money, that is it shaped values, attitudes, social relations, and the biases that informed the way knowledge would be given and received" (hooks, 2000, 178).

Struggling with these nuanced issues surrounding class often places an additional burden on students who learn to balance their class locations. Students "must believe they can inhabit comfortably two different worlds, but they must make each space one of comfort. They must creatively invent ways to cross borders" (hooks, 1994, 183). I recognized this from my childhood, but I noticed through my discussions with my daughter that she too, in spite of the same socioeconomic status, was also finding ways to cross borders.

Crossing borders was also explored by Gloria Anzaldúa (1987) as she described her concept of a "mestiza consciousness" as "spaces where the inhabitants, 'the prohibited and forbidden,' live in a state of discomfort as they negotiate between the conflicting forces in such margins" (49). People then become "border dwellers," hailing from a "borderland . . . a vague and undetermined place created by the emotional residue of an unnatural boundary" (Anzaldúa, 1987, 3). Had I made my children border dwellers? Through our discussions we learned that my notion that I could protect my children from experiencing isolation and alienation was simply an extension of my fantasy. When it came down to it, an increase in socioeconomic standing did provide an increase in some basic necessities, but it did not protect my children from racial isolation, hatred, or bigotry.

> **Nia:** If you are a gifted Black woman, it's not the struggles you're going to face and the resiliency you're going to need; that kind of transcends class. I think that's what

we've proven as mother/daughter: Outside of being gifted and black the other factors don't matter; you are still
going to have a lot to go through because of your giftedness and because of being Black.

S: In my reflections I began to wonder how much class matters,
but Nia was insistent that in other areas it was indeed helpful to be in a
higher socioeconomic class.

Shawn: Okay . . . so it seems like I was trying to provide
for you the experience I wanted, which was, you know,
to try to equalize the home component. But that didn't
really matter so it ties back into the class piece.

Nia: Yeah . . . because the things you went through I
didn't have to go through. . . . You were catching three
or however many buses . . . I didn't have to do all that
because you were dropping me off at school. It's like I
was at everyone else's level in every other way . . . you
know? I wasn't catching buses to school or anything like
that, but I was still a gifted Black girl, and being Black
was what kept me alienated.

S: One of the biggest misconceptions we had about each other
was that our different socioeconomic backgrounds meant we had different, un-relatable experiences growing up. In reality, our giftedness and
Blackness transcended our socioeconomic status.

Awareness

S: As the conversation continued, I wondered if Nia thought giftedness was an additional burden for persons of color. Was being a gifted
person allowing her to be more perceptive and oftentimes feel more
deeply? Finally I wondered if this additional awareness was an advantage or a liability.

Shawn: So is it better to be gifted or not? If you are not
gifted, you are not even aware you are being mocked.

When you are gifted you have such a high level of critical thinking that things bother you more.

Nia: Once you become aware of what's happening and
you see . . . the ways in which you're different and the
things you have to go through . . . it does suck, and it's
hurtful and painful, and you'll be angry. . . . But it's
like I would not go back to being ignorant about it . . .
for anything.

Shawn: Okay.

Nia: I'd rather know what's going on so that I can do
something about it or not take part in what's happening or whatever. So . . . in middle school if someone
would've called me an Oreo. I would have gone along
with it. . . . I would be like, "Yeah . . . sure. . . ." And I
didn't see the harm in it. But now if someone calls me
an Oreo, I am going to quickly correct that: "What do
you mean? That doesn't make sense. . . . I'm Black and
I'm also smart, intelligent. . . I can speak my mind, I can
communicate to people, etc." That doesn't mean I'm in
any way White.

N: I have no idea where I fit into the Black or gifted communities. My main objective is to collect as much information as possible to
help me navigate the world. I primarily do this by reading about others'
experiences and the difficulties they have faced. Many peoples' stories
highlight the cruelty and unjust nature of the world, which causes me to
become angry or otherwise emotional. Despite the anger, sadness, and
other negative feelings that come with awareness, I wouldn't trade it for
anything. Being aware gives me the opportunity to spread knowledge
and make sure that I don't perpetuate ignorance.

Coping and Resiliency

S: Despite valuing her experiences, Nia, like most Black women will
continue to develop coping strategies to help her navigate her complex

journey. Historically, Black women have utilized a variety of coping methods including faith, social support, body ownership, and unique defense mechanisms (Daly et al., 1995; Howard-Vital, 1989; Jones & Shorter-Gooden, 2003; St. Jean & Feagin, 1998; Terhune, 2007; Wilson, 2009). These coping methods and strategies were vital in the lives of Black women. These strategies were typically handed down generationally utilizing the rich oral tradition (Bennett Jr., 1988; Daly et al., 1995; Giddings, 1984). Hearing Nia talk, I began to wonder if I had done all I could do to help her along her journey. I thought sharing coping skills indirectly was the most useful path, but now I am not so sure.

> **Shawn:** So maybe I should have taught you more coping skills directly since I knew what you were getting into.

> **Nia:** I think we could've talked more about like the fact that I was *the* Black friend and stuff like that. I don't think I would've understood really what you were talking about. Though. so it's kind of like it almost doesn't matter.

> **Shawn**: And that's kind of, I think, the tight space you find yourself in as a Black parent raising kids in a White area. It's like how soon do you want to whisk away their joy of just being a child . . . of just enjoying life by saying other things.

> **Nia:** Yeah, and I think the issues come early, like middle school-ish and late elementary school-ish, where you start to get hints of what's going on. But it's like . . . as a kid you know when it's happening right in front of your face, but you can't grasp the bigger picture.

> **Shawn:** But I wonder if, even as a little kid, even though you can't cognitively grasp it, even if it does not

psychologically affect you, it starts to shape you . . . even though you don't even understand what's happening..

Nia: I don't think it shapes you in any permanent kind of way. . . . I think the older you get the more important it is to talk about it and realize what's going on. . . . Watching documentaries and watching MHP [*The Melissa Harris-Perry Show* on MSNBC] and stuff like that has helped me . . . reach that level of awareness.

N: I know that when I was growing up, my mom was in a difficult position. Do you let children live in ignorance and enjoy it, or do you try to educate them on some of the difficulties they will face? Even as a gifted child, most things regarding my race and giftedness went over my head. When I saw my mom get passionate about social issues, I usually passed it off as her being angry and overreacting. I needed to reach a certain level of maturity before I could understand the bigger picture of what my Blackness and giftedness meant.

Code-Switching

S: As Nia and I continued to talk, she began to describe being accused of "acting White" or "not really being Black," statements meant to make her the exception and remind her that she is being only conditionally accepted. Part of the justification of this conditional acceptance was Nia's speech. She was frequently told, since she was a small child and by extended family members, that she "talked White." Nia spent her K–5 years living outside Boulder, Colorado, but instead of chalking up linguistics to geography, people went for race.

When Nia speaks, she uses standard English. Many of her friends are expecting her to utilize more Ebonics (or Black English). Linguists have traced Ebonics back to slavery, when the need to communicate to the master and to each other demanded that slaves (from different tribes) quickly learn and use "broken English." Common language patterns were created, which were carried over for years, morphing into various dialects (such as Gullah), and reminding Blacks of our common starting place. Remnants of these dialectical differences can still be found today and have been studied and debated in academia (Dillard, 1973; Smitherman, 1977).

Many Blacks still utilize Black English today yet have learned how to code-switch out of necessity. Code-switching involves a sometimes conscious interchange of dialects that allows one to converse with various groups of people using their accepted speech patterns—whether to a Fortune 500 company or just to your friends in the neighborhood. This skill has been widely discussed as one of the tools Blacks have adopted as a survival mechanism. Through my experiences with other parents in similar situations, I realized that Black children who grow up in predominantly White neighborhoods utilized a variety of other methods to balance out their experiences. One of my friends in a similar situation sent one daughter to a predominantly White high school and the other daughter to a predominantly Black high school. Upon completing high school the former daughter went to a historically Black college/university (HBCU) while the latter daughter attended a predominantly White institution (PWI). Both were seeking that balance they felt they were missing. As Nia and I were talking, I wondered why she did not seek out additional experiences past high school to mitigate her experience.

> **Shawn:** Why didn't you go to an HBCU?
>
> **Nia:** I would have gone into shock. That's where the code-switching comes in. . . . First of all, there wasn't any HBCU that went along with what I wanted, you know, as an artist [and] everything like that. There weren't many colleges I was looking at anyway but . . . it's like I don't have an in with my Black peers. . . . It's really . . . I don't know how to explain it it's just like . . .
>
> **Shawn:** You don't have a shared point of reference?
>
> **Nia:** Yeah.
>
> **Shawn:** You don't really have a shared point of reference with White folks either?

Nia: I do on everything except for my skin color. With other Black students . . . it depends because there are a lot of other people like me—gifted, Black—that I can relate to pretty well because we came from a similar background or we grew up in similar situations or we went to all-White schools and we just can communicate more easily. But if I am trying to talk to someone who is from a city or something like that, it's just so much harder for me to communicate with them because we are from such different mindsets and different cultures.

N: Originally I was talking about how growing up, I lacked the ability to code-switch and talk to anyone from a different background than myself. As I continued to discuss, however, I brought up the fact that recently code-switching hasn't been an issue for me.

Nia: Now I am learning to do it, and I can do it with all my friends, but even if I can learn to code-switch and talk to a Black peer and then go talk to my White peers, that doesn't mean my White peers can talk to Black peers. So then it becomes an issue of "I can't combine [social] circles."

N: Most aspects of my Blackness have been removed in order for me to rise to the full extent of my giftedness. At times, I feel that the gifted community is trying to box me in and remove my ties to the Black community. My Blackness has been ignored and qualified by comments such as "Oreo" or "you aren't *Black* black." And God forbid I branch out and communicate with anyone that the non-Black gifted community doesn't understand or accept. It has happened before that I will make friends with a Black peer and not be able to bring that person into my existing circle of gifted peers. What is really upsetting about my experience as a gifted Black woman is that I am always sacrificing a bit of myself to fit into groups that never 100 percent accept me. Despite all I have given up to be a part of the gifted community, I am still thought of as "other." My Blackness has been forced out of me, yet it is still used to define and alienate me.

Going Forward

S: I am thankful for this chapter as it provided the opportunity for Nia and me to sit down and really begin to deconstruct our experiences. In this almost duo-ethnographic format, we were able to begin to understand the other's world. We had attempted similar conversations over the years, but I was more hesitant to fully engage in the dialogue out of fear of destroying her childhood. I wanted her to be innocent as long as possible. Now I realize that was a parental misstep, especially with a gifted child. I wish I would have engaged her more often about her onliness and encouraged and taught her more direct ways to push back. For parents going through a similar experience with their gifted son or daughter I share the following tips:

- Start talking with your children early (especially if they are gifted) and often about their experiences. Talking about the potential negative experiences they may encounter will not increase the chance of them having them.
- Watch documentaries and thought-provoking shows with your children. Take them to cultural events, especially if they are otherwise isolated and the "only." When we lived in Boulder, Colorado (less than 1 percent Black at that time), I worked with a non-profit organization designed to expose Black children in that area to cultural events and each other. Seek out similar programs and organizations in your area. Can't find one? Start one.
- Talk about the historical roots of code-switching. Many Black youth don't understand the historical role code-switching has played in the lives of US Blacks. Help your children understand that this now useful tool was once a must for Blacks looking to obtain upward mobility.

N: The process of sitting down with my mother and discussing our experiences has been extremely informative and helpful in my journey. I spent nearly twenty years thinking that our experiences were too different to compare, but I was completely off base. The more we discussed, the more I realized that we were both thought of as "other." We both ultimately had to sacrifice in order to embrace our giftedness. I don't think much could have been done as I was growing up to prevent or shield me from the alienation that comes from being a gifted Black woman. I think that parents can keep their children well-informed, but that's about it. Awareness comes with experience and maturity, and it takes people a long time to reach an understanding of their circumstances and how they fit in to the world around them. I see this chapter as a beginning. I am just now finding out what it means to be a Black, gifted woman.

References

Anzaldua, G. (1987). *Borderlands la frontera: The new mestiza.* San Francisco, CA: Aunt Lute.

Beale, F. M. (1995). Double jeopardy: To be black and female. In B. Guy-Sheftall (Ed.). *Words of fire: An anthology of African-American feminist thought* (146–156). New York: The New Press.

Bell-Scott. P. (1991) *Double stitch: Black women write about mothers & daughters.* Boston, MA: Beacon Press.

Bell, E. L. J., & Nkomo, S. M. (2003). Our separate ways: Black and white women and the struggle for professional identity. Boston, MA: Harvard Business School Press.

Belenky, M. F., Clinchy, B. M., Goldberger, N. R., & Tarule, J. M. (1986). *Women's ways of knowing.* New York: Bantam Books.

Bennett Jr., L. (1988). *Before the Mayflower: A history of Black America.* New York: Penguin.

Daly, A., Jennings, J., Beckett, J. O., & Leashore, B. R. (1995). Effective coping strategies of African Americans. *Social Work, 40*(2), 240–248.

Dillard, J. L. (1973). *Black English.* New York: Random House.

Early, G. (1993). Lure and loathing: Essays on race, identity, and the ambivalence of assimilation. New York: Penguin.

Ellison, R. (1989). *Invisible man.* New York: Vintage Books.

Giddings, P. (1984). *When and where I enter: The impact of black women on race and sex in America.* New York: Bantam.

Guy-Sheftall, B. (Ed.). (1995). *Words of fire: An anthology of African-American feminist thought.* New York: The New Press.

Hill Collins, P. (1990). *Black feminist thought: Knowledge, consciousness, and the politics of empowerment.* New York: Routledge.

Hill, D. K. (2009). Code-switching pedagogies and African American student voices: Acceptance and resistance. *Journal of Adolescent & Adult Literacy,* 120–131.

hooks, b. (1994). Teaching to transgress: Education as the practice of freedom. New York: Routledge.

hooks, b. (2000). *Where we stand: Class matters.* New York: Routledge.

Howard-Vital, M. (1989). African American women in higher education: Struggling to gain identity. *Journal of Black Studies,* 180–191.

Jones, C., & Shorter-Gooden, K. (2003). *Shifting: The double lives of black women in America.* New York: Harper.

Lorde, A. (2007). *Sister outsider.* Berkeley, CA: Crossing Press.

Lovecky, D. V. (1986), Can you hear the flowers singing? Issues for gifted adults. *Journal of   Counseling   &   Development,* 64: 572–575. doi: 10.1002/j.1556-6676.1986.tb01207.x.

Nelson, L. W. (1990). Code-switching in the oral life of narratives of African-American women: Challenges to linguistic hegemony. *Journal of Education,* 142–155.

Smitherman, G. (1977). *Talkin and testifyin: The language of black Americans.* Detroit, MI: Houghton Mifflin Company.

St. Jean, Y., & Feagin, J. R. (1998). *Double burden: Black women and everyday racism.* Armonk, NY: M. E. Sharpe.

Tatum, B. D. (1987). *Assimilation blues: Black families in White communities, who succeeds and why?* New York: Greenwood Press.

Terhune, C. P. (2007). Coping in isolation: The experiences of black women in White communities. *Journal of Black Studies,* 547–564.

Walker, A. (1983). *In search of our mothers' gardens.* Orlando, FL: Harcourt Bruce Jonavich.

Wallace, M. (1995). Anger in isolation: A black feminist's search for sisterhood. In B. Guy-Sheftall (Ed.). *Words of fire: An anthology of African-American feminist thought* (220–228). New York: The New Press.

————. (2004). *Dark designs & visual culture*. Durham, NC: Duke
University Press.

Wilson, H. (2009). *Our nig: Sketches from the life of a free black*. Lexing-
ton, KY: Seven Treasures Publications.

CHAPTER 12

Gifted to the World: My Passionate Journey from Urban America to Global Scholarship

Nicole Monteiro, PhD

You are young, gifted, and Black. We must begin to tell
our young, there's a world waiting for you, yours is the
quest that's just begun.

— *James Weldon Johnson*

IN THIS CHAPTER, I DISCUSS the unique and extraordinary school and
family influences that helped me blossom from a shy, intellectually,
and emotionally gifted child to a confident, socially committed scholar,
psychologist, and global citizen.

Introduction

AS A CHILD, I ALWAYS had a sense of myself, a way of understanding who
I was in a concrete and tangible way. Others would often comment that
I appeared especially grounded and steady for my age. At the time I did
not know what they meant because I was usually in my own internal
world and not really aware of how others viewed me. But I do remember as a child feeling connected to my familial roots and having a deep

perception of and sensitivity to my physical, mental, and spiritual existence. That is what knowledge of self meant to me. And that knowledge would eventually become my foundation for navigating the world as a gifted child and young woman.

At the same time, I possessed an intense curiosity about the world and myself. As young as three or four years old, I frequently asked my parents philosophical questions such as "Who am I?" "What is life?" or "Why am I here?" These moments of deep reflection were not experienced as existential crises; rather, they became a foundation for self-exploration and a way to soothe and comfort myself within the complex social and academic environment I was learning to navigate.

That deep understanding and awareness, even if not always conscious, is common for Black gifted girls that I have known throughout my life. We have a way about us. But sadly, many Black academically and emotionally gifted girls are never acknowledged or identified by their educational systems. Numerous education researchers have reported on the shameful gap in identifying and retaining gifted Black youth in schools nationwide. Those gaps are a travesty. As Donna Ford notes in her book, *Recruiting and Retaining Culturally Different Students in Gifted Education* (Ford, 2013), a colorblind approach to understanding giftedness fails Black children; more important, it misses the socially and culturally relevant indicators of giftedness in culturally diverse groups. In the end, this leads to inequity in recruiting and retaining gifted children from all backgrounds. The benefits of recognizing and nurturing multiple forms of giftedness are far-reaching for individual students, communities, and society. Denying them to specific groups, such as Black girls and boys, is an educational and epistemological crime of low expectations and even lower resources. This systemic denial of the recognition of Black boys and girls who are gifted is an impediment to the country's growth and development.

Gifted Education: Beginnings

I remember clearly when I was being assessed for and began attending MG (the Mentally Gifted program, as it was called in Philadelphia during the 1980s). A young White woman came to take me out of class so we could "play a few games together." We spent several days during class time completing puzzles, word and color games, and other fun, academic-like activities. Now, looking back through my lens as a trained psychologist, I recognize that I was being given one of the children's IQ tests that assess aspects of verbal, visual-spatial, and information-processing abilities. Interestingly, in my work as a professional psychologist, I have administered different versions of these IQ tests. Despite controversy about what some scholars view as the biased nature of many IQ tests, these tests served as my entry into better educational opportunities.

Years later, as an adult, I asked my mother how I was selected for the MG program. She replied that my first grade teacher told my parents that I often completed classroom activities quickly and with ease. The teacher asked for permission to have me assessed by the school psychologist for the MG program that would expose me to more challenging academics and an array of enriching social, cultural, and artistic experiences. Of course, my parents agreed to have me tested for the program. But had I not been singled out and tested, my parents were attuned enough to my budding intellectual capabilities that they would have likely sought out a similar school program.

Not Settling: Parents Dedicated to Crafting an Education

> Word is not the privilege of some few persons
> but the right of everyone.
>
> —*Paulo Freire*

AS I REFLECT ON MY CHILDHOOD and upbringing, I can see clearly that my parents already had their own plans to make sure I received a gifted public school education. While my parents are educated in multiple ways—both formally and in terms of global life experiences—we were not a rich family. Our financial scarcity, along with my parents' political beliefs in the importance and value of public education (my mom and dad were educated in the public schools of Chicago and Philadelphia, respectively), made them aggressively seek out and customize the best public school education. They planned, strategized, and pulled on every resource they could to avoid sending me to our regular neighborhood school. They were keenly aware of the damage that poorly resourced and neglected schools could do to their sensitive little girl. They were keenly aware that such schools often become magnets for the worse symptoms of the kind of social and economic deprivation that impedes academic progress (Barton & Coley, 2010). What my parents did, however, was enroll me in all the early education and head-start programs they could find starting when I was as young as eighteen months old. They understood the value of stimulating and awakening me during those early formative years. When it was time to enroll me in elementary school, they found a great public school in South Philadelphia called Thomas Durham School. It was at Durham that my teacher observed my academic talents and referred me to the school's Mentally Gifted, or MG, program.

Even when my parents separated and my mom and I moved to a different neighborhood far from Durham, they were adamant that I would not go to the local school in our new Germantown neighborhood. The neighborhood school, John Wister Elementary School, was a notoriously underperforming school. Even though they could not afford it, they enrolled me, briefly, in what they called a "hippy-styled" private school called The Miquon School on the outskirts of Philadelphia while they continued to search for other desirable public school alternatives. There were no charter schools then, so they needed to search and strategize anew how I was going to get the quality public education they so strongly believed in.

Miquon was a unique school with a slightly eccentric approach to academic and social learning. There were few students of color at the school, but it definitely offered a top-rate private education, and our close family friends had a son who had graduated from the school years earlier. Besides the cost and the long distance from my home (I had an excruciatingly long daily bus ride to Conshohocken, Pennsylvania), the school was a bit too unstructured and unorthodox for my parents' and my tastes. It felt like a completely unstructured learning environment geared toward students who did not function well in the traditional classroom. But that was not my learning experience. I liked the routine and rhythm of the classrooms I had been in previously—I just needed the activities to be interesting, engaging, stimulating, and challenging and the social atmosphere to be stable and non-threatening. The MG program in the Philadelphia Public Schools offered that to me.

Luckily, due to our family's connection to one of the members of the Philadelphia City Council, I was soon admitted to one of the city's top public schools. John Story Jenks School was nestled in the heart of Chestnut Hill—one of the city's prestigious neighborhoods. While the neighborhood was close to 100 percent White and upper middle class, the student body of Jenks was notably more diverse, due in part to students coming from the surrounding Mt. Airy and upper Germantown neighborhoods that were more diverse than Chestnut Hill.

I realize that it was a privilege for my family to have certain connections and, quite simply, the fortitude to exploit so many educational options and alternatives. In a perverse way, we had to seek out privileges to offset our lack of economic and racial privilege. We had to find a way through the jungle of post-*Brown v. Board of Education* de facto segregation in urban education in order to ensure my future success. (See Johnson, 2010, for a review of research on the impact of neighborhood dynamics on the academic success of Black students.)

The Formative Years

Free the child's potential, and you will
transform him into the world.

—*Maria Montessori*

I LOVED MY EXPERIENCE AT JENKS. I was immediately admitted into the MG program at Jenks after they received my records from Durham. Even though I started the school mid-year in the fourth grade, I was placed in Mrs. Rosenthal's split fourth/fifth grade class. I was one of the younger students in the class, but it took me only a short while to feel mostly at home. Rosenthal as a bit over the top and dramatic, but I had no problems with her or being in her class. Within a month, I met my BFF (best friend forever), with whom I would matriculate through my high school and undergraduate years. The following year my BFF and I were placed in Mrs. Young's science class where we became more curious about the natural world by dissecting frogs and worms and writing weekly about scientific current events.

While still in the fourth grade, I was assigned to Mrs. Robinson, an older Black woman who exuded a calm, peaceful spirit, for my MG class. Several times per week, I would leave my regular class and participate in advanced special projects and trips with a small group of students who were also identified as gifted. We went on field trips to museums, to see musicals, and to hear lectures at organizations such as WOAR (Women Organized Against Rape)—pretty heavy for nine- and ten-year-olds. We did architecture projects, social studies group discussions, and art sketching. We toyed with new ways to understand math and explored interesting books and stories that helped us develop a love of reading. I joined the orchestra where I played second violin and the theater club that allowed me to act in several school plays, including one role as the musician Prince in a comical adaptation of *Pinocchio*.

Everything we did in MG seemed to dovetail seamlessly with my parents' vision and efforts to educate me. I frequently took weekend trips with my mom or dad to art exhibitions or the local horticultural center. I helped my grandmother in her community garden and with her homemade soap-making business. I attended graduate classes individually with both of my parents. I took piano music lessons with my uncle who was a trained music teacher and drove with family friends to New York where I saw ballets (including pieces choreographed by acclaimed Cuban ballerina Alicia Alonso) and Broadway plays and sampled different ethnic foods, such as Japanese tempura and Indian dahl. I was beginning to see myself as truly of and in the world at large. In *Beloved*, Toni Morrison wrote, regarding the character Baby Sugg:

> And no matter, for the sadness was at her center, the desolated center where the self that was no self made its home . . . fact was she know more about them than she knew about herself, having never had the map to discover what she was like (140).

This passage has resonated with me for years. It is as if my parents once said to each other, "No. Our Nicole is going to know herself. She has to have a map to discover what she is like."

Self-identifying as a smart and gifted Black girl was beginning to be etched into my psyche and internalized as part of my core identity. That was a good thing because very soon I would face what seems to be a rite of passage for smart Black kids—bullying and teasing for being different or acting White (Peguero & Williams, 2013; Wildhagen, 2011). I did not get teased as badly as a few other students, but I was targeted enough to know I didn't want or enjoy this kind of attention. Taking public transportation to and from school exposed me to some of the ills from which my parents were trying to shield me. Sexualized catcalls from grown men, who viewed young girls as fair game for their lustful desires, and incessant teasing from other neighborhood children, who didn't know what to make of a shy girl walking alone from the bus stop carrying a large backpack and violin case, were part of my indoctrination into the harsh realities of an urban America shaped by persistent structural racism and sexism.

There were also overt and covert incidents of racism in the Chestnut Hill neighborhood where I attended school. My best friend and I were jeered by shouts of "niggers" by a group of teens riding by the bus stop. We often received suspicious looks from some of the clerks and owners at the shops we frequented to buy candy and trinkets after school. Being cheerful, innocent kids we mostly brushed off these incidents. Unlike many children before and after us who dealt with much harsher environments, we still experienced a general sense of safety and security. Part of my buffer was a firm knowledge and sense of self and race consciousness. Race consciousness shielded me from overt bigotry and internalized self-hatred, from people who laughed at our family's African art, and classmates whose parents did not allow them to attend my birthday party because it was held at my dad's house in the heart of the North Philly "hood" (now a gentrified area in which people are rushing to buy houses). My ideas about the world were bigger and more complex. Sneers from racists and taunts from peers were not completely erased, but those incidents took a backseat to my own evolving map of myself.

A Picture of Giftedness

THERE ARE MANY ACCOUNTS of what the gifted child looks like and how and what the gifted adult becomes. A few that resonate with me are related to the characteristic of multiplicities, sensitivity, and inner focus. According to psychologist Dierdre Lovecky (1992), some of the common social and emotional traits of giftedness include divergent thinking ability, sensitivity, excitability, perceptiveness, and entelechy (a unique type of motivation, self-determination, and inner strength). I've always possessed a deep philosophical curiosity about concepts, ideas, people, and events. I often felt that others thought these varied issues were not significant, not interesting, or just plain weird. But to me, they were topics that were always fascinating and interconnected. As I grew up, I developed a way of hiding my passions and keeping what really mattered to myself. It was a tactic to protect my interests and sensibilities, which were starting to feel different from those of many other children—and adults—in my circle. For example, I was very curious about how people in other countries lived and felt protective of respecting ethnic/racial differences and traditional practices and values. I would become deeply offended when my friends or schoolmates used anti-African and anti-Asian slurs, such as "African booty scratcher" or "Chink." At the same time, I had a deep understanding of why other kids internalized and expressed such oppressive sentiments, even before I had the intellectual framework to articulate my analysis or critique.

The other socio-emotional aspects of giftedness that I can relate to are being able to embrace and negotiate seeming contradictions, uncertainty, and ambiguity. I believe these qualities significantly shaped my life trajectory and career choice. Practices and concepts that others might see as being completely different and diametrically opposed to each other—such as being both a practicing Muslim and a feminist or being an activist and respecting and adhering to traditional practices and values—actually complement and easily evolve together when you can deal with ambiguity and opposition.

Of course, I did not always have a metacognitive awareness of giftedness, but as I mentioned earlier I always had a profound connection to myself. However, it has always felt like a dual-edged sword—a blessing and a curse—to feel very aware of myself and by extension aware of my disconnection from those around me. I often felt that I was extremely different from my peers in the depth and breadth of my interests. Many contemporary psychologists and theorists might call such belief in one's uniqueness and specialness merely a reflection of the generational narcissism of children who grew up in the 1980s (Konrath, O'Brien, & Hsing, 2010; Miller, 1997). But indeed, that may be a part of what giftedness as manifested in contemporary educational settings is about—reinforcing a division between the majority of students deemed to be just ordinary or normal intellectually and those children and students who are labeled academically and intellectually "special" or "talented" (see

Fisher's [1980] discussion of the effects of labeling on gifted children and their families). But for a young Black girl in the Philadelphia Public Schools, it is really such a bad thing to have that label and sense of specialness, confidence, and exceptionality. Despite the popular mantras decrying the rise in narcissism, I am arguing that the presence of a little more of the non-malignant upside of the narcissistic impulse, that is, an assertion of one's self and identity, is a positive development for urban Black girls.

I would describe my own dilemma as a child as being an insider to myself but feeling like an outsider to others. Looking back, I see that my perception was less aligned with reality. I had lots of friends in school and got along well with my immediate and extended family. But I also appreciate now how that perception set the stage to develop into an observer of people, situations, and outsiders. I really wanted to understand people, even if I didn't quite feel that they understood me. My growing comfort with empathy would propel me into a career as a clinical psychologist and develop in me a passion for international travel and exploration. Paradoxically, feeling out of place pushed me into the world. My strange relationships with people made me want to know and understand them on multiple levels and in various environments.

In short, my experience of being a gifted child was not only intellectual; it was also social and emotional. I was always stimulated by seemingly conflicting ideas and have been able to manage many interests and talents, even in the face of pressure to focus on one area or to stop being so flighty. I experienced feeling both very connected to and very isolated from others and being both invigorated and a bit overwhelmed by all the ideas, pursuits, and understandings that I truly love in life.

Early Activism and Social Development

IN THE SAME WAY THAT VENUS AND SERENA Williams's parents devised and carried out a plan to raise tennis stars, my parents and family were very strategic about raising a gifted child who would be engaged by and immersed in the world at large. Instead of weekly sports lessons, my parents exposed me to constant critical analysis and community activism. But like most parents, mine certainly made some missteps, like the time when I was eight years old and my dad gave me the biography of a Black labor leader to read, minus any explanation or background.

The problem was that it read like a graduate school text and I had no clue of the context or meaning of what I was reading. For a little while I thought something was wrong with me because I did not understand it, but I was afraid to reveal my shortcoming to my dad.

I attended community and political-strategy meetings in which my father was heavily involved, and I accompanied my mom and dad to rallies and marches for a variety of racial, economic, and international social-justice issues. In my family, this was just par for the course, and as a result, as an adult, I often sought out study groups and grassroots organizations in the different places where I lived as a way to connect with the people around me. As a child I was a regular at rallies and protests in New York, in Washington, DC, and at the Parkway and City Hall in Philadelphia.

The activism extended to the home classroom as well. Once, when the Philadelphia schools were on strike for several weeks, my mom homeschooled me and a few other neighborhood children so we wouldn't fall behind. Besides our daily dose of math, science, and language, we also had a racial and economic social-justice module. One of the most memorable activities was writing letters to then Republican President Ronald Reagan to ask why he was making cuts to needed social programs to poor communities. Imagine the sense of voice, agency, and empowerment a little girl develops when she writes to challenge the president.

My parents ensured the arts were also part of my education, such as in journeys to the Philadelphia Art Museum to see the latest Picasso exhibit or the Academy of Music to watch the ballet classic *The Nutcracker*. We also saw shows such as the Black musical theatre classic *Your Arms Too Short to Box with God*, and went to the Dell Music Center to see Stevie Wonder live in concert and participate in a community African dance theater ensemble. All this cultural and artistic exposure helped to balance my awareness of social justice and injustice with an equal focus on how the arts and culture are vital for holistic development. The foundation had been set to personify what theorist William Cross termed the internalization-commitment stage of racial identity development, where individuals fully appreciate their own identity while committing to advance equality and justice for their own group and in the broader society (Cross, 1971).

I participated in summer programs such as a summer internship at a highly ranked chemistry research lab at the University of Pennsylvania and a two-month summer business program at the University of Pennsylvania's Wharton School of Business where my White peers were surprised when I won first prize in an essay contest at the end of the program. I shadowed lawyers in courtrooms at Philadelphia City Hall and was active in the local Youth Are Resources (YAR) organization. The wisdom of my parents involving me in so many different activities was that I came out of my shell, I overcame some of my shyness, and I began to feel as if I could belong and excel in almost any environment.

I also acknowledge the mostly unspoken yet powerful role and impact of a family history of valuing and embodying education on both sides of my family. My maternal great-grandmother and maternal and paternal grandmothers finished high school and encouraged their children to do the same and go farther. My paternal grandfather came to the United States from the Cape Verde Islands (off the West Coast of Africa) via a brutal thirty-day boat journey with his parents and siblings. Education was always at the core of the values that he passed down to his children. My paternal uncle earned a master's degree and was a lifelong educator, my father earned a PhD in sociology, and my mother worked and completed her bachelor's and master's degrees while I was a child. What a path, what an example they laid for me.

International Leanings

> If I do not love the world—if I do not love life—if I do
> not love people—I cannot
> enter into dialogue.
>
> —*Paulo Freire*

MY FAMILY ALWAYS TALKED TO and about me in relation to the larger world. I remember my dad telling about his travels to Somalia, Cuba, South Africa, and other countries as part of his political organizing work. I remember my mom recounting stories of traveling to the World Youth Festival in Germany while she was seven months pregnant with me. When I was still a small girl, my grandmother had long-term visitors from London (a "Black Brit" as our guest called herself) and Zimbabwe (a textile artist who was doing a residency in the United States) staying at her house, exposing me to diversity in a way that no books or school curricula could come close to doing. My doll collection reflected a significant coverage of the 195 or so countries in the world, including dolls my parents bought on their travels or ones they sought out to give me a glimpse of the globe.

The height of this emphasis on internationalism came when my dad announced that he and my mom had signed me up for an international children's camp in what was then the USSR (Soviet Union). I was afraid when they told me I was going to take a plane from New York to Moscow with a group of children who also had activist parents. I worried that the plane would be hijacked or, worse, that my friends would think I was a weirdo for having parents that would send me to such a far-off place that my peers either had never heard of or had heard of only as the heart of "evil communism." But off I went. I stayed for five weeks and traveled from Moscow to the towns of Sevastopol and Yalta off the Black Sea interacting with children literally from all over the world.

As scary as the trip was initially, it ended up being one of the formative and most influential experiences of my young life. I learned in firsthand detail about apartheid in South Africa and the civil war in Nicaragua. I encountered the vast diversity of African peoples and cultures when I met kids from Ethiopia, Nigeria, Algeria, and Guinea. I was also confronted with the nasty underbelly of racial stereotyping when a couple of the White American kids in our group sarcastically asked if I had a boyfriend and joked that if I did he must be a basketball player. As isolated and embarrassed as I felt when the other members of our delegation, including Black kids, laughed and mocked me, I learned a valuable lesson in how to exude confidence and navigate others' ignorance and arrogance. Soon after I returned home, I started high school at the Philadelphia High School for Girls. I transitioned easily into honors and eventually AP classes at the prestigious and only public high school for girls in the country. My understated confidence and self-awareness also helped me to flourish socially.

On Becoming: Giftedness as an Adult

From my present vantage point, I can see clearly how my career path was also determined by my exposure to gifted education and the other gifted adults in my life. All the travel, arts trips, math, science, and civic ideals I encountered over the years developed into a keen interest in human development and the human condition. My uncle's best friend was a Black male clinical psychologist—one of a small number in the United States. My talks with him while I was a high school student further informed my interest in the scientific study of human behavior and mental processes. I knew early on that I would eventually pursue and attain a PhD in psychology. As I matriculated through school, I had an unconscious understanding that international travel and living would play an important role in my career development. Following in my mother's footsteps, I traveled to the World Youth Festival in Cuba while I was in graduate school and gained invaluable insights into race, racism, and anti-racism. I was part of the first group of students in my clinical psychology PhD program that participated in an international internship in Grenada, West Indies. I even carved out a little time during graduate school to travel to Guinea, West Africa, and Japan to study and perform with different African dance groups.

Then, to no one's surprise but many people's confusion, I applied for a prestigious fellowship (the National Security Education Program's David L. Boren Fellowship) to conduct dissertation research on the conceptualization of mental illness in Ethiopia. While living in Ethiopia to collect data for my research, I traveled all over the country and to neighboring Sudan and nearby Egypt by myself. Everyone at home thought I was nuts and worried about my going alone to chaotic and possibly terrorist states. I laughed at the idea, thinking how they were missing out on the elaborate weddings and tea parties I was enjoying in North Africa. Later, as a professional psychologist, I became involved in clinical and advocacy work with marginalized and underserved urban populations and refugees and asylum-seekers from different countries. I realize that I had created a bridge to my earlier educational and social roots. I ended up doing work in places such as Peru, Liberia, Italy, Haiti, and Senegal and presenting at international conferences in Argentina, China, and Egypt.

Eventually, I took the plunge to work abroad full-time as a psychologist, first in Bahrain and then in Botswana. I ended up being in Bahrain at the height of the Arab Spring when protests were sweeping across the Arab world. Bahrain was the only one of the oil-rich gulf countries that experienced a sustained uprising from the population. Accessible from Saudi Arabia by car, Bahrain is a small country with a population just over a million with a majority Shi'a populace ruled by a minority Sunni royal family. The political tensions erupted into full-fledged protests and a social movement. Interestingly, I witnessed much of this unfold very close to where I was living and even where I was working. The largest of the protests was about three miles from my house, and I could hear all the early-morning tear-gassing and hand and gun battles between security forces and protestors. I was nervous at times because I did not fully understand all the dynamics and how to accurately judge my safety and security in such a heightened situation, but my instincts, common sense, and experience protected me as well as helped me to study and learn firsthand about the political, social, and cultural climate of the modern Middle East.

As much I was heavily impacted by the early influences of my family and school environment, I have always been one to chart and follow my own course. From religious practice to marriage, from travel to professional development, it has always been easy to unapologetically traverse the path through life I had selected. I proudly walked the halls of Howard University, University of Virginia, Columbia University, Washington School of Psychiatry, Harvard Program in Refugee Trauma, and other places. I always felt I had something to offer in each of them because I had the map to discover what I was like.

Continuing the tradition of fostering giftedness through global citizenship, my daughter (now three years old) had traveled to Bahrain, the villages and cities of Senegal, London, Botswana, and Zimbabwe by the time she was two years old. Her first preschool experience was at an international Montessori school in Botswana, and her first caretaker was a Zimbabwean woman. Family memories and traditions run deep.

My journey from a gifted young girl to a self-assured gifted woman has been defined by Black giftedness, global exposure, and global citizenship. My sense of global citizenship was instilled early in my life and deliberately by my parents. It was also a path that I embraced and developed on my own when I began to decide who and what I wanted to be in life. My experiences shaped and finely tuned my worldview, which in turn helped me to become compassionate, open-minded, and balanced both personally and professionally. And isn't that what we hope for for our children—that their gifts and talents coalesce and allow them to contribute fully to their communities, society, and humanity? Finally, I hope that my story illustrates a model for how inculcating young people with a sense of a global citizenship is actually an effective intervention that can be applied more widely in Black communities and can serve as a potential paradigm shift for the lives of young, Black girls and boys in America.

Practical Implications and Recommendations

- *Being Deliberate and Conscientious:* It is clear from my account that mine is not a rags-to-riches story, nor is it a story of a child from great financial means breezing through school. It is, however, an account of the ways that deliberateness and conscientiousness about how to educate one's child can lead to positive short-term and long-term academic, social, and emotional rewards for the child. Parents have enormous power in shaping their children's education. Being aware and empowering themselves is an important first step in exposing their children to gifted education (either inside or outside the classroom).

- *Culture, Narrative and Identity:* Building a strong, culturally relevant individual, family, and community narrative is another essential component. Most good early education programs emphasize teaching a child early on about herself—her identity, her history, her culture. My parents understood that no school or formal educational setting could replace their influence in educating me outside the classroom and instilling my identity. When parents arm their children with a positive sense of self connected to the larger community and world, they actually equip their children with long-lasting life skills, resilience, and coping abilities.

- *Involvement and Empowerment:* Elite schools are not the only option for a good gifted education. While my experience of attending some of the best public schools in Philadelphia may not be typical, particularly for students of color, there are still options that may include select charter schools, community education collectives, and selective public schools. Ultimately, structural change in urban school systems is needed. Pedagogy that fosters holistic child development, safe and stimulating learning environments, and enlightened discovery would benefit gifted and non-gifted students alike. For parents, involvement in advocacy to improve schools can lead to increased parental empowerment and eventually better educational outcomes for their own children. As one of my mentors once asked, "What do we miss out on by not challenging the status quo?"

> No one is born fully-formed: it is through
> self-experience in the world that we become what we
> are.
>
> —*Paulo Freire*

References

Barton, P. E., & Coley, R. J. (2010). *The Black-White achievement gap: When progress stopped. Policy information report.* Princeton, NJ: Educational Testing Service.

Cross, W. E. (1971). The Negro-to-black conversion experience. *Black World 20(9),* 13–27.

Fisher, E. (1980). The effect of labeling on gifted children and their families. *Roeper Review, 3*(3), 49–51.

Freire, P. (1970). *Pedagogy of the oppressed.* New York: Herder and Herder.

Ford, D. Y. (2013). *Recruiting and retaining culturally different students in gifted education.* Waco, TX: Prufrock Press.

Freire, P. (2000). *Pedagogy of the oppressed, 30th anniversary edition.* New York: Bloomsbury Academic.

Johnson, O. (2010). Assessing neighborhood racial segregation and macroeconomic effects in the education of African Americans. *Review of Educational Research, 80*(4), 527–575.

Konrath, S. H., O'Brien, E. H., & Hsing, C. (2010). Changes in dispositional empathy in American college students over time: A meta-analysis. *Personality and Social Psychology Review, 15*(2), 180–198.

Lovecky, D. V. (1992). Exploring social and emotional aspects of giftedness in children. *Roeper Review, 15*(1), 18–25.

Miller, A. (1997). *The drama of the gifted child: The search for the true self.* New York: Basic Books.

Morrison, T. (1987). *Beloved.* New York: Vintage Books.

Peguero, A. A., & Williams, L. M. (2013). Racial and ethnic stereotypes and bullying victimization. *Youth & Society, 45*(4), 545–564.

Wildhagen, T. (2011). What's oppositional culture got to do with it? Moving beyond the strong version of the acting White hypothesis. *Sociological Perspectives, 54*(3), 403–430.

CHAPTER 13

Becoming the Sun
from a Firefly!

Rugvedita Parakh, MBBS, MD

IN THE FOLLOWING CHAPTER, the reader will discover that comparing culturally diverse individuals from across the globe should be viewed as comparing not apples to oranges but, rather, Fuji to Gala apples.

Giftedness in Youth

LOOKING BACK ON A TIME in your youth, can you share an experience or two that validated your exceptional qualities? This could be at home, school, community, among friends, etc.

My mom tells a story that when I was three years old, she asked me to fetch some medicine from my father's home-based clinic. She described the box—dark green with a black cap—and told me to remember that the label read "Paracetamol, P-A- R," she said, spelling out the first few letters. She was confident I would perfectly locate the right box even though it was among many that looked similar. She was the only one who wasn't surprised when I brought her the right one. Everyone one else looked on in awe. My mom says she knew I was sharper and brighter than most kids my age. Later in grades four and seven, I was selected among the top thirty children in the district that were awarded scholarships based on their performance on a test similar to an IQ test.

Based on what you know about your childhood, who first recognized that you were a gifted or exceptional child?

I believe my mother first recognized I was not feeling challenged enough with the regular classroom teaching. They kept pushing me to study along with children who were a few grades ahead of me.

Were you ever told your IQ? If so, how do you feel about knowing what it is?

I grew up in rural India where formal testing of IQ was neither readily available nor usually done. At the time, my academic world was limited to my school, where test scores and ranks of all children were published. Since I was routinely ranked among the top students in the class, I did not think much about it. I was also lucky to have had other gifted students in my class—some of my classmates have also received global and national recognitions—so we have had a healthy competition amongst ourselves. Now that I know about the IQ tests, I feel that knowing my IQ would have helped me think about how I compared with not only my classmates but also children worldwide.

Please describe some classroom achievements, awards, or competitions that set you apart from other children. How was such recognition accepted by them, other parents, and the community?

As I was routinely ranked among the top students in the district, my parents and teachers kept pushing me to participate in extracurricular academic and non-academic activities. I have been awarded scholarships on the basis of tests conducted by the school district in grades four and seven, ranked among the top eleven students of 150,000 candidates by the state, received gold medals for achieving top ranks in my medical education at my university, and have received awards at leading global conferences. However, the acceptance of my achievements by my parents and their reactions are distinctly different.

My father is a surgeon who left opportunities to practice in top hospitals in big cities to serve rural and underdeveloped regions of the country. I believe he is an exceptionally gifted individual. His classmates and colleagues from schools, colleges, and his medical fraternity routinely tell stories of his academic excellence and brilliance in general. Not only was he invited to medical conferences around the world, but he was also asked by top celebrities in India to make meaningful contributions to various non-academic activities ranging from cinema production to politics. He is also a poet! Whenever I communicate the news of any of my achievements to my father, he simply smiles and asks me whether I'm happy and how I'm using my ability to make a meaningful contribution to the society and the world.

My mother is an economics graduate who gave up city life and comfort to support my father. She paid close attention to my academic performance and would often push me to achieve higher ranks or grades. If I scored ninety-nine points out of one hundred, she would make me realize that I missed one point and that I should correct my learning. I also recall that when I was in grade seven, on one of the geometry tests, we had to divide a line into three equal parts. The textbook had showed only one method to do so. I used another method. My teacher gave me zero points. When my mom saw that my teacher did not grade my answer correctly, she went to the school to push the teacher to expand his understanding of the concepts.

My parents definitely celebrate my achievements, but at the same time, they make sure my focus is on learning and using the education to make a meaningful contribution to society.

As a highly gifted/highly bright child, were all your classroom experiences with teachers positive? If so, please describe the experience that stands out the most today. You may also describe negative experiences.

My classroom had the brightest students in the school district. One of my classmates went on to win the top prize in the world in mathematics; another classmate has a number of patents on bio-medical instruments credited to his name; and yet another is a leading businessman. Most of my teachers were passionately devoted to teaching. As a result, teachers had their favorite students. I recall once that my classmate friend was ranked higher than I was on an exam. (He scored a few points higher in mathematics.) My biology teacher felt sad; she bought an advanced mathematics book from her meager salary and came to our home to give it to me. She had tears in her eyes. I remember consoling her and promising her that I would do better next time.

Since my school was in a rural part of the country, some of the teachers were not experts in their subjects. For example, a Hindi teacher was not always a native Hindi speaker. At our home, however, we spoke three languages—Hindi with my mom's side of the family, Marathi among the siblings, and Marwari with parents and grandparents. When Hindi was introduced as a subject in grade five, it wasn't new to me. In one of the poems we studied, a Hindi word, *jugnu*, was used. It means firefly, but my Hindi teacher thought it meant peacock. I argued with my teacher about the meaning until finally he asked me to prove I was right. This was the pre-Internet era, so I went to the library to get a book that would clarify the meaning of jugnu. My teacher admitted that I was right. Leaving his ego aside, he explained to the whole class that jugnu did, indeed, mean firefly.

I was fortunate to have had such dedicated teachers in my school. As a result and over time, my school became one of the most sought-after schools in the town.

Fitting In/Social Isolation

Please describe experiences where you may have felt like an outsider or socially isolated from your young age-mates/peers because of your exceptionalities or how you preferred to spend your time.

I loved reading books. One of the first books I read before I began school was a biography on Abraham Carver. The book completely moved me and has influenced me in my life. I realized early in life that being different—whether because of race, gender, nationality, or for any other reason—meant facing discrimination and possibly even social isolation. As I had to wear glasses, I looked like a nerd. As I spent more time with books than with other children, I was often teased by other girls in the class for not being interested in the latest fashion trends or for not being interested in gossip.

My mother was a homemaker, but she was a lateral thinker. She spent more on our development than on her clothes or jewelry. She went years without buying new sarees, but she made sure that we were learning right things and looking at things from different perspectives. My mother used to tell me that I should never worry about pleasing others and should be comfortable with being myself. She would often say, "A lion lives alone with its family, not in a herd, and yet it's the king of the jungle—those who are in herds are sheep. Become the king! Seek to be powerful within. Be fearless." It was possibly my resulting confidence that got me elected as class president (and best looking) later in university.

Bullying is always problematic whether one is a child or an adult. Were you ever bullied in school because of your high intelligence? If so, how did you manage to stand strong and accomplish your schoolwork? Please feel comfortable sharing an experience.

I grew up in a large joint family. My parents, siblings, grandparents, uncles, and cousins all lived under one roof. It was a household full of ten children, all competing and fighting for limited resources and limited attention. At extended family gatherings, the number of children would grow to over twenty-five. In my family, my older brothers were five to six years older than I was, and they were high achievers—top schools, scholarships, top ranks, and high grades. They'd often throw tough challenges at me, such as solving Rubik's Cubes, running fast, or figuring out complex concepts. Dealing with the kids in school was much easier. Moreover, my parents were of great support. I quickly learned not only how to deal with bullies but also how to protect other girls in the class from bullies. I recall an instance when I was troubled by some kids who snatched my lunch box and tried to demean me, but then my parents asked me to think about a scenario in which a strong girl would defend such attacks in a graceful way. I could recall the book *Little Women*. Thanks to my reading about different scenarios and interacting with a number of children in my immediate and extended joint family, I learned to defend myself, either by taking help from friends and teachers or distracting the bullies, confronting them, or even ignoring them.

As a gifted child, did you have a role model, and that is, someone whom you looked up to and believed you could achieve as much as? Where is this person today and have you shared your successes with him or her?

My father has been my role model. As a curious child, I often accompanied him and saw him tend to medical emergencies and even make house visits at odd hours and in remote places. Even though he practiced in a small town, he regularly acquired the latest skills to bring new techniques to his practice, such as the endoscopic surgery. My father is highly respected, not only in the town but also in the whole region. He brought together other medical professionals in the region to solve critical problems by setting up a non-profit blood bank and a free tuberculosis-and-AIDS treatment center. Being a witness to my father's work, I had the opportunity to see firsthand how a devoted doctor can touch many lives and transform communities. He has also contributed to reviving theatre and drama in the region, helped production of movies in the regional language, successfully led election campaigns, and raised funds to rehabilitate people struck by natural calamities, such as earthquakes. He lives a simple yet purposeful life, full of rich memories and varied experiences. He is a constant source of inspiration for me as I share my accomplishments and successes with him. It's a great feeling of unparalleled joy and happiness when I see him talk about me to others with pride.

Have you ever felt that your giftedness was misinterpreted or discounted because of racism, classism, or some other factor?

As a child who spent more time with books than with people, I felt that whenever I asked my teachers or other members of society difficult questions, they felt I was being too direct. Some even labeled me a rebel. I was unwilling to accept rules and regulations blindly without questioning the rationale behind them. Sometimes I had to pay the price for confronting such norms that I did not agree with by not getting the grades, awards, recognition, or ranks that I deserved. Once, at a cultural event, I had prepared a short play based on Abraham Lincoln's letter to his son's teacher. The main purpose was to bring together the girls who wanted to perform but never got a chance to be on stage. This was because of a fixed pattern of selection of plays and students from one class. The teachers responsible for selecting the shows for the event discouraged me because it was competing with another routine show from my class; each class could submit only one entry. I contested and took up the issue with the principal. Everybody was initially upset with me, except my dad. He said, "You think ahead of today's times, and it will take a huge effort, but stay firm on your beliefs, and people will change." True enough, I did not win the trophy, but we got a standing ovation from the entire school after the performance.

From today's perspective, what are the major achievement obstacles for high-ability/gifted children who are racially, ethnically, or culturally different?

The major challenge for high-ability/gifted children that are racially, ethnically, or culturally different is the confusion caused by the pressure to assimilate with others and the necessity to foster their intellectual curiosity that questions conventional wisdom. In our society, there is much pressure to get along with others and appear normal. By the very definition, gifted children are not normal; their IQ is at least a standard deviation higher than the mean. Further, when they are racially, ethnically, or culturally different, it makes them feel further isolated. The family can play a crucial role in making the child believe in her individuality and become comfortable with who she is. My grandparents had migrated to the region from another state; we spoke a different language, ate different food, celebrated different festivals, and my grandparents even dressed differently from most others. At school, I was often teased for being different, yet my parents and family put things in the proper perspective. Even though my parents had limited financial resources, they made sure we travelled to different parts of the country to realize how what's considered abnormal in one place is considered normal in another. They taught us that being different is not necessarily bad.

Family Life

WHAT WAS THE SINGLE MOST important lesson you learned from a family member that you too will pass along (or are presently passing along) to your children or others if you do not have children?

The most important lesson I have learned from my father is how to bounce back and achieve success, even in face of extreme adversity. I was in grade twelve when my mother met with a severe accident. She was hospitalized. My father was the only earning member of the family, and his medical practice suffered as he had to look after my mother and pay her medical bills. He had no savings, as he had only recently left the joint family, giving away his entire life's earnings to his brothers who had suffered major business setbacks. My father discussed the challenges in a calm and composed manner with me and came out with solutions to address each day's problems. Finally, my mother miraculously recovered, and my father was able to pay off the medical bills, as well as college fees for my brothers and me. I accompanied my father and helped take care of my mother while studying for my grade twelve exams, on which I scored among the top eleven out of 150,000 students. The most important lesson I want my children to learn is to face unforeseen challenges, digest failures, and spring back in the face of extreme adversity.

From your adult perspective, what role did your parents play in nurturing your gifts and talents?

I became fond of reading, and my parents encouraged me to read. My father brought me translated books from different cultures, such as Russia, Korea, etc., and my mother encouraged me to read books on varied topics. She even gave me cuttings of interesting articles from newspapers. With reading came curiosity, and I was quite vocal in asking questions and expressing my opinions. My parents encouraged me to argue, debate, and participate in various competitions. Among three siblings, I was the youngest and the only girl child. In rural India, girls were often discouraged from speaking up, but my parents always treated me equally and encouraged me to stand up for my beliefs. When I was presented with stressful situations or preparing for critical exams, my father was my firm support. He would even stay up all night only to give me company. My parents taught me to digest failures sportingly and even bounce back to achieve success in face of adversity. Thus, my parents have been role models, guides, and conduits to sources of knowledge and opportunity.

Please describe your family of origin and how you all spent your time together when schooling was not involved. Were there family socioeconomic challenges? If so, how did these impact your future life choices?

My grandfather migrated from Rajasthan to Maharashtra when he was only twelve years old. He had lost his parents and had no family support. Working as a porter at an early age, he was an honest and hardworking businessman who went on to establish various businesses, such as a textile factory, trading company, tile factory, and construction company. Against the convention in typical Marwari business families, he encouraged my father to study and become a doctor. However, after my grandfather retired, my uncles could not manage the businesses properly, and our family ran into financial troubles; our joint family house had to be mortgaged. Under the economic stress, our joint family broke into nuclear families. My parents had to leave the house and live in my father's small clinic, which became our house. Suddenly, we had no TV, refrigerator, car, etc.

My parents showed us how it doesn't take a lot of money to enjoy life! They would spend time with us to share their perspectives, tell us stories, celebrate little occasions, and build memories. When we came home from school, my mother and brothers would play interesting educational and recreational games with me. My parents also took time each year during the holidays to take family vacations to different parts of the country. My parents believed in giving us the basic framework of being good citizens in life, but encouraged us to follow whatever interested us in our careers. My life became rich and full of varied experiences as a result.

Based on your experiences, what do you believe all parents and teachers should do to support their gifted children? What shouldn't they do?

Gifted children are not normal, and the parents and teachers should avoid forcing them to fit the mold and should instead teach them to become comfortable with who they are. My seven-year-old daughter has been selected in the 2E gifted program. She is a child of Indian origin in an American school. I encourage her to learn about different cultures and teach others about the Indian culture. Now she asks me to dress her in sarees or traditional Indian clothes at the school's cultural events! Parents and teachers must also encourage the gifted children to freely explore areas of their liking and stimulate the intellectual curiosity of children. Parents and teachers must spend more time with gifted children and guide them through emotional ups and downs.

Motivations

WHAT MOTIVATED YOU to achieve at a very high level as a child, and has this changed now in your adulthood?

As a child, I heard stories about how my parents had been high achievers, and then I saw my brother do well in school. Early in life, I felt I wanted to do well, like my parents and brothers, and I found it was quite easy to do so. As I grew up, the competition in India became intense; stakes were high. I had witnessed how my father's education helped us overcome financial difficulties. My parents had shown me how material possessions could be lost, but nobody could steal the wealth of the knowledge one possesses.

As a merit rank holder, I was among the few fortunate students in India who could choose any field of study. My brothers said they chose engineering and management careers because they thought that a doctor's life would be tough—working hard and dealing with the sufferings of others. I disagreed. I always found it interesting to talk to patients at our clinic and enjoyed staying up late at night to study. I always thought becoming a doctor would be immensely satisfying, as I had seen how doctors shoulder the responsibility of looking after the health of the society and the society in turn respects doctors. Patients put tremendous faith in doctors, and doctors make a direct impact on people's lives. I was further fascinated by the field of medicine because it is a student's paradise and I enjoy learning. In the field of medicine, each case is an opportunity to learn and then apply what has been learned. Moreover, going into medicine was also an opportunity to follow my dad's footsteps and make him proud. The choice was clear: I had to become a doctor.

The medicine programs in India provide a solid foundation of the basic subjects. For me, it was a great place to realize that I enjoyed pathology among all subjects. Early in medical school, I became fascinated by tissue diagnosis and the basics of pattern analysis. As I studied pathology more in depth, I could see myriads of research possibilities. Naturally, I received the gold medal in pathology and became eligible to apply for a pathology residency. Post-graduate training involves original research, which is best achieved through collaboration, creativity, and contemporary technology, for which US programs are best known. Therefore, I considered applying to the residency programs in the United States and signed up for the USMLE (United States Medical Licensing Examination). It was a personal challenge as I now had two children and had to compete with fresh graduates, but that was also a motivating factor. I'm now further excited and driven by the opportunity to do original research and make meaningful contributions to the field of pathology

To what extent are you motivated by challenges? Please explain.

I love challenges and find them motivating. I'm lucky to have a family that encourages me to take risks. My husband has an exceptionally high IQ, and so do my in-laws. They know I get motivated by challenges, so they push me even though they know it makes me anxious sometimes. They have always been a great source of support and inspiration.

Doing well on my USMLE exam was one such challenge. It is considered among the toughest exams in the world, and I needed a lot of preparation because I had been out of the academic environment for a long time. Moreover, I had to look after two children, my consulting work, and my family. I also wanted to get back in shape after having had my second child. My brother put it as a time-management challenge, said he would take me out for a nice dinner at a restaurant if I could find one hour every day for six months to work out at the gym. When I spoke with my husband, he pushed me to accept the challenge. He requested my in-laws come to the United States, and they were kind enough to do so—leave their comfortable lives in India for six months to look after my newborn and help me prepare for the USMLE. With their help, I was able to achieve my two goals—shed twenty pounds and score among the top 1 percent of the USMLE participants. I demanded that my brother take me out to the restaurant as promised. It was one of the toughest challenges I have undertaken, and I feel so proud and motivated that I keep asking my brother to set new challenges and goals for me.

What role does historical tradition or country of origin play on you selecting your current career?

Colonial India has provided an interesting twist to the educational system that exists in India even today. It introduced lucrative employment to the people who learn English and could take care of white-collar office work. The most secure, high-quality, and high-paying jobs were in medicine, engineering, mathematics, and law. To enjoy the political and socioeconomic power, the middle-class and lower-class mindsets were lured into this built-in educational hierarchy. Even as time progressed, the majority of educated people in India preferred jobs that were from the STEM fields, hence the cut-throat competition to get jobs and a huge emphasis on academic education, being gifted in a particular academic field, and total ignorance toward emotional intelligence. My family did not follow the set pattern, yet we siblings ended up being STEM graduates out of our genuine interests in the field.

PART V

Navigating Self:
To Belong or Not to Belong

CHAPTER 14

Unleashing the Fire: No Longer Ashamed of Being Gifted

April J. Lisbon, EdD

To be young, Black, female, and gifted in a predominantly White society can take its toll on the psychological, emotional, physical, and spiritual needs of the gifted child. Coupled with a lack of understanding of what it means to raise, nurture, and educate children who are identified as gifted, families and peers often find themselves becoming even more confused about executing best practices toward the gifted child of color. The confusion starts at the beginning, for current academic literature seemingly lacks consensus on defining what giftedness means. Renzulli (2011) suggested that gifted and talented individuals have "above-average general abilities, high levels of task commitment, and high levels of creativity" (87). Individuals identified as being gifted exemplify a unique quality of learning and development all on their own. Yet for some young students participating in gifted education programs, the experience can be quite lonely—especially if one's peers are unaware of the unique qualities that identify the student as gifted. Many gifted students might find themselves in a place where they stand out from their peers, as they simply do not fit the status quo at their age and grade level (Peterson, 2006). In essence, the intellectual processing of gifted students are vastly different from students with average ability. Therefore, gifted students are at greater risk of experiencing significant discomfort at school when they perceive that their peers, teachers, etc. are unaccepting of their unique talents and knowledge.

This chapter focuses on my life as a Black female who participated in gifted education programs. It is organized into three sections. The first gives a background and history: when I was identified, the gifted education program I participated in, and how this influenced my tween and teenage years. The second section shares my perceptions of myself as a young adult, hiding my giftedness in my twenties, chronicling my life as a graduate student, and then working as a professional in the field of school psychology. The final section centers on how I came to terms with myself as a gifted adult, learning to embrace my identity in my thirties.

Black, Gifted, and Loss of Identity

THE IRONY OF MY LONELINESS as a gifted child is that it is common condition in the academic literature on giftedness. The loss of identity experienced by gifted students, especially Blacks, is well-documented. According to Grantham and Ford (2003), Blacks who are identified as being gifted find it challenging to develop healthy self-concepts. More specifically, the authors concluded that "these students frequently face negative peer pressures relative to doing well in school; they are often accused of 'acting White'; and they are frequently alienated and isolated from Black and White students alike" (27). Moore, Ford, and Milner (2005) suggested that teachers must nurture friendships, feelings of safety, a sense of belonging, and identity in conjunction with challenging the gifted mind cognitively and academically. To focus only on the latter could mean that gifted students of color will perform below expectancy because of "the unique social and psychological issues they bring to educational settings related to their culture" (168). To be young, gifted, Black, and female can take an emotional toll on a person if she is not nurtured and cultivated properly. This is my story.

At the Beginning

I AM THE PRODUCT OF A SINGLE-PARENT HOUSEHOLD where my mother, a college-educated professional, worked tirelessly to support me in every area of my life. As a Black female, my mother struggled to find a job in her degree area, medical technology. She worked various jobs while on partial welfare. Even with all her personal trials, my mother always instilled in me the idea that in order to excel in life I needed two things—an education and good manners. I always tell people that I am a military child whose mother was not in the military.

Growing up, it seemed as if I was always living in a new location. Before the age of fifteen, I had already lived in New York, South Carolina, Connecticut, Florida, and the United States Virgin Islands (USVI). Constantly moving, I found it challenging to establish friendships, as I never knew when my next move would be. I attended nine schools (public, private, and parochial) from the ages of five to eighteen. Yet, despite my transient life, and perhaps because of my mother's resolve, education, especially reading, was something I excelled at.

I was *that* student—the one who knew she was smart, the one who would earn awards for academics and for citizenship. However, it was not until my sixth grade year, while attending my first public school in the USVI, I finally felt I was acknowledged as a smart student. My sixth grade teacher was as tough as nails, pushing me to excel. My mother's recollection of this time helped me better understand this critical period in my life. She shared that although I was not actively recruited for the gifted program at this school, my teacher always treated me as a gifted child, ensuring that my mind was always stimulated while moving through the curriculum. It was because of that teacher's belief in me, pushing me towards my highest potential, that I learned that it was okay to be bright.

After my sixth grade year, I moved to Charleston, South Carolina, for one year. It was there, at age twelve, that I was initially identified and invited to participate in a gifted education program. The Charleston County Public Schools (CCPS) Gifted and Talented program (GT) has since changed how students are identified; however, in the late 1980s, selection was not based solely on cognitive (IQ) tests.

I do not recall ever being pulled out of class to be evaluated for any types of programs. However, it doesn't mean I wasn't assessed. Most current models now rely on a range of assessments to determine gifted-ness. My mother and I do not have memories as to how selection choic-es were made. Based on the current standards and practices, combining high test scores, good grades, and a nomination from teachers, our best guess is that my reading skills, my seventh grade English teacher's rec-ommendation, and national normed tests determined that I qualified for admittance to the gifted program. During the time I was identi-fied as a gifted child, the pre-Internet age, the only way Black families were aware of gifted education or had knowledge of gifted education opportunities required them to rely on teacher advocacy, informal net-works, or other community resources (e.g., church) (Grantham, 2005; Olszewski-Kubilius, 2003). Not all Black families had such awareness. Unfortunately, depending on whether or not their child's school com-munity has a deficit-thinking mentality with regard to the identification of Black children in gifted programs, many parents/guardians even to-day may be unaware of how their child is—or can be—initially selected for gifted programs: "If a deficit orientation is present among educators, they may not communicate with minority families about gifted educa-tion services and opportunities" (Ford et al., 2001, 55). I am grateful that my teacher saw my potential and provided information about the gifted education opportunity at my school to my family and me.

Whatever the selection process that was in place at that time, I do vividly remember my seventh grade reading teacher telling me that I would be in a new class. While I loved reading and thought a new class with a reading focus would be lots of fun, I was conflicted. I had finally established a few peer relationships. Where would my friends go? Would they be coming with me, or would I have to make new friends once more? Initially, it was challenging. I was scared to start all over again making new friends. However, when I realized it was for one class and I still could see my friends in other classes, it made the move a little easier—or I thought it would.

I realized immediately that I was the only person of color in my gifted education group. It was a lonely experience. Most of the students had participated in the program for several years and had established friendships. I found it challenging to connect with some of my peers since I did not look or speak like them. This was the first time I recall feeling the only way I could fit in was to act White in my gifted class and Black when I returned to my regular classes. I changed my behaviors to meet the expectations I thought others had of me. As an adult, I can see I was a child who desperately wanted to be liked and, as a result, started to lose a sense of my own identity. Unfortunately this habit of downplaying my authentic self sabotaged who I was as a gifted student and person and has impacted me for more than twenty years after I was initially identified.

Tween to Teen Years: An Identity in Crisis

DESPITE THIS IDENTIFICATION AND RECOGNITION of my academic strengths, my tween to teen years were the toughest times in my development. I remember it as a time when the social debate centered on whether light-skinned Black girls or dark-skinned Black girls were prettier. As a "beautiful but didn't know it" chocolate-skinned sister, I always felt left behind in my social circles. Adding to my anxieties, I had a flat chest, a big butt, a Jheri curl, braces, and glasses. I was a nerd. Looking back, it was not a pretty combination.

My mother's drive to find the best schools or best opportunities meant that our constant moves impacted my peer relationships. Friendships were short-lived, and I learned not to get too close to people as I might not be at the school the following year. All my energies were focused on school and being ahead of everyone else. I think this drive, this sense of competition of me against everyone else, stemmed from the fact that I felt I was ugly.

The move to Charleston in 1987 was a transition not just from the United States Virgin Islands but also of families. My mom sent me to live with her sister and her three children. It was an interesting experience, as I went from being the only child to suddenly living in a house full of "siblings." I had no clue how to handle this change. I was used to being by myself. I was in a new place, and I had a new competitor—my big cousin, who was as smart as or smarter than I was. She was as sharp as a tack and very pretty with light-colored skin and long hair. People loved her. And we both attended the same middle school where she was a grade ahead of me.

During this time in middle school in Charleston, I was blessed to have a few girls befriend me, one of whom I've recently reconnected with through social media. Most of them had attended the same elementary schools, so their willingness to take in an awkward-looking girl and accept her as a part of their crew provided me with the social bond that I needed. I now had individuals to call my friends. We all had the same classes, and we were all smart (if not all gifted) and loved learning. I felt I had finally found my place in school.

While I initially thought the GT label would only place me in advanced English classes, in fact, my whole schedule changed And thus, my social circle changed with my classes. My usual set of friends, my crew, was not in the gifted program. Instead, I was in a class with several White girls whom I had never met before. So my way of fitting in with these smart White girls was to emulate their behavior. In short, my solution was to start acting White, even if it meant I was no longer representing my authentic Black self. Fordham and Ogbu (1986) indicated that Black students carry the burden of choosing to remain authentically true to their Black self or striving to be academically successful, which for some members of the Black community requires an individual to conform to White societal norms (Tyson, Darity, & Castellino, 2005). I chose the latter as I learned from my elders that if I wanted to be somebody, I had to work twice as hard in my life to get half as much as White folks. I had no other choice but to start mimicking their every move. I learned to better articulate standard English, walk like them, and watch some of the same television shows they liked in order to fit in. I even started to lie about my home life so it could appear to be as good materially if not better than their lives. If they lived in a beautiful home, our family lived in a mansion. If their parents had nice cars, we had several nice cars in the backyard. Whatever they had that my family didn't, I had no problems lying—I wanted to be accepted at any cost.

Of course, my lies could be discovered, causing me to give up even more of my identity. I remember when our teacher broke our class up into teams of two in order to create a major project based on a book we had read. My partner and I chose to act out *Charlotte's Web*, as we both loved the story and felt it would be a good fit. I chose to play Charlotte the Spider, and she chose Wilbur the Pig. In order to put this little production together, we would have to spend time on the weekends to build our set and create our costumes. When I learned this, I freaked out. Everyone in class would know that my story about my family and our living situation was simply not true. So, anytime we had to work on our project, I would always go to her house, and her mom would drop me off at my aunt's friend's home. I simply could not get caught in my lies about my living circumstances and become, in my mind, the laughing stock of my class. I was sure that no one would want to be my friend any longer. As a middle school girl, I felt that the culture of the gifted class was quite upwardly mobile, or what we called at that time "uppity." It seemed to me that the only people who were deemed smart were those who had money and were White (Beilke & Burney, 2008; Mickelson, 2006). In retrospect, this was the origin of my feelings that I was living a dual life—a so-called White girl living in a Black girl's body.

Further Transitions

I WAS IN THE GT PROGRAM for only one year. Then I moved in briefly with my Nana in Connecticut to attend private schools in the fall of 1988. My Seventh Day Adventist grandmother's strict rules were a challenge. Then a teen, I enjoyed watching TV, eating meat, and hated going to church on Saturdays as I knew it would destroy my social life if I ever had one. Even there, I struggled to meet the expectations others had of me. I eventually moved back to the Virgin Islands, living with my mom until I went to college in 1993. I maintained the mentality that when I was around White people I had to be White and when I was around my own kind I was free to be me but just not overly smart. To this day, people state that I sound White when I speak on the phone or when I am in professional attire but show more of my Blackness when I am around people who are not White. I am unable to see this, as I simply perceive it as me just being me.

I stayed in the Virgin Islands attending parochial schools until Hurricane Hugo struck in 1989. In reflection, if Hugo had not hit the island, I believe that my gifts and talents would have been better developed, based on the consistency of attending one school and having stable peer relationships. I think the constant moving contributed to feelings of isolation and awkwardness that I felt as a child into most of my adulthood.

After Hugo, I found myself in a new location, again making new friends. This time, though, in Florida, I found friends that were smart, cool, *and* Black, just like me. We all had the same advanced classes together. This group helped me realize I didn't have to tell people that I was gifted, as everyone within my circle appeared to be gifted like me. But my transient education continued, and I moved one last time back to the Virgin Islands to complete my last three years of high school. Those last three years I feel were the best of times and the worst of times.

I attended a private school, having earned a partial scholarship. I loved my friends, and even though I had not attended the school since preschool as many had, I felt a sense of belonging. They saw me as the girl with the loud mouth who was smart. It was as though I finally struck a balance in my life. I was in AP classes for most subject areas except math, providing both challenge and stimulation. There were times, however, when I felt I had to dumb down my performance on tests and projects because I just wanted to be average. Being average meant being normal and, more important, being liked by my peers. Normal students got a B or a C, especially Cs, so I would underperform every now and again so that when asked by peers how I'd done I could say I had earned a lower grade. This warped perception I had about being normal and needing to appear normal not only lowered my GPA but also impacted my ability to be considered as a serious candidate for valedictorian or salutatorian. In attempting to be normal, I was sabotaging my own best interests. These misperceptions regarding education, friendships, and my intellect were further convoluted when I went to college.

Faking the Funk: Repercussions of Trying to Fit In

I HAD ALREADY MADE UP IN MY MIND that once I got to college I was going to be as normal as possible and be as Black as possible. I planned to be like everyone else on campus. This self-constructed image meant that I just could not be smart because I'd learned as a Black girl, when I allowed myself to be seen as smart, I would be accused of trying to be White. Henfield, Washington, and Owens (2004) said, "Attitudes toward Black students who 'acted White' were far more negative" (19). I decided that since I was now in college I simply didn't have time to be isolated from my people. In my mind, this was simply a non-negotiable stance.

To minimize my smartness, I told myself over and over again that I had to "fake the funk," that is, pretend to be someone I was not in an effort to gain acceptance, no matter how it impacted me or those around me. I had to change my perceptions of who I was as a person and what I could do academically. So I downplayed my intelligence. I convinced myself that it would be okay to earn Cs as this was acceptable in college and I would be more Black. As Rascoe and Atwater (2004) found, individuals who shift their perceptions of their academic abilities from time to time will also notice changes within their academic achievement. To be embraced by the Black community at school, I would blame my professors for any grades below Bs. This would be my ace in the hole and my excuse to be an average student. No more pressure to be smart—I had left my mother on the island, and she could no longer monitor my academic progress.

I attended a college that was predominantly White. Like most teenagers leaving home for the first time, I found myself in the land of freedom. I could do what I wanted to do, say what I wanted to say, and act like a complete fool. And that's just what I did. As an undergraduate student, I found it easier to make friends. Many of our common bonds were based on where we were from. I had lived a lot of places, and I met people from South Carolina and the Virgin Islands. It was a perfect blend of home and friends, and these friendships have lasted over the years.

I partied as if the world was going to end, and I didn't have to be smart if I didn't feel like it. More times than not, I slacked off academically because I was simply tired of getting good grades. I felt I had proven I was smart where it really counted, in high school. All I had to do in my four years in college was enjoy life, earn Bs, and get into my desired program of study, which at that time was speech and language pathology.

Unfortunately, my self-sabotage to fit in meant the goal for future studies would have to change. I'll never forget the day I went to speak with one of the advisors in the Speech and Language Pathology Department to see how strict they were with the minimum grade point average (GPA) of 3.0. By the time I left her office, I vividly remember hitting myself in the head and calling myself stupid over and over again as I felt I had messed up my life over some odd, lethal combination of teenage rebellion and a Black authenticity crisis. While the student manual indicated that you needed a minimum GPA of 3.0 for entrance, the school was looking for students who had a 3.25 or better. I had a 2.75. Yet, in my mind, my re-emerging competitive spirit meant I needed to complete my degree in just three years, as my "smart, if not smarter" cousin had. I needed a workable plan.

I laugh now because I realize my hunt to find a major that would accept my GPA was a key step to my current career as a school psychologist. However at that time, I only sought a major that would allow me to graduate on the timeline I wanted. I remember searching through the undergraduate course handbook to find majors where the minimum GPA for acceptance was a 2.5 or lower. I thought with my 2.75, I was sure to get in when compared to someone with a 2.5. Although I had played around, I still wanted a major that would be challenging. I found a program where I could help people and be accepted with my GPA. After exhaustively searching for over five hours, I found the major: rehabilitation services. I had never heard of this program before and I was nervous because I had to interview in order to be considered as a potential candidate. But it fit my two criteria, and it was worth a shot.

My coursework in the rehabilitation services program was instrumental in helping me understand the lives of individuals with disabilities and appreciate all my gifts and talents. Working through this program made me realize that if I wanted to change the world, I had to change myself, and the first start was improving my GPA. During my last two years, I earned As and Bs. My GPA increased to that 3.0 mark, and I graduated in three years , albeit with student loans. I was off and ready to start a career . . . or so I thought. No one ever told me you needed experience in order to get a job. I was on the hunt once more to find a graduate program in order to make money. And once again, I would be the lone minority, trying to fit in.

Life Is Not a Bed of Roses: Solo Is So Low

I found myself in a depressed emotional state. Overly critical of myself, I was a perfectionist and should have known better. I should have done better. White (2011) wrote that gifted individuals are highly sensitive, which often leads to feelings of disappointment and self-ridicule when things fail to develop as anticipated. This, in turn, may lead to feelings of emotional brokenness and isolation, making it challenging to recuperate from setbacks (White, 2011). To be young, Black, female, and gifted in a setting where I was the only person of color in my graduate program or one of only three Black women among twenty-two school psychologists at my job was pretty tough. I found myself constantly trying to prove that I was just as good as or even better than my White peers and colleagues. This is a common occurrence in Black, gifted individuals (Ford & Grantham, 2003).

Graduate school was less of a choice and more of a necessity to secure employment and begin to pay off student loans. I had never been a stellar test taker, and as I got older, I developed test-anxiety issues. Now I can see that it was due to my internal need to be perfect. Both my scholastic aptitude test (SAT) and graduate record examination (GRE) scores failed to show my true abilities. In fact, I was rejected by every graduate program I applied to, except for my undergraduate alma mater, Florida State University. I was accepted into the school psychology group as the first Black in their 1996 Education Specialist (EdS) program.

It should have been an honor being told that I was the first person of color to be accepted into the EdS program. But I had no clue what a school psychologist was when I applied, and I applied only because I read the average salary was forty-five thousand dollars yearly to help children. The money was attractive (especially as a college student living on student loans), and I knew I would be helping children. Knowing I'd managed similar situations before, I was excited about being the only minority in my program.

My first year in my program was quite challenging, reminding me of when I was in Charleston and the only person of color in my GT program. I found myself questioning if I was really good enough for the program and if I could excel like my White peers. Forgoing being Black, a skill so thoroughly embraced as an undergraduate, I reverted to my "White girl" performance. I wanted to sound educated and intelligent like the other people in my class. This is because I felt my first graduate professor, who was still working in the field as a school psychologist, seemed hostile towards Black people. She always highlighted the work of my peers and would respond to their questions without hesitation. When I would ask questions, she would either diminish the importance of the question or defer it to someone else in the class. It made me angry because I was just as smart as or even smarter than many of my colleagues and I felt I was simply being ignored because I was the only person of color in the class.

I found myself working hard in her class simply to prove that I deserved to be there, but it came at a cost. Working so hard in the class, along with an equal fervor in my other classes, was mentally and emotionally draining. I was ready to quit the program. I began to feel that it simply was not worth compromising my sanity. My boyfriend at the time was a source of encouragement. He told me not to give up and never to allow White folks to make me feel I was inferior to them. I took his words to heart. I kept pushing forward while attempting to minimize my Blackness, as I had in middle school, fearing I would not get far in the program if I did not. I had no other choice but to act White in order to be accepted by my professor, feel validated in my abilities to be successful in the class, earn a decent grade, and get out of the class. My strategy worked for that class and subsequent classes thereafter. I successfully completed my program with high marks and was off to start my career as a school psychologist.

Professional Years

AT THE TIME THIS WRITING, I have worked for fourteen years as a school psychologist, predominantly in districts where the majority of school psychologists were White and female. The toughest years in this career were my first four where out of approximately twenty-two school psychologists I was one of three Blacks in my first place of employment. Two of us worked full-time and one worked part-time. There were no Black males in the district when I first applied in 2000 and after I left the second time in 2012.

I found it very challenging to work in a school district where there were clear demographic boundaries regarding race and where it seemed the divide included how resources were allocated, including where and how quality teachers were assigned to schools and classrooms. I worked primarily on the Black side of town. It was confusing to me as a school psychologist that a school district with a high concentration of minorities failed to recruit more Blacks to work in teaching, administration, and related services roles. I often reflected on my graduate program, as it was a reminder that there simply weren't a plethora of minorities, especially Blacks, pursuing careers as school psychologists. I discovered that many of the positions I obtained had previously been held by older White men. And I found myself working twice as hard because some staff members at my school sites believed I was not qualified or effective in my role as a school psychologist. They thought I was unable to work effectively with Black children from lower socioeconomic statuses because I sounded White. I had to fight the perception that I somehow was inauthentic or incapable because of the dual identities I had cultivated over the years.

In fact, during my first two years, I found myself having to justify my Blackness to some of my colleagues and students' parents. At times, I was defensive. Earlier in my life I was never quite right—I was not Black enough or too Black, not smart enough or too smart, and now again, I was too smart and sounded too White (not Black enough). I was so frustrated that I was ready to quit after my second year. I came to realize that my ability to enunciate clearly in standard English, use both specialized nomenclature customary to the field and parent-friendly language in meetings, and meet the needs of families I advocate for had nothing to do with how Black or White I was. Instead, it was indicative of the ways in which the negative connotations of Blackness and the positive connotations of Whiteness had become internalized in multiple ways by both White and Black Americans. But with the support of my colleagues and family, I realized that how other people viewed me was something I couldn't control.

I had a job to do: to ensure that all students, especially minority students, were appropriately assessed for special education services. In my earlier days as a school psychologist, I saw how school personnel would, with very limited evidence, repeatedly refer minority students to special education services. This practice infuriated me. It seemed that school personnel were often prepared to easily and quickly conclude that Black children were not good enough to excel at the same level of their White peers. I made it my mission as a school psychologist to ensure that all children received due diligence regarding the quality of educational supports received before I would test and/or identify a child with an educational disability. Knowing that any label, being it gifted or disabled, put a child outside the range of normal, I didn't want these children to experience the same sense of identity loss I had felt for so many years. For too long, I believed that no one wanted to be around individuals who were different, who were not the norm.

Black, Gifted, and Beautiful

Over the course of life, we eventually have to decide what is most important to us. Do we succumb to the pressures born of not fitting in, of not being a part of the norm? Do we forgo our identity, simply blending into the shadows, to be accepted? Or do we fight like hell to reclaim our identity? Ford and Whiting (2010) wrote that many gifted Blacks find themselves at crossroads, feeding themselves negative affirmations about their "personal worth, academic worth, and their social worth as human beings" (149). When these negative affirmations seep into the minds of an individual, internal destruction may be inevitable. The individual either succumbs to these negative messages of destruction or rises to change these messages into positive affirmations of happiness and health (Ford & Whiting, 2010).

Living the Golden Life: Happy in My Thirties

My newfound purpose means my thirties have been good to me. Having a steady job and motherhood has been key. Even with all the ups and downs of personal relationships, I have always been on my grind, struggling to financially support my children as a divorced mother. I think that's one of the reasons I decided to go back to school. I wanted to—better yet, I needed to—prove to myself that I had what it took to be successful once again. Furthermore, I needed to prove to my children that I would do whatever it took to ensure they were always provided for, no matter what it cost me.

In my thirties, I pursued both a master's in business administration and a doctorate in education. I always thought both were out of my reach. Once again there was the gifted child inside me who was always ready to set false limits on my abilities. I never thought I could earn an MBA: I hated math and always struggled in the subject. But I persevered and earned mostly As in courses filled with mathematical applications and calculations. I was really proud of myself, once again showing that if I applied myself I could achieve any goal. As the sole Black in my EdS program, I never felt I could keep up academically with my White colleagues. They seemed to earn more As and receive more teacher accolades than I did. However, completing my MBA at Tiffin University and doctorate at Northeastern University gave me a sense of scholarship and true accomplishment. I finally felt I was good enough and smart enough to compete with my White colleagues while remaining steady in my identity as a Black woman.

Unfortunately, these feelings are often tenuous. It is amazing how one bad experience, my first class in my school psychology program, reshaped how I felt about my abilities. Looking back, all I can do is think about how overwhelmed I was by life at that moment. I was working on two degrees at once. During my last full year of my MBA program, my children and I moved from the West Coast to the East Coast so I could provide a healthier and more stable life for my boys. I started a new job and had to, once again, re-acclimate to another area. It was tough but doable. Then I started my doctoral program, working on two degrees simultaneously for an entire year. I was determined to earn those degrees. By the time I finished my MBA, I was in full swing with my doctoral program. I successfully completed my program three years after I initially started. I can truly say it was only through my faith in God that I survived this period in my life.

Now that school is finished, I am learning how to develop friendships. Recently, through social media, I have been able to reconnect with peers from elementary, middle, and high school. I am still working on creating friendships within my local area. However, this is quite challenging when I wake up before the sun rises and return home after it sets. I am still learning what it means to have stable friendships, as for so many years, the pains and trials of life created high levels of anxiety in my willingness to allow anyone to get to close to me for fear of my leaving them or their leaving me. Feeling secure in relationships is a work in progress. Having said that, if nothing else, whether it's motherhood, being gainfully employed, being a student, or connecting with friends, my thirties have shown me it's not about how smart or gifted you are that determines your level of impact in your field or in your relationships. It's who you are as a person and how you present yourself that makes all the difference.

Final Thoughts

MY CONCEPT OF SELF, which was labeled as a gifted individual at an early age, came with a price. I felt no one would accept or appreciate me because I was different, even if those differences should have been viewed as a positive, for I felt no one would want to be around a nerdy girl. The emotional and mental warfare I put myself through caused me to sabotage not only my academic performance in high school and college but also my happiness. I couldn't ascribe value to my own gifts. Instead, I saw them as liabilities. Christopher and Shewmaker (2010) found that the "flexibility of thinking and the ability to see options allow the [gifted] child to develop skills that can benefit him or her in the problem-solving process when faced with the inability to achieve perfection" (28). I created a negative flexibility, changing myself instead of seeing those options. If I had seen more options and been able to embrace different perspectives, I more than likely would have spared myself years of self-inflicted criticism about not being good enough.

In allowing myself to relive memories of my experiences as a gifted individual in writing this chapter, I shared intimate details of my perceptions of being identified as a gifted child and how for many years I hid my unique qualities from most of my family, my peers, and my colleagues. The following is what I learned and what I perceive are very important for parents and educators to understand in order to efficiently and effectively support the needs of Black, gifted children.

For parents, it is important that you provide your children with positive affirmations that it is okay to be Black and intellectual. It is important that parents clothe their children with their history, with the contributions of Blacks and Browns to American society, so children believe they are capable of making change within their environment. I also recommended that parents recognize there is a lot of pressure associated with being identified as gifted, which may create significant emotional and psychological difficulties. Therefore, it is important that parents provide their gifted children with counseling services either at the school or community level, so they never feel they have to change their identity or deny their intellect to fit in with others who may be of another race or ethnicity, or of the same race and ethnicity.

For educators, it is imperative that you realize gifted children require counseling services to help them develop positive self-concepts outside their gifted status. Minority children, in particular, will need to understand that being Black or Brown and gifted is just as normal as being White or Asian and gifted. School personnel should work closely with parents to help develop activities at home and outside school that will help support the emotional needs of the gifted child at school.

Further, it is suggested that school districts implement or continue providing parents of gifted children with support groups or workshops to connect them with other gifted parents.

Today, as you read my story, I want you to know that I have embraced my gifted identity because I have learned to accept me, flaws and all. Rather than fitting others' expectations, we can be our authentic selves, accepting who we are, and people will tend to accept us. Instead of finding fault, I will continue to love me first and spread this love to those I am blessed to encounter. The self-reflection spurred through writing this chapter has highlighted that if I do not want my children to experience the same type of pain I did, I must let go of negative thought patterns and teach them to do the same. Here's to future years that will be filled with more love, peace, happiness, and more creativity that stems from the gifted mind I am proud to call mine.

References

Burney, V. H., & Beilke, J. R. (2008). The constraints of poverty on high achievement. *Journal for the Education of the Gifted, 31*(3), 171–197.

Christopher, M. M., & Shewmaker, J. (2010). The relationship of perfectionism to affective variables in gifted and highly able children. *Gifted Child Today, 33*(3), 20–30.

Ford, D. Y., & Whiting, G. W. (2011). Beyond testing: Social and psychological considerations in recruiting and retaining gifted black students. *Journal for the Education of the Gifted, 34*(1), 131–155.

Ford, D. Y., Harris III, J. J., Tyson, C. A., & Trotman, M. F. (2001). Beyond deficit thinking: Providing access for gifted African American students. *Roeper Review, 24*(2), 52–58.

Fordham, S., & Ogbu, J. U. (1986). Black students' school success: Coping with the "burden of 'acting White.'" *The Urban Review, 18*(3), 176–206.

Grantham, T. C. (2005). Parent advocacy for culturally diverse gifted students. *Theory into practice, 44*(2), 138–147.

Grantham, T. C., & Ford, D. Y. (2003). Beyond self-concept and self-esteem: Racial identity and gifted African American students. *High School Journal, 87*(1), 18–30.

Henfield, M. S., Washington, A. R., & Owens, D. (2010). Gifted to be or not to be. *Gifted Child Today, 33*(2), 17–25.

Mickelson, R. A. (2006). Segregation and the SAT. *Ohio St. LJ, 67*, 157–199.

Moore III, J. L., Ford, D. Y., & Milner, H. R. (2005). Underachievement among gifted students of color: Implications for educators. *Theory Into Practice, 44*(2), 167–177.

Olszewski-Kubilius, P. (2003). Do we change gifted children to fit gifted programs, or do we change gifted programs to fit gifted children? *Journal for the Education of the Gifted, 26*(4), 304–313.

Peterson, J. S. (2006). Addressing counseling needs of gifted students. *Professional School Counseling, 10*(1), 43–51.

Rascoe, B., & Atwater, M. M. (2005). Black males' self-perceptions of academic ability and gifted potential in advanced science classes. *Journal of Research in Science Teaching, 42*(8), 888–911.

Renzulli, J. S. (2011). Kappan classic: What makes giftedness? Reexamining a definition. *Phi Delta Kappan, 92*(8), 81–88.

Tyson, K., Darity, W., & Castellino, D. R. (2005). It's not "a black thing": Understanding the burden of acting White and other dilemmas of high achievement. *American Sociological Review, 70*(4), 582–605.

White, S. (2011). Too sensitive? Thanks for the compliment! High sensitivity in gifted and talented individuals. *Gifted, 162*, 12–16.

CHAPTER 15

Too Smart for My Own Good: The Journey to YoungGiftedandFat

Sharrell Luckett, PhD

"WHY DO I HAVE TO RESPECT ADULTS?" This question forcefully fell out of my five-year-old mouth in kindergarten, and I wanted an answer. My young, White kindergarten teacher at Mt. Olive Elementary School in East Point, Georgia, knelt down at eye-level as she asked me to repeat the question. So I asked her again, this time with more urgency. "Why do I have to respect adults?" Her response: "Because they're older than you, Sharrell." I looked at her with my deep-set eyes, furrowed my inquisitive brow, and retorted, "But my brother is older than me, and I don't have to respect him." My fragmented memory tells me that the teacher ignored my response and walked away or maybe just laughed at my response. Nonetheless, I did not like the fact that the logic behind respecting my elders did not make sense. I was never told to respect my nerdy brother who was four years older than I was, fighting him tooth and nail and calling him disrespectful names whenever I deemed it necessary. At five years old, I did not yet understand that older people may have more wisdom and that I should listen to them—sometimes. This is where my story of being young, Black, gifted, and eventually fat begins.

From an early age, I have been highly inquisitive. Since I could not find a sensible answer to the question I had posed to my kindergarten teacher, I began to view adults as my equal, as peers. I wanted equal respect in the classroom and an explanation for everything. I was a critical thinker before I knew how to define critical thinking. However, my critical thinking and combative nature towards authority often led me to both in-school and out-of-school suspension. I was labeled a smart, mean girl with a flippant mouth. When rules did not make sense and no one could explain their logic, I would let my grievances be known. In hindsight, I was simply a smart child who needed some specialized care from my elders.

When I entered first grade, I was identified as a student who should be tested for the Talented and Gifted Program (TAG). On the day of TAG testing, an incident between the teacher and myself upset me. To punish my teacher I decided not to take the TAG test. I simply refused. The school phoned my mother, but she informed them that I was stubborn and if I said I wasn't going to take the test then it probably wasn't going to happen. The teacher, a dark-skinned Black lady with a Jheri curl, probably in her mid-fifties, urged me to take the test. To isolate me, she moved my desk next to the classroom door and instructed me to take the test. I remember looking down at the test and easily knowing the answers to the questions that were set before me, but I wanted to prove a point. I never took the test, and I was never enrolled in TAG.

But something special happened. Instead of turning a blind eye to my unruly giftedness, my teachers, for the remainder of my formative years, chose to believe in my talents and nurture my strengths, rather than focus on my misbehavior. Their guidance and wisdom led me to eventually become a theatre professor, thriving within a professional outlet where I could act out whenever I felt the need.

In this essay, I will poetically and demonstratively share how my elementary, secondary, and university teachers nurtured my giftedness. Simply put, TAG was for the gifted and well-behaved, not the gifted and eccentrically curious. I have incorporated various poems throughout this narrative that will highlight elements of my artistic development, the impact of my most influential teachers, and how their actions propelled me from a perpetually misunderstood Black, gifted child to an eventually successful life as a Black, gifted adult. For example, I was recently honored as the doctoral marshal and keynote speaker during my graduate studies ceremony at the University of Missouri-Columbia. I am the first person on both sides of my family to earn a PhD. I am truly the academic fruits of their labor. Finally, I will share an excerpt of an interview with my mother, my first teacher, as it pertains to my youth and an excerpt from the world premiere of my one-woman show in which I reflect upon my giftedness and struggles with weight, titled, *YoungGiftedandFat*.

With my use of performative writing, a methodological approach to documenting research that incorporates poetic and unconventional literary devices on the page, I pay homage to my educators and their witty ways of helping me unveil my unique, intellectual vigor. I employ performative writing in this essay to not only "expand the notions of what constitutes disciplinary knowledge" (Pelias, 2005) but also highlight the artistic text as a framework for the way I choose to contribute to the fields of education and performance.

Elementary School

Kindergarten, or a Question

Dear Ms. Hunnings, why you shun me?
My question you see
With your long honey-blond hair
Too tall so you knelt down for my inquiry
Why don't I have to respect my brother?
No answer for me
Caused me all types of confusion
And my ability to separate the rules from the muck
Made it a bad childhood
In school
Just mess
Agitating the teachers
While excelling in English
If rules are made to be broken
I broke them, with a smile

First Grade, or My Gifted Rejection
I remember that Jheri curl on Ms. Williams
And those black slacks so clearly
U and me
Same skin tone
Us running from your pinching fingers
When we did something wrong
Me sitting in the desk
Arms crossed
Refusing to take the test
I'm the boss.
I won.
No talented and gifted for me
Began to train in privacy.

Second Grade, or a Whale of a Tale
It was the whales. A whale of a tale.
The story of whales were on the screen
And I wrote an essay just for me
So I thought . . .
I took it to school and showed it to Mrs. Carey
She was excited and insisted
I read it in all of the classes in the hall
There I was, my first speaking engagement
Class to class to class I went
Assured my time was being well-spent
The teachers applauded my two-page
Essay about the whales
Greatness in the making
You still tell me this story
Me watching the story of a whale
Took out my pencil and paper and
Decided to share what I had written
Now how did this little young me know
That I could turn visual knowledge
Into something tangible and solid
On a piece of paper

Guess it was from lots and lots of reading
So I wrote and wrote and wrote
And you did what any good teacher would do
You made me share and share and share
My essay to the entire second grade
I knew you were proud
Of my often high scores
That whale and me, that whale you see
Got me presenting and writing
Today, happily.

Third Grade, or an F on My Paper
An F on my paper
Me moving too fast
Completing that worksheet
My eyes surpassed the directions
Read the directions
What do the directions say?
Follow directions
Following anyone has never been my strong suit
I am a leader and leaders break rules and ignore directions
Sometimes
As my young mind did on this day
A group of words that I must unscramble
Knew them so fast, so quick
Done in a few minutes
Up outta my seat to turn it in
Once again, faster than all my friends
Ms. Woods with her full yellow cheeks
And flurry black hair wrote an
F so fat on my worksheet
And gave me a stare
But I got them all right
My li'l brown lip quivered
Sharrell, my dear, remember
Read the directions
As my eyes met the top of the page

I now understood the seat of her rage
Alphabetical order was also requested
But those unscrambled words just
Rested in disorder
And that F, that F, never saw the light of day again
Not on my work at least
I always read the directions now
Following them when I get ready
Leadership, my strong point.

Fourth Grade, or Smarty Pants
Placing me in the smart group
Even though I was a bit uncouth
Cuz Ms. Ward knew I was great with fractions
And to my non-diagnosed-ADHD satisfaction
The moving from class to class helped.

It was in fourth grade that I first noticed my teachers were privileging my intellect. At this time, the fourth grade teachers were group teaching, and at times, TAG students from my class would switch with students from the class across the hall. Ms. Ward was a slender Black woman with a medium-caramel complexion. She was a nice lady who wore her ear-length hair in big curl swoops. When the gifted group of students began to switch classes, Ms. Ward would let me switch with them sometimes. And the times when I didn't switch I would ask to see the gifted students' worksheets. I remember thinking that gifted work was so easy and wondering why only gifted students were allowed to participate in extra fun, intellectual, and creative activities.

Fifth Grade, or Mrs. Kleckley
I wanted to run and hug you
That last day of fifth grade
I felt my heart imploding
As you ushered me on my way
You said, "Go on, now!"
"Go on, Sharrell!"
And I just walked away and

Waved
At your wonderful brown face
That apple tree was no joke
And you stayed committed to your rules
I always knew you meant well
Always
You made me a better teacher
Showed me the actions of someone who really cares
From giving me a platform to speak with the principal
To checking on me at PruCare
Not sure how the bond was created
But it is there
So sad you left me, us, so sad.

It was in fifth grade that I was really embraced and nurtured. I adored my fifth grade teacher. Her name was Mary Kleckley. I can remember her voice and her authority as if it were yesterday. She was a tall, slender, beautiful, dark-skinned woman. She mostly wore pencil skirts with muted-toned blouses. She had a nice smile, but I don't remember her laughing much. Mrs. Kleckley urged me to be responsible for my actions. She also empowered me to question authority in a respectful manner.

Even though I never officially enrolled in the TAG program, by fifth grade, all my teachers at my elementary school acknowledged my young intellect and began instructing me on how to deal with adversity. For instance, during my elementary school spelling bee, I out-spelled over forty students to compete for the grand prize. The other speller misspelled the word "apologize." At that moment I knew I was going to win—or so I thought. When I stepped to the podium, I spelled "apologize" correctly, but the principal announced that it was incorrect. I was baffled but was too afraid to challenge him in front of the entire school. I remember seeing my former teachers' faces in the audience looking perplexed as well. The humor in this is that I ended up losing because I misspelled "bacon." Now that seems really "ungifted," right? Not really. I'm a visual learner. I can spell virtually any word after I see it once. But my family rarely ate bacon. I clearly remember being on stage in that moment, visualizing opening my refrigerator, and searching for the bacon in my mind. I could not find the word, it was not there, and I spelled bacon, b-a-c-k-o-n. The other girl won. I was defeated in front of the entire school, having to retreat back to my classroom. What happened next affected me more than the loss. I informed Mrs. Kleckley that I had spelled "apologize" correctly, that I had won before I misspelled "bacon." Mrs. Kleckley requested the principal's presence. He came to my classroom, and I spoke with him in the hallway. He said he was sure I had spelled apologize with a *y* and not an *i*. We talked, and the situation was over. Although he didn't change his opinion, he did listen to me. In that moment with the principal, I learned that I could respectfully question authority. My fifth grade voice was respected, and I could express myself.

Mrs. Kleckley also had an apple tree, a two-dimensional tree tacked to the wall. All students had an apple with their name on it. At the beginning of the week, all apples were placed in the tree. If someone misbehaved, depending on how bad the offense, her or his apple would begin to be lowered out of the tree. If by Friday a student's apple reached the ground, that student did not receive a treat at the end of the week. The treat was usually some form of candy. That apple tree meant so much to me, and there were so many times that my apple hit the ground by the end of the week. I would go to Mrs. Kleckley with my sad eyes and ask if I could still get a treat, and she would nicely tell me no and that I could start again Monday. Mrs. Kleckley held me accountable for my behavior. She insisted that I learn about consequences but also taught me that second chances were possible. She would also assign me extra work to complete when I finished the regular classwork. Mrs. Kleckley had heard about me and how I had refused to take the TAG test. Still, she made sure that I succeeded in the school system and supported my giftedness, regardless of my non-enrollment in the TAG program.

My chubbiness also became a problem during fifth grade. At this time, I noticed a recurring dating trend among my chubbier female peers. They all had chubby boyfriends. Yes, we were dating in fifth grade, sort of—mostly phone calls and little love notes to one another. But I wasn't attracted to chubby boys. I had the biggest crush on a male classmate. He was simply adorable. He would sit in the back of the classroom, complete his work, and was quiet as a mouse. I never had the courage to tell him I liked him. But I did become sad because I was taller and bigger than he was. These issues with my body size would later resurface during early adulthood and during my PhD studies.

On the last day of fifth grade, as Mrs. Kleckley took us to the departing area where I would hitch a ride home with a friend, I remember I was about to cry. I was becoming emotional and went back to hug her, and I guess she sensed I was about to cry, so she turned me away. She said, "Go on, Sharrell. Go on!" Mrs. Kleckley was a really special teacher whom I am grateful for. She knew the importance of ushering me on my way to begin my middle school journey.

I enrolled in Woodland Middle School for the sixth grade. The school had a majority Black student population. This is the year I knew that I was extremely different and gifted. My heightened maturity and sensitivity were activated, and I knew that something about the school wasn't right. I just couldn't explain it to my mother. The daily chatter was usually about what was on television the night before and who was about to get into a fight. But I didn't watch network sitcoms, and I wasn't interested in physical altercations. I watched the Disney and Nickelodeon channels. Now that I'm older I realize that Woodland did not provide the artistic outlet that I needed.

Woodland Middle School

Sixth Grade

HELL NAW!

Lo and behold I found out about our county's Majority to Minority (MtoM) program. To help diversify schools, a person who attended a school in which her or his ethnicity was the majority could apply to be a minority student at another school in the same county. This program was also implemented due to the significant disparities between the educational opportunities of North Fulton County and South Fulton County, Georgia. North Fulton County consisted of mostly white students, while South Fulton County consisted of mostly Black students. The North County schools had more resources than the South County schools. So, I begged my mother to let me apply to a middle school in North Fulton County.

I remember calling Fulton County schools at the tender age of eleven and inquiring about the MtoM program. The assistant on the phone told me the steps I needed to take to apply, and I relayed that information to my mother. Later that year, before seventh grade, I was accepted into the MtoM program and received my school assignment. I was to attend Ridgeview Middle School in Sandy Springs, approximately thirty miles from my home and over an hour bus ride with traffic in the mornings and evenings. My family and I were willing to make this time-consuming sacrifice in order for me to receive a better education.

Ridgeview Middle School, or Anger Management
Mistook my giftedness for anger
Made me swim twice a week to tame
The eccentric ingenuity
Within me
He threw Checkers' burgers at us and worksheets
That meant nothing
All you had to do was ask me not to curse
Around the teachers
Or make jokes about their prostitution
My mama hung her head
And said what is wrong with my child
Mama ran me
No more sadness for her
Fine, I will behave
And pass me the scalpel so I can dissect this frog
Cuz my lab partner is too afraid
Of the juice.

The first time I had ever been in an educational environment with white classmates was at Ridgeview Middle School. My behavior problems also increased during seventh grade, partly because I was bored and partly because I was a preteen who still did not understand why I had to respect authority and seniority. My misguided behavior was usually directed at the teachers. I got along with my peers just fine. But I would often curse around the teachers or tell a joke to make my classmates laugh. To combat my behavioral problems, my teachers would comment on how smart I was or suggested that I could be a great leader. But I didn't care. The tests were too easy. I was a far better writer and reader than my peers, but I was just bored at Ridgeview. Week after week I was sent to the assistant principal's office. I was often assigned in-school suspension, and after that I would receive out-of-school suspension, and every now and then they would threaten to send me back "down south" to South Fulton County, but that never happened. I believe they allowed me to stay "up north" in North Fulton County because of my high test scores. Ultimately, I was one of the highest achieving students who had been identified by teachers as gifted but was not enrolled in a program. Instead, Ridgeview enrolled me in an anger management program in which we swam twice a week and I was offered a meal from a local hamburger restaurant.

In retrospect, I would not classify my issues as anger management issues. I did not quip at the teachers because I was angry, and I know the teachers were not afraid of me. I was simply bored, as gifted students can quickly become. While the class took two weeks to read a certain book, chapter by chapter, I would finish the book in two days.

When I decided to return to South Fulton County to attend Tri-Cities High School for the Visual & Performing Arts, I was following in the footsteps of my older brother.

Ninth and Tenth Grades
You wrote on the board in chalk from top to bottom, DR. SCOTT and
You insisted that we call you doctor
Mrs. slipped out time and time again and you would
Stop time and time again
And insist on doctor cuz u wrote a book, a dissertation
I had a 64, failing
I could do much better and u knew it
U also knew I deserved an F cuz I wasn't doing
The work
Worked it
Into my head that I was ahead
Of my class
Behind cuz of sass
But then u reached me
Asked me to write a poem.

The assignment was to poetically describe an inanimate object, and this is what I wrote at age fifteen:

Submissively engaged in your body's movement. As you dance steadily,   my new words are erased, and I am rushed with the capacity of the   ocean's floor. My tears endure your vivacious strokes as my pure juices   caress the many unknown secrets of your world. Throw me, drop me,   break me. I don't care. My purpose is to wait for you. While flushing the   impurities of your bosom away, you sing me sweet songs; knowing our   time together won't be long. Acting as if you are ashamed of me, you set   me on my pedestal, and I wait. Wondering when will you be back to share   with me the scent of life.

> Celebrated its brilliance
> Class couldn't guess it
> SOAP, hahaha, the power of poetry
> Unfolded
> And I finally decided to
> Do the work
> It didn't hurt
> 64 to a 98
> Then u asked why I wasn't in honors classes
> And it was cuz of my behavior
> And u knew I was telling the truth
> But I never forgot that doctor lesson
> Your name in big bold chalk
> A big deal
> Just thinking bout how to pass
> Ninth grade English.

> **Drama, or Freddie Hendricks**
> With finesse and skill
> U directed the ills of the world
> From no page to the stage
> Tapped into your brilliance
> And now I'm reveling in it
> And my own too
> Taught me how to direct
> Set, strike a picture
> Thank you for sitting me in the audience

Blocking
Directing is a gift
I can see backwards
I really can.

When I enrolled in the drama magnet program at Tri-Cities High School in East Point, I had finally realized my love for the arts. I began writing plays and directing, and soon after, I enrolled in college where I was co-producing, writing, and directing musicals.

Two of my most influential professors who nurtured my gifted abilities were Shirlene Holmes and M. Heather Carver of Georgia State University and the University of Missouri-Columbia, respectively. Holmes is a tall, Black, regal lady who assisted me in my undergraduate education, and Carver is a tall, White, gregarious woman who realized the harsh reality of being a Black female navigating academia and made it her business to guide me through the perils and joys of my PhD studies. Both of these strong women helped to make my dreams a reality, and I'm sure they protected my educational path in ways that I am both aware and unaware of.

Dr. Shirlene Holmes

What a magnificent, grand being in every way
Told me to get my feet off the theatre seats
Focus
She believed in theatre
I believed in theatre
Good Company
Always listening and then
How do you know those
Big words?
She spoke
You will know them too one day
Dr.
Too
Someday
Dismissive, all of nineteen
I couldn't imagine

Big words?
Just "lights up"
And "black out."

Dr. Heather Carver
You laugh and laugh and laugh
I just look
Relatable, taller, I look up to you
Heart and ambitions on the page
See you on the stage
Realize that my story has its ways
Supportive day by day
Write, you say
I did and wrote some more and wrote some more
Performance studies I adore
Because of you
Grateful, honored, elated
To have studied with you.

Both Holmes and Carver maintain careers as professors and solo performers. Thus, it was a natural progression for me to tell my story of childhood anguish connected with being young, gifted, Black, and fat in a solo theatrical piece. After losing nearly one hundred pounds in my late twenties, I was happy with my weight-loss success but didn't fully understand the implications and consequences of my survival as a performer until I moved from Atlanta, Georgia, to Columbia, Missouri, to begin my PhD studies. While enrolled at the University of Missouri-Columbia, I was cast as the lead actress in *Holding Up the Sky*, a play adapted from folklore and tales from across the globe. In the play, a married couple survives a devastating war and proceeds to build a new life. Being surrounded by all new people and a new environment, my recent weight loss remained a secret, but although I was much smaller in size, I was still mentally living in the space of a morbidly obese person. My work on this role led me to suffer from psychological and physical stress because of my history as an obese person and my lack of experience on stage in a newly transformed, smaller-sized body. For instance, I started to experience extreme anxiety when I was told that my costume would reveal a large amount of skin. Also, I was to be lifted up in the show twice. I was so scared that my cast mates would not be able to lift me that I promised them I would not gain weight during the rehearsal period. I also had to simulate sex on stage with an orgasm. Fat actresses are rarely portrayed as sexually desirable, rarely lifted, and surely don't have orgasmic sex on stage.

As I worked to understand the stress and extreme anxiety that I was experiencing during the rehearsal and performance process in *Holding Up the Sky*, I decided that I wanted to further explore the implications of mentally living as a morbidly obese woman while maneuvering in a slender body. This began my auto/ethnographic study of a weight-conscious, Black woman and her body on the stage. In my dissertation, I employ auto/ethnography as both a method and a methodology, highlighting the experiences of Black women on stage with issues around size through analyzing my personal experience.

If it hadn't been for Carol T. Scott and Shirlene Holmes ingraining in me that I, like them, could and would earn a PhD one day, I don't know that I would've ever visualized myself as doctoral material. Furthermore, it was Heather Carver who recognized early in my doctoral studies that I could become bored quickly, so she invited me to work with her on her research and helped me find opportunities on campus to become more involved in my studies. But the strongest driving force behind my educational attainment was the everlasting support from my mother, Rev. Beverly H. Luckett, and her endearing commitment to providing me with great educational opportunities. She laid a strong, supportive foundation for me, and even during her heroic battle with cancer, she skipped a chemotherapy treatment so she could travel to the University of Missouri-Columbia to attend my graduation and witness my commencement speech. A month later, she passed peacefully surrounded by loved ones.

This final section includes an interview with my mother, as it provides a small peek into the type of parent she was and how she viewed my giftedness and my size in my formative years. This interview clip is then followed by an excerpt from my solo show, *YoungGiftedandFat*, which addresses my issues with being gifted and fat.

The Interview

Mother: You were about nine years old when I started realizing I had to buy a little larger sizes for you, and I didn't see it as a real problem at the time, and actually I've never felt it was a real problem for me. But as you entered your tween years and then your teen years, with the mocking and harassment from classmates and neighborhood kids, I realized that it [fatness] was a problem, a big problem for you, and of course since it affected you, it affected me because you were a beautiful little girl with pretty hair, beautiful skin, and I really didn't understand it. It really upset me when you would be the victim of meanness, and . . . there were situations where you retaliated and quite a few kids got beat up for their disrespect of you with words.

Sharrell: Was it easy to find clothes to fit me for my age?

Mother: After you started getting into your tween years, I realized that I would have to incorporate the services of my seamstress, who had done quite a bit of alterations for me to outfit you for special occasions, such as Easter and other holidays. She made you very pleasing straight-line , and that was a godsend for me because actually you never cared for frills. You always looked nice.

Sharrell: Let's talk about my weight-loss journey. How many diets do you think I was on as a teenager? Does it seem like I was always dieting?

Mother: Of course I didn't keep up with the number of diets you were on, Sharrell. I do know that I saw that the weight was really bothering you, and like I say, that was when it became a real bother to me, and I knew you were always a brilliant child, and I was afraid that your weight would impede the expression of your talents and gifts that God had given you. . . . Even before you started your weight-loss programs, you were achieving, and now you seem even more determined since you're more pleased with yourself now with your substantial weight loss. I see even more enthusiasm, and that makes you more well-rounded. For that I'm grateful.

Sharrell: Let's talk about me on stage as a big person during my fat years. What did you think about me as a big girl on stage through high school and early college in general?

Mother: I really admired your tenacity. Being your mother, as I've said, and being overweight myself, you know there were a lot of things that I did not take upon myself to do. You know, I too am very talented, but you know [my weight] was a drawback for me. But you impressed me with your determination to kick down barriers, and that's the way I see you now. You know, you are a person [that] when you come up against something you tackle it. I don't have that type of stamina, and I don't feel bad about it because that's just the way I am. Our personalities are so different. You know you always say that I am a very laid-back person and that I am not aggressive. I'm a subtly aggressive person, ah passive-aggressive. And you're definitely not that. You are aggressive-aggressive, aggressive-aggressive-aggressive, and it serves you well in facing some of the obstacles that you come upon in your life.

Sharrell: Do you remember how my behavior was surrounding my weight while I performed in graduate school as a slender person?

Mother: You were very happy and excited—and excited for me to see you that way. For some reason, you always felt . . . because of your weight you were not good enough for me. . . . But that's never been, like I said, an issue for me. It was an issue for you. And I really do recall why I believe you felt that way. You told me stories about how your classmates always said, "Oh, your mama is so pretty. Why you don't look like your mama?" and you got a lot of that. . . . But now that your beauty has evolved with your substantial weight loss, you are more comfortable with yourself. I think your peers always compared you to me, myself being a lighter-skinned person and you being darker-skinned like your father. Your peers were always comparing. And even as you got older, I'm sure your more mature peers thought the same thing but didn't say it. But like I've always maintained, it's never been an issue for me.

Sharrell: Anything you want to add?

Mother: I appreciate this opportunity to interview with you, and in my maturity in life, I've learned to let go and let God, and I want to be as honest as I can in responding to your questions, and I hope I have. May God's speed continue to be with you in your endeavors and your positivity about life and your sense of contribution. Thank you.

Sharrell: Thank you.

Mother, or You Birthed a Fighter
You birthed a fighter
head on your bosom
held on to her in the darkest hours
she found herself in you
Reflection
bedroom eyes
chiseled mind and cheekbones
You birthed a fighter
dark-wine rivers intertwine, your energy like no other
God. She sees Her in you
'tis the season to reach for the stars and fly above and beyond them
with you by her side; her everything
shouted for her because she had
Purpose
planted a seed, nurtured it, and prayed over it
Your flower has wonderfully bloomed
sunshine and glistening streams, she just needs yours
no stopping us now

You birthed a fighter
a beautiful bird song; a rose
"Rose"
transcending time and space; you knew all along
she would find her way
light her path and she will see
lead her and she will follow
name her and she will become
You
birthed a fighter.

As stated earlier, my mother passed away in the summer of 2012. With amazing family and friends I have found the strength to continue my artistic and intellectual journey in life. In June of 2014, the rolling world premiere of *YoungGiftedandFat*, my solo show, was produced at California State University-Dominguez Hills to sold-out audiences. This show was borne out of my dissertation studies, and the script is a culmination of my journey, of living and being Black, gifted, and fat. The following is a short excerpt from the show in which I speak about my invisibility as a child and teenager as it relates to my giftedness and my size.

When I was a child, I would close my eyes and really think that I was invisible. Just stand up against a wall in broad daylight and black out. Now you see me; now you don't. The darkness became so familiar. At my lowest point in life, I would make myself invisible so frequently that I forgot how to use my light. Searching the darkness with my fingers, pulse, my breath, and my eyes darting from one crevice to the next. No light switches anywhere, so I adapted to the darkness. Made a big comfy bed in it and slept in it every night. Face wet and salty and supple. Drowning in the black abyss. In deep, no longer searching for switches or motion-activated lights. In the coastal south, you're supposed to stock up on candles and flashlights for hurricane season. My mama was always good about that. She put a flashlight and a candle in every room in the house, and when it began to thunder and lightning really bad, my mama walked fast through the house, lighting the candles, preparing us for the storm. But she couldn't figure out how to light the candles during my storm. And by the time I was a teenager all of the batteries in the flashlights had run out. So my mama would just sit with me in the darkness and change the wet pillowcases and assured me that the only reason I know it is dark is because I have experienced my light.

Now that I have reclaimed my uniqueness and giftedness, which I term "light" in the previous excerpt, I am taking it upon myself to nurture my gifted spirit and to allow myself to be artistically different and advanced in every way. As a professor, I gravitate towards the gifted, misguided children, and I expose them to the arts. As an artist, I perform and write works that speak to the gifted experience. And as a Black, gifted adult, I work to join forces with other gifted adults to make sure our voices are acknowledged. This essay is a testament to the profound honor and challenge of what it means to be young, gifted, and Black.

References

Pelias, Ronald J. (2005). Performative writing as scholarship: An apology, an argument, an anecdote. *Cultural Studies ⊠ Critical Methodologies*, 5.4, 415–424.

CONTRIBUTORS

NADIRAH ANGAIL, MFT, is an independent writer/editor and interviewer. She is a Marriage, Family, Therapist graduate of Drexel University (Philadelphia) and lives in Kansas City, Missouri.

MARQUIS BEY is a PhD student, studying contemporary African American Literature at Cornell University (New York). He has published on the subjects of Black women abolitionist feminisms, racial fugitivity, atheistic Black radical feminism, and the criminalization of Black bodies. His areas of research are literature, Black feminist thought, and transgender studies. He lives in Ithaca, New York.

SARA DEL MORAL, MA, Environmental Studies, is a senior performance auditor at the Washington State Auditor's Office in Olympia. She leads research teams to carry out performance evaluations aimed at improving government processes and services. She lives in Olympia, Washington.

TRACI ENGLISH-CLARKE, PhD, is a postdoctoral research associate at the University of Illinois-Chicago. Her research focuses on the roles of family, culture, and race in math learning and identity. She is currently writing about mathematical and racial-mathematical socialization. She lives in South Bend, Indiana.

ASEGUN HENRY, PHD, is an assistant professor in the Woodruff School of Mechanical Engineering at the Georgia Institute of Technology. He completed his bachelor's degree at Florida A & M University in 2004 and his master's degree and PhD at MIT in 2009. Henry's research is centered on the development of a solar-based, grid-level, electrical power generation technology that can compete with fossil-fuel-based technologies. His research involves two major thrusts, namely high temperature concentrated solar-power engineering and atomistic-level, thermal-transport physics. He lives in Atlanta, Georgia.

DIANA SLAUGHTER KOTZIN, PHD, is Constance E. Clayton Professor Emerita in Urban Education, University of Pennsylvania (Philadelphia). She lives in Los Angeles, California.

NEERAJ KULKARNI, MBBS, MD, PHD, is a doctoral candidate in biomedical engineering at Drexel University (Philadelphia). He completed his medical degree at Shivaji University in India and MS in bioengineering from Penn State University. He is concurrently working in a medical resonance imaging company, Fonar Corporation, and researches cell biology, nanotechnology, medical imaging, CSF flow dynamics, water, and biology. He lives in Washington, DC, and Philadelphia, Pennsylvania.

APRIL J. LISBON, EDD, is a school psychologist with the District of Columbia Public Schools. Her academic research area is special education. She is currently co-authoring an article focused on twice exceptional African-American students, identified gifted and emotionally disturbed. She lives outside the Washington, DC, metro area.

SHARRELL D. LUCKETT, PHD, is professor of Performance at California State University-Dominguez Hills (California). Her research interests focus conceptually on performance theory and women's issues. Luckett is the author of *YoungGiftedandFat*, and is the co-editor of an upcoming anthology about Black acting methods. She lives in Los Angeles, California.

Ruben Martinez, PE, SE, is president of Martinez Moore Engineers, LLC (Texas). His firm provides structural and civil engineering services for commercial and institutional projects. He lives in Austin, Texas.

Nicole Monteiro, PhD, is founder of CHAD, Center for Healing and Development and visiting professor, Masters Clinical and Counseling Psychology, Chestnut Hill College, Philadelphia. She is the co-editor of *Pain without Boundaries: Inquiries across Cultures* and author of *Global Insights and the Zen of Travel: Musings on How to BE in the World*. Her research area is global mental health and the socio-cultural context of mental illness. After living abroad for more than four years as lecturer at the University of Botswana, she currently lives in Philadelphia, Pennsylvania.

Rugvedita Parakh, MBBS, MD, is a permanent resident of the United States, originally from Ichalkaranji, a small rural town in Western Maharashtra, India. A trained pathologist with a focus on genitourinary pathology and oncology, she joined the Pathology Department at the University of Washington-Seattle in 2015. She lives in Medina, Washington.

Jennifer Quamina, MPhil, is a business entrepreneur as a jewelry designer (Euphena Beaded Jewellery). She lives in London, England.

Shawn Arango Ricks, PhD, is associate professor in Rehabilitation and Human Services and chair of the Department of Human Services Studies at Winston-Salem State University. She lives in Winston-Salem, North Carolina.

Nia Ricks, BFA, is daughter of Shawn Arango Ricks. She is currently pursuing a master's of education degree at Winthrop University in Rock Hill, South Carolina.

JOY M. SCOTT-CARROL, PhD, is executive co-founder with the International Gifted Education Teacher-Development Network (IGET-Network, LLC) and visiting professor in the School of Education at the University of the Witwatersrand (Johannesburg). Her research areas and interests are in cultural diversity and gifted education, neuroscience cognition, and giftedness among gifted youth, adults, and the elderly. She lives in Bellevue, Washington.

TIA SHAFFER, EdD, is Fine Arts Department chair in the Atlanta Pubic Schools (Georgia). Her dissertation centers on how participating in theatre impacts life skills and psychological needs in youth. Shaffer is co-editor of a groundbreaking anthology centered on Black acting methodologies. She lives in Atlanta, Georgia.

ANTHONY SPARKS, PhD, is a writer and assistant professor of Television and Film at California State University, Fullerton. He has also taught at Occidental College and the University of Southern California. As a scholar-artist, Sparks has also enjoyed a successful, award-winning career in theatre and television. His credits as a television writer-producer include *The Blacklist* (NBC), *Undercovers* (NBC), *Lincoln Heights* (ABC Family), among others. Originally from the south side of Chicago, he now lives in Los Angeles, California.

ABOUT THE EDITORS

Joy M. Scott-Carrol

Joy M. Scott-Carrol, PhD, earned her bachelor of science degree in psychology from Creighton University-Omaha, Nebraska, master of science in counseling education from the University of Wisconsin, and doctorate of philosophy in educational leadership and policy studies/ higher education administration from Loyola University-Chicago. Her dissertation research on early-identified gifted Black college students concluded that the academic achievements, as measured by comparable high school to college grade point averages, declined absent support systems such as enrollment in honors program and continual account-ability from parents and academic/support counseling.

Scott-Carrol has both national and international university teaching and administrative experience. Since the late 1980s, she has presented at national and international conferences (e.g., NAGC, AERA, and WCGTC), authored and co-authored peer-reviewed, published articles related to gifted/talented learners, and mentored numerous graduate students. Her last teaching position, about which she is most proud as a seasoned academician, is visiting professor in the School of Education at the University of the Witwatersrand-Johannesburg, South Africa. In 2007, she co-founded the International Gifted Education Teacher-Development Network (IGET-Network, LLC). She is a member of the National Association of Gifted Children and the World Council for Gifted and Talented Children.

Scott-Carrol lives in Washington State with her husband, Paul. They are parents of two adult children, a daughter and son, and two adorable grandchildren.

Anthony Sparks

Anthony Sparks, PhD, is a writer and assistant professor of Film and Television at California State University, Fullerton. He has also taught as a faculty member at Occidental College and the University of Southern California. In addition, Sparks is an award-winning television drama writer-producer with credits on hit shows, such as *The Blacklist* (NBC), *Undercovers* (NBC), and *Lincoln Heights* (ABC Family), among others. For his television work, Sparks has been nominated for two NAACP Image Awards, and he received two Sentinel Awards from the Norman Lear Center.

Hailing from Chicago's south side, Sparks is a graduate of the Chicago Public Schools Gifted and Talented program at the nationally renowned Whitney M. Young Magnet High School. As a high school student, he participated for two years in Northwestern University's School of Education NU-Horizons program for gifted and talented economically disadvantaged youth. This program was directed by Joy M. Scott-Carrol. Sparks went on to earn his BFA and MA degrees from the University of Southern California. He also earned his PhD from the University of Southern California in American Studies and Ethnicity.

Sparks is married to Anita Dashiell-Sparks, a Broadway veteran, director, and theatre professor. They have three young children and are based in Los Angeles.

APPENDIX A
Screening Survey

Survey to Help Establish Selection Criteria

1. Gender: Male _____ Female _____

2. Age: 24-28 ____ 29-33 ____ 34-38 ____ 39-45 ____ Over 45 ____

3. Racial/Ethnic group in which you identify (select only one):

    a. Black/Brown-African, Caribbean, Pacific Islander
       or North American _____

    b. Bi-Racial Black/Brown _____

    c. Latino/a, or Hispanic Brown/Non-African descent American*
       _____

    d. Other Black/Brown American (please specify) _____

    e. International or foreign born _____

4. When you were selected to participate in a classroom or program for gifted and talented children, were your parents (or guardian) USA citizens or in the process of applying for citizenship?
   Yes _____   No _____

5. At what age were you identified as gifted or selected to participate in a gifted class or program? _____

6. If later required, will you research and provide the authors with information on the selection criteria used to determine your eligibility?
   Yes _____   No _____

7. If applicable, at what age were you accelerated a grade level? How many grade levels accelerated? _____

8. Check all subject areas in which you were most academically abled.

   a. Science _____

   b. Technology (computer science) _____

   c. Math____

   d. Verbal ability (writing, reading) _____

   e. Art, music, theater, photography _____

   f. Other _____

9. Full name and location of the gifted program you participated in: _____
   _____
   _____

   a. Approximately what academic years were you enrolled in this
       program? ___to __ (example, 1999-2003)

   b. How many years (or grade levels) did you participate in the
       above program? _____

10. Name of school district (private or public) of the gifted and talented
    program: _____

11. Your current educational attainment:

   a. High school diploma _____

   b. BS/BA _____

   c. Master's degree _____

   d. Doctorate ___

   e. Professional degree _____ (lawyer, medical doc-
       tor, pharmacy, dental, etc.)

   f. Other _____

12. Are you currently employed or self-employed?
   Yes _____   No_____

   a. In what industry or profession: _____

13. Marital status:

   a. Married_____
   b. Single never married _____
   c. Widow/er _____
   d. Divorced _____
   e. Other _____

14. Did you have a mentor during, after, or beyond high school?
   Yes _____ No _____

   a. Were you and your mentor of the same gender?
        Yes___   No_____

   b. Were you and your mentor of the same ethnic group?
        Yes _____   No _____

15. At the time you were identified as gifted or selected to participate in a gifted program, your family's socioeconomic background may have been considered:

   a. Poverty (homeless, living in a shelter) ___
   b. Lower income_____
   c. Lower middle income _____
   d. Middle income _____
   e. Upper income_____
   f. Upper income ___

16. How many siblings lived in the same household as you when you participated in a gifted and talented program? _____

    a. Where did you rank among your siblings? _____

    b. How many of your siblings also participated in a gifted and talented program? _____

17. Please indicate your household configuration at the time you participated in a gifted and talented program.

    a. Mother/father _____

    b. Single mother _____

    c. Single father _____

    d. Grandparent _____

    e. Foster parent _____

    f. Other _____

18. Do you have a strong opinion about gifted and talented programs in general and specifically as it pertains to Black and Brown children?
Yes _____ No _____

19. Now, reflecting on all of the above questions, the time you spent in gifted programs, and your life story as it may relate to the choices, opportunities, and so forth in life, do you have a compelling story to share about your journey as a gifted child selected to participate in a gifted and talented program and now as an adult navigating through life as a Black or Brown gifted individual? We know that being gifted does not go away.
Yes _____ No _____ Maybe _____

Briefly explain only in one or two sentences: _____

_____

_____

_____

_____

_____

_____

Fictional accounts will not be accepted for this book. Unless your life or the life of others are at risk for being harmed, we kindly require that names and locations are actual. Additionally, manuscript submissions must be returned to us in final format. Contributors should return manuscripts already edited. We suggest consulting a proofreader before sending.

Screening survey developed by Joy M. Scott-Carrol, PhD, IGET-Network, LLC (2013).

APPENDIX B

Interview Questions for Highly Accomplished Gifted Adults

THE FOLLOWING INTERVIEW PROMPTS AND QUESTIONS were developed by Joy M. Scott-Carrol (2015) and presented to chapter contributors.

The purpose of this interview is to include your manuscript as a chapter in the book *Running the Long Race in Gifted Education: Narratives and Interviews from Culturally Diverse Gifted Adults*, edited by Drs. Scott-Carrol and A. Sparks. Individuals selected to contribute interview chapters have in common that they have been identified as gifted or participated in gifted and talented programs in their youth. However, we know very well that depending on where one lives, both here in the United States and in other countries, some highly gifted individuals had been recognized by teachers and others but never officially identified as gifted when they were children. As such, only a few of the questions will apply to them.

The following interview questions will greatly assist us in offering our readers insights from highly gifted adults who were: (1) identified for their achievements or accelerations, by educators and others, as gifted when they were children; (2) identified as gifted in adulthood by some measure of intelligence (e.g., qualifying for Mensa membership); (3) never officially identified but recognized as gifted and did not participate in gifted classroom/programs based on lack of gifted program offerings in one's country of origin. [Individuals fitting number 3 and selected as interviewees were on the recommendations of narrative chapter authors.]

We kindly ask that you include your responses in a narrative format (11–13 pages) or provide detailed responses directly underneath the questions you choose to answer. We strongly suggest that you respond to questions marked ** as these will give readers contrasting perspectives. Please feel comfortable elaborating on any topic that may come up and adding an additional question if necessary. We discovered from many of our narrative chapter contributors that they had not thought about some childhood experiences until now. So, please feel comfortable sharing the details about what you now feel is important to talk about or want to share with readers from your country of origin or elsewhere.

Our book is intended to be used in college and university classrooms across the United States and abroad, so if in the process of writing you discover an emergent topic that could be a lesson to pass onto teachers, students, parents, or anyone else, please do not hesitate to share.

To begin, please provide demographic information (1–3 will appear in the book) as follows:

1. Full name: (how you wish to appear in the book)
2. Credentials: (example, MD, PhD, etc.)
3. Affiliation, title, location (name of university/business, full address, telephone number, and position)
4. Email address
5. Age
6. Nationality (include in interview)

Questions are not listed chronologically.

Giftedness in Youth

1. Looking back on a time in your youth, can you share an experience or two that validated your exceptional qualities? This could be at home, school, community, among friends, etc.
2. Based on what you know about your childhood, who first recognized that you were a gifted or exceptional child? **
3. Were you ever told your IQ? If so, how do you feel about knowing what it is?
4. Please describe some classroom achievements, awards, or competitions that set you apart from other children. How were these accepted by them, other parents, and the community?

5. As a highly gifted/highly bright child, were all of your classroom experiences with teachers positive? If so, please describe the experience that stands out the most today. You may also describe negative experiences.

Fitting In/Social Isolation

1. Please describe experiences where you may have felt like an outsider or socially isolated from your young age-mates/peers because of your exceptionalities or how you preferred to spend your time. **
2. Bullying is always problematic whether one is a child or an adult. Were you ever bullied in school because of your high intelligence? If so, how did you manage to stand strong and accomplish your schoolwork? Please feel comfortable sharing an experience.
3. As a gifted child, did you have a role model, that is, someone whom you looked up to and who believed you could achieve and accomplish all that you set out to accomplish? Where is this person today, and have you shared your successes with him or her?
4. Have you ever felt that your giftedness was misinterpreted or discounted because of racism, classism, or some other factor?
5. From today's perspective, what are the major achievement obstacles for high-ability/gifted children who are racially, ethnically, or culturally different?

Family Life

1. What was the single most important lesson you learned from a family member that you, too, will pass (or are presently passing) along to your children or others if you do not have children? **
2. From your adult perspective, what role did your parents play in nurturing your gifts and talents? **
3. Please describe your family of origin and how you all spent your time together when schooling was not involved. Were there family socioeconomic challenges? If so, how did these impact your future life choices? **

4. Based on your experiences, what do you believe all parents and teachers should do to support their gifted children? What shouldn't they do? **

Motivations

1. What motivated you to achieve at a very high level as a child, and has this changed now in your adulthood? **
2. To what extent are you motivated by challenges? Please explain.
3. Please finish this sentence: As a child, when I failed at something I really wanted, I typically _____.
   In your answer, please describe whether this holds true today.

Accomplishments

1. What has been your highest tangible accomplishment as an adult? In your answer, please indicate whether this accomplishment could have been achieved had you not been gifted. Was it easy? Did it require a lot of work, effort, time, etc.? **
2. What would you now consider your greatest accomplishments on a personal level?
3. What are other accomplishments have you not mentioned up to this point? Don't be afraid to brag. In fact, we'd like you to!

Career

1. What is your current profession? Please describe how you got there (education, promotions, challenges, etc.) **
2. How many other persons of your same race, gender, or nationality share the spotlight with you at your place of business?
3. In situations where you are the only person of color, how does your high intelligence help you to cope? **

Beliefs: True or False **

1. In general, children identified as gifted continue to apply their gifted talents and abilities in similar ways as they become adults.
2. I would be where I am today in my career had I not been identified as gifted or participated in gifted and talented programs.

3. Participating in gifted and talented programs taught me how to be competitive in the workplace and aspire toward advanced education.
4. I believe intelligence is a combination of genetics and environment. Please explain or provide an example.
5. I believe, spiritually, there is a higher power every single individual can draw upon to tap into his or her individual gifts and talents. Please elaborate.

Thank you again for agreeing to include a chapter in this book. Your chapter will appear as follows:

Title (please provide ASAP)
Author (your name)
Affiliation (your place of business)

Post Narrative Survey: Author Perspective on Being Identified as Gifted

Five- to seven-minute survey—all multiple choice. The purpose of this post-narrative survey is to collect data from chapter authors. Data collected will be included in the book's introduction. Our descriptive summaries will not identify authors by name or other characteristics.

1. What was your perception about the impact of being identified as gifted on your life, before writing your chapter?
   - o Big positive impact
   - o Somewhat positive impact
   - o Neutral (neither positive or negative)
   - o Somewhat negative impact
   - o Big negative impact

2. What was your perception about the impact of being identified as gifted on your life after writing your chapter?
   - o Big positive impact
   - o Somewhat positive impact
   - o Neutral (neither positive or negative)
   - o Somewhat negative impact
   - o Big negative impact

3. In general, children identified as gifted continue to apply their gifted talents and abilities in similar ways as they become adults.
   - o Strongly disagree
   - o Disagree
   - o Neither agree nor disagree
   - o Agree
   - o Strongly agree

4. Gifted children from culturally different backgrounds (race, ethnicity, language barriers, etc.) are as successful in life as mainstream children who are also identified as gifted.
   - o Strongly disagree
   - o Disagree
   - o Neither agree nor disagree
   - o Agree
   - o Strongly agree

5. I would be where I am today had I not been identified as gifted or participated in gifted and talented programs in my youth.
   - o Strongly disagree
   - o Disagree
   - o Neither agree nor disagree
   - o Agree
   - o Strongly agree

6. Participating in gifted and talented programs taught me how to be competitive in the workplace and aspire toward advanced education.
   - o Strongly disagree
   - o Disagree
   - o Neither agree nor disagree
   - o Agree
   - o Strongly agree

7. What do you think are the major obstacles for gifted children from culturally different backgrounds even if they are identified as gifted when young?

8. Please rank the subject areas in which you were most academically abled as a child.
   - ___ Science   ___ N/A
   - ___ Math   ___ N/A
   - ___ Verbal ability (writing, reading)   ___ N/A
   - ___ Art, music, theater, photography ___ N/A

9. Are you male or female?
   - o Male
   - o Female

10. Current age: _____

11. From which of the following racial/ethnic groups do you identify?
    - o Caucasian
    - o Black or African American
    - o Hispanic (Latina/Latino)
    - o American Indian, Native American, Alaskan Native, First Nation
    - o Asian
    - o Native Hawaiian or other Pacific Islander
    - o Bi-racial
    - o Foreign born
    - o Other (please specify):_____

12. Which of the following best describes your current relationship status?
    - o Married
    - o Widowed
    - o Divorced
    - o Separated
    - o In a domestic partnership or civil union
    - o Single, but cohabiting with a significant other
    - o Single, never married

13. What is your highest educational attainment?
    - o Bachelor's degree
    - o Master's degree
    - o Doctorate or completing doctorate
    - o Professional degree (MD, JD, pharmacy, dentistry)
    - o Other (please specify): _____

14. Age identified as gifted or began participating in gifted programs
    ○ 6 months–3 years
    ○ 4–6 years
    ○ 7–10 years
    ○ 11–15 years
    ○ Over 15 years

15. With whom did you live with as a child and at the time you participated in gifted programs? _____

   _____

16. When you were a child, your family's socioeconomic background may have been considered:

17. Your current annual household income:

   _____

18. Current position/professional title or homemaker:

   _____

19. We welcome your comments:

   _____

INDEX